Italian N ve Design

by Andrea zi

foreword by Arata Isozaki

THAMES AND HUDSON

Front cover: *"Metropole" clock, George Sowden, Memphis, 1982.*

Back cover: *"Dalila" chair, Gaetano Pesce, Cassina, 1980.*

Picture research by Piercarlo Bontempi
Design by Anthony Mathews
Translation from the Italian by C.H. Evans

First published in Great Britain in 1984
by Thames and Hudson Ltd, London

Printed and bound in Italy

Contents

Foreword by Arata Isozaki   4

Introduction   8

I   From Form to Reform   12

II   Unity in the Building   17

III   The Futurist Metropolis   27

IV   The Rationalists   33

V   Italian Design in the Fifties   39

VI   Pop Realism   50

VII   Radical Architecture   63

VIII   The Joyful Science   73

IX   Mass Creativity   80

X   Dress Design   86

XI   Design "Primario"   96

XII   Colour Design   102

XIII   The Active Surface   109

XIV   Decorative Design   115

XV   Banal Design   122

XVI   The Metropolitan Scene   128

XVII   The New Handicrafts   136

XVIII   New Design   142

         Biographies   151

         Index   156

Foreword

In the mid-1960s, it became apparent that the "avant-garde" in architecture and design was no longer functioning as it had in the early period of the Modern Movement. In the mid-1980s, it is clear that the avant-garde is no longer performing its role of instigating new movements in any cultural arena. Thus passed a mechanism contrived by modern society in order to perpetuate itself—a mechanism that was an integral component of our conception of progress.

This book by Andrea Branzi is testimony to the fact that the various experiments in design that have taken place over the last twenty years have contributed to the demise of the avant-garde. There is an insinuation of something catastrophic and traumatic as Branzi ventures into the boundless, unknown wilderness.

Modern architecture, since its beginnings, has sought to develop technology and attain utopia, and the avant-garde was given responsibility for steering its course. After the early 1960s, however, the avant-garde could no longer fulfill this responsibility. At that time, young architects from Tokyo, London, Vienna, and other centers were creating utopian technical proposals for the city of the future. My own career as an architect was launched via such proposals. But some of these architects had already become aware that the future would not be rosy, that technology could become destructive, and that the "utopian" residences they were planning were only congested places where people would swarm like ants or bees. It became apparent that serious questions had to be asked about the fundamental tenets of modern architecture. And so they were.

At that time I was caught between two forces. While in Japan I sympathized with the radical tendency that would culminate in the "abandonment of art"; on the other hand, I was making full use of technology in assembling a robot, to be displayed at the Milan Triennale of 1968, which abstracted the hidden violent character of technology. But despite its intent, my work was denied because I was associated with the regime of the established industrial society that ruled the production and distribution of design.

Borrowing a Zen term, this denial was a strong *coup* to me. In Zen training, the master imposes on his trainees various difficult questions to help them attain a new realization of the world. The purpose of the questions is to trap the trainees in paradox. In this way, the master asks the trainees to empty their minds. But in most cases, because candidates are limited by knowledge gained in the past, they cannot attain the real void. At such times, the master, sometimes through verbal means and sometimes through physical violence, delivers a strong blow, whereupon some trainees come to feel emptiness and to free their minds from knowledge based in the past. I received such a liberating *coup* in 1968.

I consider the course of modern architecture pioneered by the avant-garde to have been changed definitively and qualitatively by the confrontation resulting from the occupation of the Triennale exhibition building in 1968, which was in turn part of a cultural revolution whose origins were in Paris. I later came to regard the year of the Triennale as a cultural watershed, comparable to 1527 when the Sack of Rome helped to stimulate Renaissance architecture. At the time, however, I was too much a hostage to immediate events to have any perspective on the situation. Recovering from that *coup*, I signed the agreement for the occupation. I remember the name of Archizoom among the list of signatures, but I did not know at the time that the author of this book, Andrea Branzi, was a member of this group.

After being struck by the *coup* of confrontation, I turned my attention to the work of architects who were actively engaged in destroying the canon that had supported modern architecture. Among such architects, I found two groups who, breaking off relations with former avant-garde thought, presented an attitude of extreme radicalism. Both groups were based in Florence: Superstudio and Archizoom.

What their work shared in common was a fundamental criticism of the established concept of architecture. Superstudio, to strip the designed object of its own immanent meaning, adopted the strategy of covering the object's entire surface with a continuous neutral grid. And then they extended this grid beyond the city, beyond the earth, even to cosmic space, calling the result a "Continuous Monument".

Archizoom also developed a project of infinitely extended neutral architecture: this was the "No-stop City", where parking, residential space, and offices were arranged in layers of artificial space, strung out like groceries in a supermarket. Because it abandoned any dependence on natural light, "No-stop City" went on growing into a strange assemblage beyond the usual limits of architecture. The composition of elements and the forms of production, conjunction, traffic, and distribution were to be the last direct product of the rationalism that had supported the development of modern architecture. The result was the terribly homogeneous city that would emerge when the naturalistic constraints that work to keep these elements in balance were removed.

Superstudio adopted the means of sanctifying an architectural object by eliminating its details. Their continuous architecture is very similar to the Nirvana sought by the Flower Children. Here architecture becomes united to nature and is submerged. Archizoom's "No-stop City" presents the utmost extremity of modern rationalism, where any kind of fantasy is forbidden. Using a nasty trick, they turned our present situation inside out, a development driven by a rationalism that was now extended to the production system also. One must acknowledge a certain black humor in this.

The aspect of a city formulated according to these proposals, whether it reaches a saturated state or a state of super-homogeneity, is never the naturalistic utopia that modern architecture sought. Rather, such proposals should be perceived as fundamental criticisms of modern architecture through the presentation of an instantaneous glimpse of the nightmare of the future.

There is concealed in both the "Continuous Monument" and the "No-stop

City", I believe, the memory and experience of the great flood that visited Florence in 1966, which must have had a profound effect on the members of Superstudio and Archizoom who were graduated from the University that year. During the flood, the center of Florence, a symbol of urban culture since the Renaissance, was submerged. This abrupt invasion by an alien substance buried the well-balanced city of beauty and elegance. Just as the flood was symbolic of the destruction that could level physical culture in an instant, the "Continuous Monument" and the "No-stop City" are architectural concepts that might launch a destructive attack against the city; at the same time, both are endless objects that might plot a homogeneous, untamed, reckless invasion. Are they not analogous to the violent conditions of the flood in this sense? Indeed, both projects may well be regarded as metaphors of the flood, whose impact on the young designers was comparable to the *coup* of Zen.

Since the mid-1970s, Andrea Branzi has been involved in new design experiments with Ettore Sottsass Jr., Alessandro Mendini, and others. These experiments exhibit the same characteristics that were featured in "No-stop City"—an endless expansion reaching toward insanity and meant as an offensive attack against established norms. Concretely, the products of their design encompass all the elements that compose the environment, such as technology, objects, surfaces, colours, materials, clothes, and furniture. They reduce each of these elments to its original state and then try to understand it from a new point of view. They adopt, as the most effective clue, a critical method that I wish to call "constraint-free rationalism". As the concept of design was actually born in the Modern Movement of architecture, so it is deeply supported by rationalistic thought. Therefore, when we intend to criticize modern architecture or design, we cannot avoid the difficulty of having only the rationalist way of thought at our command. This is tantamount to the contradiction posed in another sphere of thought today, namely, that in order to criticize the compositional logic (logos) that supports language, we have no means of criticism other than the very language that is the subject of the critique. Andrea Branzi and his colleagues release the objects produced rationalistically from the frame that has confined their rationality, and extend this rationality to the furthest reaches and beyond. Here it is expected that the excess or the border incursion will occur. It is clear that the activities of Memphis and Alchymia have already been influential beyond the borders of Italy.

It seems to me that these movements have passed beyond the labels "avant-garde" and "radical". They have progressed to a stage that might be called "critical rationalism". My wish, however, is not to limit what they are doing to the parameters of this term, but rather to relate what issues from Andrea Branzi and others in this book to the more eloquent, fluid, and fundamentally invasive idea of the flood.

Arata Isozaki

"Look,
I fill this
sacred pipe with
bark from the red willow;
but, before we smoke, let us see
how it is made and what it means:
this eagle's feather represents the thoughts of
man and how they should soar high like the eagles."

Black Elk

Introduction

This book assembles in critical and narrative form a particular series of experiments in design and in the elaboration of an underlying theory that have taken place over the last twenty years. These experiments have been carried out by workers with whom I have had an intense exchange of views and in many cases collaborated directly. Some critics have found the experiments that make up this current of research to be so disparate that they have been unable to discover any link between them. In reality there has always been a common vector, consisting in the effort to test and actively stretch the limits of design: the aim in fact has been to set up a new frame of operation, more in touch with the social and cultural changes taking place in the world around us, which would allow some active influence over these same developments. Our efforts have always been directed towards a greater realism, i.e. closer adaptation to a changing situation, even if this was often achieved by means of apparently unrelated methods and illogical shifts in direction.

One should not be deceived by the fact that this book has more to say about design than architecture or town-planning, for it also sets out to question the traditional distinction between these three disciplines, and in any case the dimension of a new metropolis is a prominent factor in all the experiences of design described. The origins of Italian "New Design" lie not in a disciplinary revolution limited to the design of industrial objects, but rather in a new way of looking at both architecture and town-planning and in an examination of the priorities on which such intervention is based and of the effectiveness of the canonical instruments of planning in general.

It is no coincidence in fact that the generation which underwent its apprenticeship in the climate of the upheavals of the late sixties and under the influence of radical architecture has shifted its center of attention, from around 1972 onwards, away from great metropolitan themes to the design of objects and to working in a critical manner within *industrial design*.

We see design, therefore, as a site for the rebuilding of architecture: not in the sense of mere additional growth, "from the spoon to the city" as Ernesto Rogers would have it, but rather as an attempt to find, amidst the dramatic epistemological crisis in modern architecture — a crisis which has threatened the very existence of the modern world — a point from which a real link between man and the system of his objects could be forged. To design a chair or a colour has meant to start again from scratch, in search of a utilitarian culture that is not worn out, and on this basis to discover, not an impossible unity of design, but merely that lost grace of making simple things, without which it becomes futile and dangerous to make such big ones as houses and cities.

Taking the argument over large and small things to its logical conclusion, one arrives at the paradoxical claim that the whole debate over the linguistics of the Modern Movement, from its birth to the present day, has revolved around models of chairs: the only truly complete work carried out by modern architecture is represented by the collection of chairs that it has turned out uninterruptedly as theoretical models of composition and as critical analyses of structures of habitation. Gropius, Le Corbusier, Rietveld, Loos, Mackintosh and Morris spring to mind: the history of modern architecture seems to coincide with that of the modern chair. But the route that should have led from chair to city has always been cut short; when it has succeeded in crossing the threshold of the house it has often come up against a failure of town-planning. It could be said that there is not a single modern urban model that has not failed or is not on the road to failure. The same cannot be said of the chair, which has been the only structure of habitation to undergo a complete though separate revolution; even the house has undergone much less radical and significant modification of its morphological structure than the chair. It has even been found necessary to define habitation as the space "around" the chair, understood as a perfect and totally controllable minimal structure, the ideological copula of the universe, a place of dynamic stasis and a model for understanding the revolution in architecture.

It has been pointed out correctly that from the 18th century up to the present day, that is ever since the beginning of the Industrial Revolution, all emerging cultural movements have claimed for themselves a greater "realism" than contemporary aesthetic thought. This is true of Romanticism and Neo-classical culture, Rationalist thought and 19th-century eclecticism and the post-modern with respect to the Modern Movement today. In effect the changes caused by the processes of industrialization over the last three centuries have been so rapid and profound as to force a continual re-examination of the foundations of the theory and praxis of aesthetics in order to avoid their being left definitively on the sidelines of history.

This continual transformation of the historical context has resulted on the one hand in the institutionalization of the "avant-garde" as a breathing space free from the trauma of modern culture, and on the other in a diametrically opposed attempt to get away from experimentation in order to reach a stable threshold of security that would allow culture to contain, but not to formalize, potential mutations in social behaviour. This schizophrenic attitude has kept on re-emerging: the Modern Movement responded to the avant-garde currents of the beginning of the century by proposing a methodology based on the lasting certainties that emerged from a rational analysis of necessities; the radical movement reacted to this in its turn by placing the scrutiny of instruments and the limits of the project at the heart of the problem. Finally the post-modern has tried to get out of the crisis area by opening itself to the certainties of historical memory. Culture seems to have been generated more by the stimulus of a "permanent crisis" and the overthrowing of false historical certainties than by a linear expansion of its own theoretical foundations.

In some ways design has never had an independent history of its own; it has always been seen either as industrial culture or as social decor, if not merely as a curious chapter in the history of customs. Currently the design project is credited with the role of a minor, applicative part of modern architectural culture — a disciplinary setting for the final steps of a more ambitious project taking its cue from the metropolis. It is expected to confine its attention to the utilitarian object and to realize that unity of human technologies within the "project" so dear to the Modern Movement. But this type of operative unity between design, architecture and town-planning, based on a rigid hierarchy of decision-making, broke down some time ago, giving way to a common antagonism among the three disciplines, each one of which now claims not only its own total autonomy but even the need to set itself up as a complete alternative to the others.

Over the last twenty years we have found ourselves operating in a historical context in which all the factors of cultural disaggregation have been exacerbated, in the sense that any unified hypothesis of design, as method or as language, has disappeared. The present post-industrial model of society reveals a world in which industry has come to the end of its period of heroic growth, characterized by a rationalist and internationalist culture, and in which the homogeneous society of equals has been replaced by an assemblage of minorities, of conflicting groups no longer founded on different productive, economic and social functions but on different cultures, religions and traditions. A world which is seeing the return of culture, the transcendent and the traditional as great historical forces. As a result the myth of reason and egalitarianism, so vital to the whole of modern culture and architecture, has entered a period of crisis. The myth of the unity of all languages and technologies in the project has given way to a "narrative" process of discontinuity and partiality. The disciplines of planning have undergone separate processes of growth and demand their own autonomy and operative supremacy. Taking Argan's famous 1958 definition of industrial design as a starting point, we can see just how far the experiences of the avant-garde have diverged. Argan wrote that industrial design produces prototypes for industry which will lose none of their

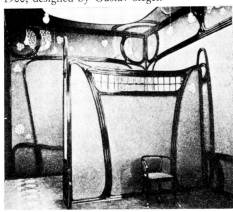

1) Köhn pavilion at the Paris World's Fair in 1900, designed by Gustav Siegel.

semantic values in mass-production. This definition, in its clarity and simplicity, hints at the means rather than the ends of industrial design. To put it another way, it delimits the sphere of action that architecture and town-planning would have to take over. But over the last twenty years there has been a progressive expansion of the theoretical and operative limits of design: light, colour, fashion, materials, decoration and sounds have become the instruments of a new kind of design aimed at the creation of a more habitable modern metropolis. The cosmesis of reality is no longer considered a diversionary or remissive action, but part of a plan for the transformation of the world.

This book discusses Italian design; this is more of a convention than anything else since, although the illustrative and documentary material is drawn from that country, the critical arguments and the contents of the research itself form an integral part of a much wider international process in which Italian designers have participated at every stage. Even the bibliographies bear witness to this, showing that the circulation of ideas and exchange of experiences have never been limited to a national set of problems, a concept that is in many ways artificial. It remains true that in the overall picture of international attempts to deal with these problems, Italian design represents, if not the most advanced stage, at least an experimental laboratory of exceptional interest, in which a large number of foreign architects have often worked. For a complex series of reasons the culture of architecture in Italy represents something more than a mere professional discipline; throughout the long post-war period an entire class of intellectuals has recognized in the debate over design an opportunity for revitalization of the country and for cultural forces to participate in its reconstruction and development. This hope has been largely dashed, just as a panorama of modern architecture has never been realized in this country. But the democratic battle for the conservation of historic centers and the heritage of art, for a new planning policy and for a rational solution to the problems of modern technology has involved not only those directly engaged in these works, but all intellectual and political forces. Even the linguistic terms of our discipline have become the patrimony of the entire educated class.

Italy is a country where too much has been built and badly — or too little and excessively well — and it is also the country where the greatest theoreticians and historians of architecture live, where some of the best international reviews of the sector are produced and where as many books on architecture are sold as in the whole of the United States. This is only an apparent contradiction: the very fact that it has remained theory has often transformed this research into a sort of pure intellectual force. Hence there is in Italy today an identification between the culture of design and the culture of opposition, almost to the point of their becoming synonymous.

It could be said that one of the peculiar characteristics of modern Italian architecture is the way its own discontinuity is taken as a preliminary condition of the project itself. Whereas in the rest of Europe modern architecture was almost always born as the last formal act in a complex balance of urban and social standards that had already attained stability, ranging from the presence of traditional and proven patterns of housing to widespread forms of social welfare, to which the project gave historical and territorial continuity, modern architecture in Italy has always had to fight for its place in a hostile setting and in a socio-political situation demanding challenge, first under Fascism and then during the thirty years following the war. The individual project, far from being an element of continuity, has been the symbol of an alternative approach and evidence of opposition: its lack of continuity with the current situation has become an indication of its quality. Hence the essentially polemical nature of modern Italian architecture, whose foundations seem to rest more on opposition than on equilibrium. It is a history, therefore, in which names figure more than schools, individual works more than units of territory.

Likewise the historical struggle of Italian design has followed a course riddled with contradictions. In spite of all the academic definitions and the experience of other countries, relations between Italian design and industry are anything but simple and straightforward. This is not so much, or not only, because of problems over areas of operation or questions of quality, but a consequence of the fact that the culture represented by the designer in Italy has never really been that of industry; on the contrary, the critical code to which the Italian designer owes his allegiance led to his work showing all the signs of active contradiction, stimulated by an oscillation between integration and denial, between consensus and opposition. The great expressive and experimental richness of Italian design is born out of this conflict. This is an unresolved contradiction and perhaps one that is, fortunately, incapable of resolution. The broad experimental vista of the fifties showed at once that Italian design did not belong to the tradition of international functionalism, and that the false certainties of an industrial culture based on the myth of the infinite series and the definitive product were alien to it.

Italian design, in contrast to the punitive extremism of the Rationalist tradition, or to the commercial excesses of the American one, developed an original equation of its own, poised in unstable equilibrium between the culture of consumption and that of production. Thus it was able to mediate between the two opposing utopias — definitive products and perpetual mutation of products — in search of a solution that was never final but always provided a drift, a perfectible error and the possibility of further development. Technology has always been used for its expressive possibilities, whereas fashion was always analysed to find out whether any of its components might prove to be lasting.

Italian design has experienced its years of brilliance since the war, without ever having produced a school or a museum or an official history, and the full significance of this fact should not be underestimated. All the attempts made in this direction have only succeeded in so far as they have been presented as parts of the picture, as passing tendencies, and never as all-embracing and definitive institutions. If one thinks of a school of design like Domus Academy, of regular events like the Triennale, Eurodomus and the Compasso d'Oro competitions and of the reviews and exhibition catalogues, all these instruments have fostered a debate with the outside but have never managed to encompass the whole phenomenon of Italian design; the consistent success of the latter throughout this long period is due precisely to its capacity for regeneration through direct experience in the field, in direct contact with industry and with the experimental "super-handicrafts." Such a hypothesis is not wholly naive, given the history of all the crusades that have been proposed to promote design in those countries where it did not already exist, and where it has always been spurned just because it was promoted by a centralized culture.

The state of historical amnesia to which design is prey, i.e. its ability to stand as "history in the making" and not as a tradition of itself, as action and not as reflection, has been its strength up to now. It may be that this "radical" capacity is being sidetracked today, with the current re-discovery of historicism as the foundation of modern culture. One can escape from this kind of digression in two ways: by accepting the presence of history as "style", i.e. as already codified language, or by identifying a new strategy of growth, accepting the present as our field of action and drawing comparisons with the past. The latter is the road we are taking; "the hot house" is still the ideal place to start looking for a way of making our cities and buildings habitable. All our efforts are aimed at extracting from the corners of a domestic world a renovated and credible culture of living that can serve as the practical basis of a new architecture.

In the opening chapters of the book an attempt has been made to trace the thread which links the experiences of a part of the Modern Movement, and still earlier of the old applied arts, to the Bauhaus, the Futurists and the Italian Rationalists; this is done not in search of historical justification, but as a contribution towards a different interpretation of the complex relationship which both binds together and fragments modern architecture.

Many experiments of the Italian New Design are still in progress, and no-one is interested in a premature attempt to find a place in history for them; nor is this the aim of the book. As a worker in the field I am interested not in writing history but in modifying it, putting forward a strategy of interpretation and action at this moment of work on the present.

From Form to Reform

I From the second half of the last century onwards the Great Universal Expositions gave the public their first chance to weigh up the achievements of the emerging industrial civilization. These were not mere trade fairs, but rather the first comprehensive demonstrations of what was taking place, as a result of mechanical production, throughout the West. For the first time individual products and machines were placed side by side, making it possible to examine the present state and potential of the industrial project as an all-embracing design for the transformation of the world. This design was being put into practice as a comprehensive and unified undertaking that transcended all the conflicts of free competition and the limits of individual industrial enterprise.

It is well known that the enthusiasm that these expositions aroused not only among businessmen but also in the public, which flocked to visit them in great numbers, was not shared by intellectuals, artists or shrewder minds in general. Despite the fact that the Universal Expositions were accompanied by some of the earliest examples of modern architecture (Paxton's Crystal Palace or the Eiffel Tower in Paris, for example), the aesthetic and cultural value of industrially manufactured products was so low, at times absurdly so, that a bitter argument arose over the question of the relationship between industrial production, culture and society — a controversy that is still of fundamental importance in modern design.

The debate over this set of problems was a totally new phenomenon, in part because this was the first time questions were being raised not so much about different artistic stands, or new styles and tendencies, but about the use and function of mechanical and economic devices, indeed of industry as a whole, as sources of social and cultural processes that would form the basis of a new kind of criticism.

Over the course of the 19th century, the applied arts, previously viewed as minor arts, gradually came to play a leading role in an extremely advanced debate and were made the subject of new critical attention.

2) Frontispiece of *The Art Journal* (London, 1851), with the catalogue of products displayed in the Crystal Palace at the first Universal Exposition.

It is interesting that this occurred at a time when production in the sector of the applied arts was going through a phase of great decline, accompanied by a striking deterioration in quality. But despite this profound crisis — or perhaps as a consequence of it — the applied arts became the most significant symptom, the crux of an extremely broad range of problems that concerned the most fundamental aspects of industrial production and its role in civilized society. Unlike the so-called major arts, and even architecture, the applied arts were exposed to all the negative effects of industrial production: industrially manufactured goods were presented as a mechanical reproduction of hand-crafted products. The result was that handicrafts were subject to attack on two fronts: on the one hand commercial competition from industrial products, and on the other the most vulgar exploitation of their formal patterns. By imitating the work of the craftsman, the machine humiliated him and swept away all the expressive values implicitly contained in the handmade products.

Moreover, handmade articles for the home, such as chairs, cupboards, clocks and vases, were naturally suited to manufacture by machine; initially the goal of the industrial product was to break into the market of handmade products, but without, at least in the beginning, giving rise to any new patterns of consumption. On its first appearance, the industrial product took the form of a physically limited and morphologically imitative single object, manufactured by simple machines and not by assembly lines, and for an absolutely traditional market.

Hence any discussion of the applied arts and their revival meant examining the possibilities of a new function for industrial activity in society: this is the reason for the absolutely central role the minor arts came to play in the 19th-century cultural debate.

Throughout the century, theoreticians of art were in agreement on one fundamental point: the decadence of taste and the arts was a direct consequence of the decadence of the society of which they were an expression. Discussing art meant making a judgement about the historical conditions of society and putting forward an alternative model. As the relations between art and society were uncovered, it became clear that theory could take two possible directions, and this remains valid today: one stressed social problems as the basis for any revival of art, while the other saw art as an instrument for the reform of society.

Pugin, Cole, John Ruskin, William Morris and Viollet-Le-Duc were convinced that all artistic reform implied putting forward a comprehensive model for society. In this sense, the Gothic Revival was not a mere stylistic exercise involving mediaeval idioms, but the proposal of a style historically derived from a social organization which was seen as a model of great import; on this they were all agreed, although they gave it different nuances, ranging from the ethical and religious commitment of Pugin and the spiritual aestheticism of Ruskin to the embryonic socialism of Morris.

Eclecticism became a method of design that incorporated social criticism as well: a radically different model to contemporary society was being put forward as an alternative to the line of development that led from the Renaissance to the Enlightenment, and that had brought about the current crisis. The eclectic rediscovery of the Gothic was also a response to the demand for a style which society was on the way to losing for good. Religious purity, freedom of imagination and social cohesion: only mediaeval society appeared to have succeeded in realizing these values, and the Gothic cathedrals were the highest testimony to this. The deliberate revival of mediaeval forms was an affirmation of a desire for reform that aimed to salvage, through art but for society, those values that had been lost in the decadence of the new industrial age.

The certainty that art and society were profoundly linked led to an exploration of the functional nature of art, in the broadest sense of the term; that is it encouraged an analysis of artistic forms in relationship both to their structural functions in the environment and to their significance as a testimony to man's creativity and labour. In 1907 Ruskin wrote: "Ornament... has two entirely distinct sources of agreeableness: one, that of the abstract beauty of its forms,... the other, the sense

4) Cast iron chair in rustic style manufactured by G. Collison of Doncaster.

3) View of the east side of the transept of the Crystal Palace during the exposition.

The objects exhibited in the first Universal Expositions were thoroughly eclectic in their styles, using printed decorations, industrial materials and craftsmen's models. This cultural hotchpotch appeared to its critics as the outcome of a deep rift within society between artistic creation and the realities of alienated industrial labour.

13

The young English reformist critics toured the world as sensitive dandies, seeking the aura as well as the styles of antiquity: the patina of the old stones of the cities. They then tried to fill their eclectic code with the greatest possible number of elements and memories.

of human labour and care spent upon it." The function of art is not just that of creating beauty, but also of allowing social fulfilment of the creativity of the individual; human labour and creativity are still seen as an indispensable vehicle of the spirit, a fundamental condition for the happiness of the individual. Hence happiness remains the goal of art, both for its creator and for its audience, and when it no longer has this aim, it is bound to fall into decay.

Thus the degeneration of man's labour in industrial civilization, its transformation into slavery and confinement, lies at the bottom of the crisis in art at that time.

Pugin described the earliest industrial products in 1843 as follows: "A firescreen is a sort of battlemented rampart with a gate at each end, the poker ends in a very sharp point and the tongs in a statuette of a saint." In 1853 Redgrave said about the Universal Expositions that manufacturers look on good taste as an impediment to sales; their attitude could be summed up in the fundamental principle:

7) Pompeiian decorative patterns (from R.C. Racinet, *Handbooks of Ornament in Colour*, vol. 3).

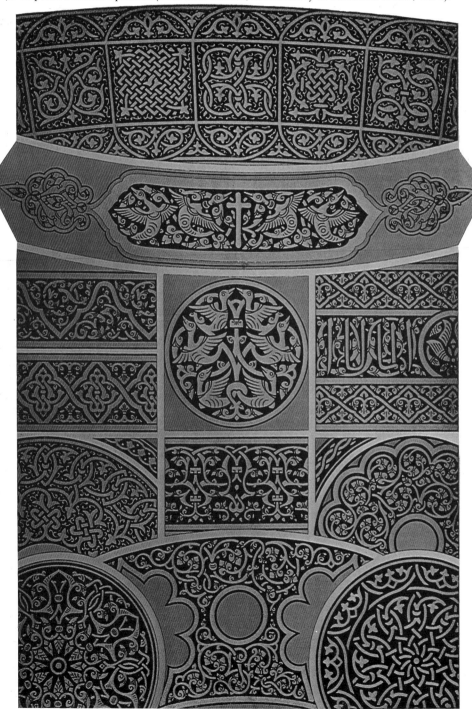

5) John Ruskin: "Detail of St. Mark's in Venice".

6) Self-portrait in charcoal by John Ruskin.

The encyclopaedic knowledge of the decorative codes of different epochs and countries gave decorators and builders a vast quantity of signs and languages which could be freely employed in the environment and on products, including industrial ones.

what is best is what sells best. The utilitarian view of beauty, seen solely as a function of sales, formed part of the industrial mentality of the era; as Engels put it: "Today anything that does not make money is stupid, out of place and idealistic."

Ever since Carlyle's work *Signs of Time*, published in 1829, the 19th century had seen the growth of a increasingly deep-rooted opposition to the use of machinery and the division of labour, to which the neo-mediaevalist model was held up as an alternative.

The argument became more and more wide-ranging, going beyond the scope of the initial controversy to become, on the one hand, political and social criticism and, on the other, a dispute over the proper use of the machine itself. William Morris, while a great paladin of the battle against machines, wrote: "If the necessary reasonable work be of a mechanical kind, I must be helped to do it by a machine, not to cheapen my labour, but so that as little time as possible may be spent upon it.... I know that to some cultivated people, people of the artistic turn of mind, machinery is particularly distasteful... (but) it is the allowing machines to be our masters and not our servants that so injures the beauty of life nowadays."

Thus the revival of handicrafts was at one and the same time a restitution of the value of manual skill from its humiliation in factory labour, a defence of cultural values and an attempt to rescue household objects from the uniformity of mass-production.

Human labour had ceased to be a constituent element of the object itself and

Decoration, destroyed by the budding industrial culture, still reigned in certain social circumstances as witness to refined habits that refused the constriction of the masses.

8) Foyer of the Ritz Hotel in London.

9) Alfonso Rubiani: table lamp (from *I veri e i falsi storici*, Galleria d'Arte Moderna, Bologna).

10) Carlo Bugatti: wood and enamel seat.

11) Carlo Bugatti: chair with writing-desk.

The attempt on the part of some to retain a creative individuality led to extreme cases such as that of Carlo Bugatti, a craftsman and ebony worker who created neo-mediaeval pastiches.

Within the framework of Italian neo-mediaevalism, "Aemilia Ars" directed by Alfonso Rubiani was founded in Bologna in 1898 under the auspices of Count Cavazza. This was the first attempt in Italy to reform handicrafts and the applied arts by introducing Renaissance and mediaeval models along with the nascent Art Nouveau style, all within the sphere of the local Emilian traditions.

12) Alfonso Rubiani: designs for public clocks (from *I veri e i falsi storici*).

was demoted to mere energy of production: the object was no longer a cultural vehicle but only a reproducible image of itself. The transformation of artisanship into pure and simple labour force had robbed man of direct control over his own means and models of production: the industrial system brought to a conclusion a broader and more radical change in society, taking over, through "wages", management of the economy and, through industrial products, the shaping of cultural patterns.

Hence the battle over the applied arts took on the significance of a battle for redemption of the positive value of human work; these battles produced the theoretical foundation for a potential revival of environmental culture, and this had an effect on architecture as well. Historically speaking, the whole debate over a new architecture emerged in those years out of the defence and reinstatement of the minor arts.

Decoration as a system of signs, symbols and patterns, overlaid on the individual object or architectural structure, became a sort of linguistic veneer, still capable of differentiating the object or the "cultural" site of simple static structures or buildings. Decoration is evidence of a freedom of invention, an indication of the high moral and cultural value of man's labour, that traces its dense mesh of symbolic references, rich in suggestions and citations, on structural surfaces. Style, decoration, superfluous shoots or caryatids combine as elements of culture and painting to indicate a physical reality that would otherwise be bare, reductive and devoid of any cultural meaning. They constitute the last line of defence against an intrusive, subterranean and hollow reality to which man, the artist, opposes his web of cultural memories, his right to the superfluous as evidence of an unshakable freedom of invention and of work.

Unity in the Building

II

At the beginning of the century William Morris wrote: "I find it disgraceful that there exists a class of mere artists... who supply ready-made designs to those whom you call executive designers, who have hardly anything to do with the project, but are occupied solely in what you call heavy labour." By this time it was clear that the content of design had been taken out of the hands of the artist, who found himself on the one hand operating as a mere technician subject to the logic of the division of labour, without any responsibility for the product, and on the other becoming more and more detached, providing decorative schemes and samples of improbable patterns to be applied to an ever wider range of merchandise.

But the last vestiges of the argument over the use of the machine in the production of art, still hotly debated by the group around Muthesius, were now giving way to a gradual rethinking of critical attitudes and a shift towards a new conception of design that relied on the use of a new range of tools. At the first meeting of the Werkbund, Theodor Fischer declared: "It is not the machine that is responsible for poor quality work, but our incapacity to use it effectively."

The new positivistic theories influenced doctrines of aesthetics as well, laying the philosophical foundations for an acceptance of modifications in style deriving from changes in the historical situation: it was now possible for culture to break out of the traditional mould of humanism and to start operating within the new logic of industry and mechanical work, without abandoning its function as a testimony to civilization.

The process of renewal in the applied arts that went on throughout the 19th century was a struggle aimed at conservation of the cultural environment and the dignity of the home; Morris's Red House can be taken as a symbol of this. At the beginning of the 20th century the battleground shifted to the field of architecture, which appeared to present an opportunity for the construction of a new civilization. In this connection, Giedion wrote: "By the 20th century the movement was from handicrafts to architecture and not from architecture to handicrafts."

In an attempt to set the minor arts on a par with the so-called major ones, a unification of all creative forces was sought in architecture: "The ultimate goal of all the figurative arts is the complete building. The adornment of buildings was once the most noble function of the arts; they were indispensable components of great architecture." Gropius wrote this in 1919, in his manifesto of the *Staatliches Bauhaus in Weimar*. He went on to say: "Architects, sculptors, painters, we must all get back to the craft. Art is not a profession. There is no qualitative difference between artist and craftsman. The artist is only a craftsman writ large."

Handicrafts ceased to be an independent category, testimony to an indispensable set of civic values opposed to the coarsening of industrial civilization, and became part of a more wide-ranging project, a sort of feeder for industry, indeed its experimental precursor.

The modern view was that handicrafts were a specialized phase in industrial design and presented an opportunity for the creative use of machines, though the latter were to be utilized in accordance with a cycle that would permit total control, in all phases of the work, over the experimental prototype. An infinite number of copies of this prototype would then be reproduced by industry.

In the Bauhaus, design models were no longer sought in the world of literary and figurative culture outside the factory and foreign to the spirit of the machine, but were looked for instead within the profound logical structure that shapes and organizes the world of work. Thus, at a time when culture was adapting itself to the historical logic proclaimed by industrialization, it gave up being a critic outside the system in order to become an operative force inside its circuit, and its

13) African female figure.

The discovery of African art during the twenties represents a sort of indirect confirmation of the existence of a natural rationality that coincides with the neo-plastic language of primitive creativity. The so-called minimal arts thus lead to purity as the threshold of human expressiveness, in coincidence with an extremely effective and synthetic linguistic code destined to have an important influence on the nascent proto-rationalism.

Cubism represents the adoption of the logic of the factory on the part of design and the figurative arts. It implies a deep interiorization of the logic inherent in assembly-line production.

14) Fernand Leger: "The yellow stairs", 1913, Kunsthaus, Zurich.

efforts were channelled into keeping a check on aberrations.

The factory, however limited and partial with respect to a still largely mercantile and agricultural world, was already claiming a universality of its own, putting itself forward as a universal model for a rational and economic logic. In this way the relations between culture and industry began to change, and a comprehensive plan of collaboration between them was set up, aimed at launching a programme of cultural regeneration and re-evaluation of industry as a tool and pivot capable of altering the world according to a rational design.

This is where modern design was born: it assumed the role of transforming necessities of production into "rational values" and in the process dug up and re-examined all the experiments of the artistic avant-garde, reducing them to simple tests of language and turning their subversive content into an analytical and rationally exploitable force.

In this manner the semblance of a perfect coincidence between cultural revolution and industrial revolution was created. The liberating effect of the former, its bias towards a new way of handling aesthetic models and towards their absolutely relative character, was used as a demonstration of the radical logic inherent in industrial production.

In design, the destruction of culture showed up as an effort to reveal to production its own secret rationality, to the point of making this rationality an autonomous factor in the production of design itself: furthermore, its effort to take the pro-

15) Kurt Schmidt: "Man + machine", ballet scenery, circa 1924.

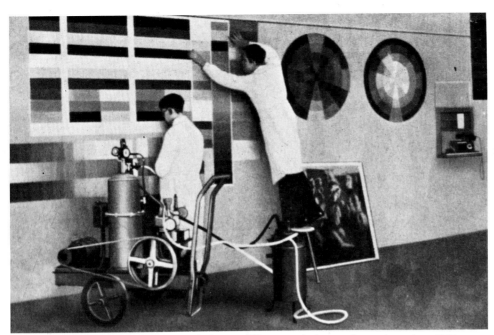

16) Mural-painting workshop: tests relating to different techniques of spraying, circa 1927.

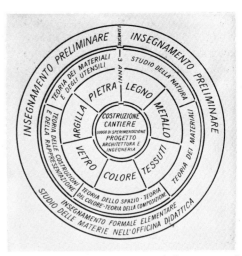

17) Schematic representation of the course of studies at the Bauhaus.

In the Bauhaus there were seven laboratories for working stone, wood, metal, terracotta, glass, colour and fabrics; old crafts were taught alongside structural analysis and formal composition. Research undertaken in the laboratories did not lead to mass-designed objects but to universal models that could be used as guides for production.

18) Moholy-Nagy and Dell with apprentices and workmen from the metal workshop, circa 1924.

Bauhaus students set out from a basic training that insisted on a code made up of elementary geometrical figures, such that objects were reduced to simple elements which could then be machine-produced.

duct to the highest level of quality, in both technical and aesthetic terms, laid the foundations for industry's drive towards the utopia of the "definitive series", beyond time and space, in a society made uniform by consumption.

The universality of art became the universality of the product. In those years design's interest in minor arts developed into an obsession with "minimal" arts, such as that of Africa, to which the whole of the cultural avant-garde was turning its attention as a source of primitive and essential, but extremely expressive forms.

By taking the role of intermediary between industrial manufacturing technique and the market, design tended to transform objects into elementary data and simple geometrical figures, in order to facilitate their processing by the machines that were to reproduce them. All the vast heritage of mediaeval revivals, decorations, ornaments and literary quotations vanished to make way for a stark form, coincident with an elementary and spare structure of objects that was at one and the same time consistent with function and an autonomous linguistic code.

The applied arts were gradually swallowed up by architectural design, becoming part of a general ergonomic system; the great wealth of variety among objects was lost by linking their destiny to that of architecture. Eccentricity, the possibility of choice and the "freedom" of invention of which Ruskin spoke gave way to a critical operating awareness, to a terse capacity for synthesis.

It is in this manner that the aesthetics of the machine tended to rigidify into a closed circuit. Design solutions tended to become absolute and exclusive, based on finding, indeed on discovering rather than inventing, the "natural" coincidence between the form of the object and the production processes necessary for its industrial manufacture. Yet by doing this, design was envisaging an impossible role for industry: that of a mechanism for producing definitive objects, i.e. ones which were not fated to be replaced in time, in that they belonged to a category not subject to taste or even history - a sort of naturally rational product. Hence produc-

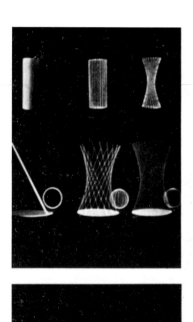

19) Teaching exercises with solids of rotation and joints.
20) Introductory course by Moholy-Nagy and Albers: study of equilibrium.

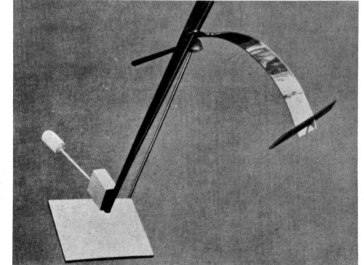

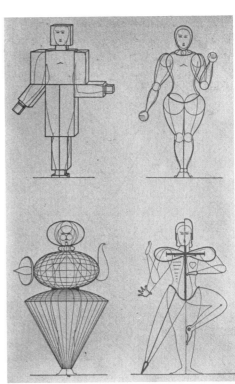

22) Oskar Schlemmer: characters from the "Triadic Ballet", 1922.

21) Kurt Schmidt: puppets for the show "The Adventures of the Little Hunchback", circa 1924.

The human figure is made to fit into an elementary geometrical figurative code that seems to reflect in formal terms the new mechanized civilization with its rational logic of production.

23) Portrait of Oskar Schlemmer.

24) Oskar Schlemmer: Figures from a ballet.

Picasso's people are less absolutely changed than uncertain, as though they were hiding behind masks larger than they are.

tion seemed to become a fixed-term, temporary operation, the simple filling of the void formed by needs; once this void has been filled, no more than simple maintenance operations should be required, and never ones of renewal or replacement.

In fact the Modern Movement believed that the new man emerging from the "civilization of the machine" would be the man who adopted the laws of production as his own intimate nature (Cubism) and who saw the rationality of the machine as a scientific instrument for the reorganization of reality (design). Only in this way could the relationship between factory and society become a natural law. The "wholly production" man would sacrifice all to it: he would sublimate his own bourgeois ambitions in an *Existenz-Minimum* surrounded by object-tools.

Design seemed to be the instrument of demystification best suited to those market processes induced by industrial production, but the liberation that it brought about served to channel all the energies of the individual into the development of his own productive potential. In this profound sense the effect of proto-design turned out to be a repressive one: the maximum integration of labour envisaged the freedom

The "U Theatre" of Molnàr is a good example of the power of the geometric code to contain a world of experience and signs; the other more radical Bauhaus theatrical line created scenes in which rows of empty rooms contained only manikin figures seated at empty tables. Breuer, in his youth, also imagined a sterile world of strictly useful objects without any linguistic connections which were not tied to the use of "industrial" materials.

25-26) Pablo Picasso: maquette for "Le Manger Français", 1917.

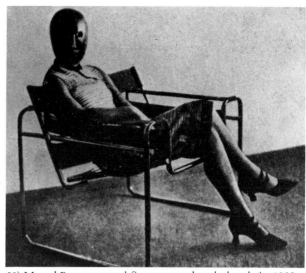

27) Oskar Schlemmer: "Table-companions", oil on canvas, circa 1923.

28) Marcel Breuer: seated figure on early tubular chair, 1925.

29) Farkas Molnàr: "U theatre", circa 1924.

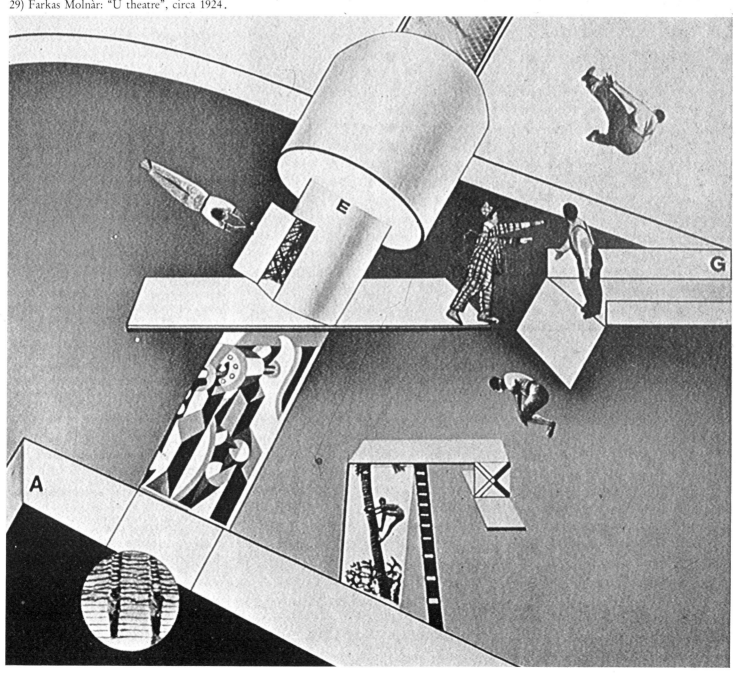

of the worker from the bourgeois condition. The process of stripping away stylistic accretions from the object carried out by proto-design did not serve so much to guarantee a greater autonomy from myths, but led rather to a renunciation of the objects themselves.

The Modern Movement appeared to be committed to defining the condition of the worker as a primary one, devoid of the cultural myths typical of the middle class, and wholly committed to the logic of the factory, in which the working class would recognize a powerful device with which to challenge the morality of the bosses. Thus the working class would spontaneously identify with the condition of the factory, seeing in it a future civilization wholly committed to efficient production and spurning consumption as irrelevant to production. "Production and not consumption" seemed to be the new revolutionary ethic, in contrast to

30) Model house built at Weimar for the Bauhaus exhibition of 1923.

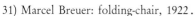

31) Marcel Breuer: folding-chair, 1922.

Furnishings disappear and are replaced by containers and cupboards that hide everything. Decoration will be considered superfluous for the next sixty years.

the bourgeois state that on the contrary consumes but does not produce.

The growing difficulties encountered by the Bauhaus in Germany and the crisis of rejection experienced by the Modern Movement throughout Europe were born out of the advent of the great dictatorships and the spurning of the reformist ideas sponsored by the movement on the part of the middle classes. But there were still deeper reasons for the isolation that the ideology it promoted met with in its direct confrontation with reality. In a way, one could speak of a two-fold failure of the Modern Movement's working hypotheses. The hypotheses it formulated were rejected by both sides of the social conflict. In fact the working class has always seen the factory merely as an instrument for the organization of its own struggle, which is a struggle against the condition of the worker, that is to say against poverty and exploitation, and even a struggle against work itself through use of its alternative, the strike. The working class adopted the mechanism of consumption as an indication of its own social rise, and destroyed all the political equilibria attained during development of the system. It took the middle class as the measure of its own growth, and by replacing it destroyed it, along with its cultural values. It rejected design as a model for behaviour in that its political import was based on an urge towards imitation and not on an alternative culture. Even Capital rejected the model of design: production and its logic require not the disappearance of consumption, but on the contrary its progressive increase. A satisfied consumer is also a better worker. Indeed, in an advanced industrial society, production and labour must remain a marginal factor, taking a back seat to consumption, which lends meaning and purpose to the activity of production, ennobling it. It is not society that should resemble the factory, but the factory society. If the identification between Capital and its society is genuine, there ought to be a coincidence between Capital and the spontaneous contents of society. And it is consumption that provides the plan of action for this spontaneity; its continual renewal guarantees a renewal of production models and their constant movement towards an unattainable utopia of prosperity.

Culture has to put consumption to good use and not repress it by creating a system of transitory patterns of behaviour; culture might then lose its unifying features and be replaced by thousands of partial utopias. No therefore to the radicalism of the Bauhaus; yes to the experimentalism of artists like Picasso.

33) Ludwig Hilberseimer: proposal for a city.

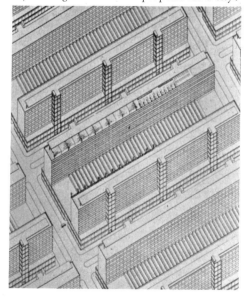

32) Herbert Bayer and Rudolf Paris: wall decorated in collaboration with the Bauhaus mural-painting workshop, 1923.

It is interesting to see how architectural elements such as the window and the radiator tend to fit into one and the same figurative range made up of quotations from the neo-plastic and proto-rationalist codes.

The Futurist Metropolis

III

34) Umberto Boccioni: "Morning", 1909.

In 1922 a series of pictures was exhibited by Moholy-Nagy at Der Sturm gallery in Berlin: they had been executed by a designer of sign-boards, to whom he had instructions over the telephone. This is a good example of how the exponents of the Bauhaus, faced with the growing difficulties of collaboration with industry and the impossibility of reconciling complex social themes within design, threw themselves more and more into a sort of immanent idealism, that is to say an a priori application of their whole range of ideal ready-made forms before the work was even begun. In this way the gap between industry and culture widened instead of diminishing; collaboration was reduced to an abstract confrontation between the individual problem and an Olympian pantheon of idea-forms.

So it was that the creation of a style became the most obvious result of the effort to overthrow all styles, and the destructive and utopian impetus of the Bauhaus gave way to a sort of mirror image of itself; here was the cradle of Art Deco, which achieved great success by proposing a chic modernism to a middle-class hankering after a renovation of style, but not of life. Art Deco resulted in a renewal of the forms of interior decoration, in which the only role for craftsmanship was in the elegant construction of luxurious prototypes; the sophisticated research into materials carried out by the Bauhaus was replaced by a taste in which high-quality materials were used as one component of style, in the name of elegance and attractiveness.

As a result the Franciscan poverty of proto-design came into currency only when, with its reformist tendencies inactivated, its presence could be accepted as "modern" style. The building, from which the new culture was to have erupted into society,

Within the metropolis, a conflict arises between public and private, technics and feeling: Signora Massimino's drawing-room is invaded by a swarming, growing city that appears to have no limits.

36) Umberto Boccioni: "Portrait of Signora Massimino", 1908.

35) Carlo Carrà: "Brawl in the Arcade", 1910.

37) Paul Citroën: photomontage "Metropolis", 1923.

38) Umberto Boccioni: "The rising city", 1910.

39) Carlo Carrà: "What the Tram Told Me", 1917.

became its prison.

On top of this, the direction taken by industry was different from the one based on design that the Modern Movement had assumed. In order to grow, the consumer market demanded a continual transformation of its own points of reference and models; its field of action could not be confined to the excessively uniform, rigid and limited one of the building but had to expand into a much larger and more mobile area — that, in fact, offered by the modern metropolis.

As a concentration of buildings the metropolis has always guaranteed a very high level of communications within the market-place and society, constituting a sort of jungle in which goods and information circulate naturally and acquire value, driven by internal differences of potential in the urban fabric; the urban shock stimulates individual creativity and lends meaning to all patterns of behaviour, burning them in order to regenerate them.

At the end of the first decade of the 20th century Futurism brought about the first definite shift in the focal point of cultural and aesthetic production away from

The Futurist painters expressed themselves in abstract terms that were an immediate reflection of the experience of the modern metropolis.

27

The Futurist architects still followed the traditional view of a city made up of monuments, which now included those of the modern world: power stations, factories, railway stations. Their general approach to the city was traditional in its use of perspective. It was the individual architectural features that underwent change.

nature and the home, to the theatre of the metropolis. Ever since the Universal Expositions and the Bauhaus, the production of goods for the home had been seen as the area with the greatest potential for a renewal of culture, but the Futurists took the city as their point of reference, seeing it as a structure open to modification and variation. Here the active surfaces of structures and buildings acted as technical and social scenery for a now irreversible fragmentation of society, in which design merely sign-posts the vortices of differing and diverging impulses.

Public and private, architecture and city, intimacy and technical development enter Futurist culture as the terms of an irreconcilable contradiction. If architecture and design served the Bauhaus as models for research into a potential unification of technology and human experience, for the Futurists the metropolis would be the only real setting for an experimental existence, for a way of life based on the practice of a heroic existentialism. So a historic turning-point was reached in these years: if at the beginning of the century "the movement was from handicrafts to architecture", as Giedion put it, it changed direction from this moment on and began to go from the metropolis towards design, and from there to the territory, passing through an architecture that was increasingly uncomfortable in its double function of private place and public structure.

Even the concept of the city itself underwent a profound change in those years and began to overstep the canonical bounds of planning. The city or metropolis is no longer a unitary place in which a civilized and physical balance is attained between the different parts of society and that special coming together of history and environment. The metropolis of the 20th century differs profoundly from the historic model of the city: completely different conditions of urban life have been created there. Until the last century the urban fabric and its architectonic symbols formed a medium that was totally comprehensible to its inhabitants; that is to say, a proven equilibrium existed between travelling times, visual spaces and the height at which architectonic signs were placed in the perspective space of the city. Architecture fitted perfectly into the urban fabric; indeed the city was inconceivable except in terms of architecture, which formed both its premise and its logical synthesis. But this equilibrium was now shattered, and in place of the space of perspective within which the great cultural structure of architecture was consumed, there was a direct relationship, an integrated perception, devoid of empty spaces, a completely filled space in which no hierarchical examination was

40) Virgilio Marchi: Futurist architecture, 1922.

41) Antonio Sant'Elia: "Theatre", 1914.

42) Antonio Sant'Elia: study for a building, 1915.

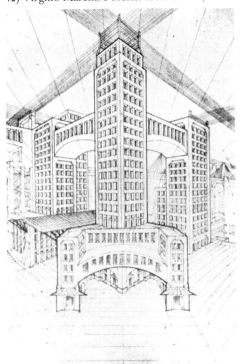

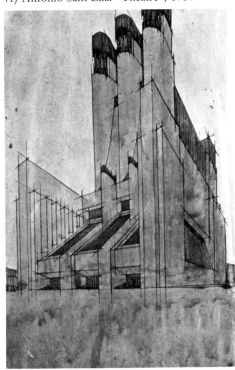

43) Giacomo Balla: painted screen, 1918.

44) Giacomo Balla: "Project for a Lounge/Show-room with Furnishings", 1918.

45) Giacomo Balla: "Project for a Bridge of Speed", 1913.

46) Fortunato Depero: interior of a Futurist cabaret, Rome, 1922.

Giacomo Balla was the first to transfer Futurist dynamism to environmental design, bringing structures and the individual, aggressive sign into head-on confrontations, obliging language and functional definitions to measure up to each other.

The Futurist transformation of the universe gave rise to a number of "manifestos" that were programmatic declarations of what had to be done in every sector of human activity. In 1921 Marinetti published a manifesto on "Tactilism" in which he proposed an art that was entirely bound up with direct bodily experience.

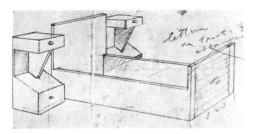

47) Fortunato Depero: design for a cot with bedside tables/cupboards, 1920.

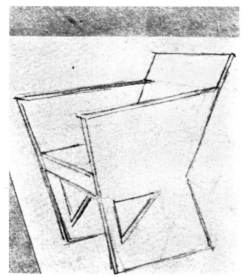

48) Fortunato Depero: design for a chair, 1920.

49) Fortunato Depero: vase, 1922.

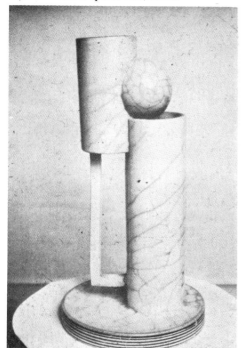

possible, only a bodily consumption of reality.

The Futurist painters, rather than Sant'Elia, were the first to point out that the harmonious distance between interior, architecture and town-planning had vanished: man lives the urban experience as a complete alternative to his own private condition: "We are killing the moonlight," as Marinetti had said in 1909.

And so the city no longer possesses an external and an internal space, just as there no longer exists any territory without connections to the mechanical system.

It is within this new situation that architecture experienced the first crisis in its function and message. It remains a form of cultural communication which requires space for its interpretation, a preparatory distance from its user: it stands witness to a unity of forms that has already been overthrown. The system of communication on which its message is based is still that of allegory or at least of direct visual experience.

In his manifesto of 1913 entitled "The wireless imagination", Marinetti wrote: "Futurism is founded on the total revolution in human sensitivity that has taken place as a result of the great scientific discoveries. Those who make use today of the telegraph, telephone, gramophone, train, bicycle, motorcycle, automobile, transatlantic liner, airship, aeroplane, cinematograph and daily newspaper, do not realize that these different forms of communication, transport and information exert a decisive influence on their psyche."

The stratum of the city really used by the individual is made up of disjointed sequences of images, crumbs of that image of the city and of those building complexes of which the historical city is formed. The Futurist artist sees the metropolis as an abstract and compact system, which "rises" dynamically like a vortex of integral experience.

As Kevin Lynch was to say much later, the urban experience of the modern city dweller is made up of strictly private tunnels of memory, ranging from luminous street signs to individual elements of the urban fixtures. The composition and texture of the facades, however, are no longer able to form a framework of stable references.

The urban dweller's experience of his city extends as far as the perusal of street posters, signs, shop-windows, displays of merchandise, hydrants and traffic lights;

In his "House of Art" at Rovereto, Fortunato Depero created a programme of futuristic applied arts leading to a neo-plastic language later developed by the budding Rationalist movement, starting with the well-known decoration of the Zampini home designed in 1925-26 by the "Futurist" Ivo Pannaggi.

50) Fortunato Depero: scenery for "Il Mercante di Cuori", 1927.

above this height the city is outside the range of his perception. The skyscraper is not, as is commonly believed, a super-monument but an undifferentiated pile of cubic metres able to reach vertiginous heights; it no longer "figures" in the urban experience of the inhabitants, but forms instead an abstract "fin".

Out of the new dimension of the metropolis arises the first real conflict between modern architecture and its city. The response of Italian architecture to the new situation is significant: faced with the impossibility of containing urban growth within a unity of form, and at the same time incapable of conceiving a city without architecture, it resorted to the creation, through the "900" movement, of a sort of point-based system of conventional architectonic signs within urban systems that no longer have any real continuity with the traditional conception of the city.

Unable to overcome even conceptually the architectural limit of the metropolis, architects chose to create a network of tiny references that would still permit the exercise of judgement, even if only a visual one. Lots of small features and disconnected quotations were put together: flowers in vases, benches on motorways, fountains in entrances, frontispieces on prefabricated buildings, in an attempt to simulate the existence of a visual and historical continuity.

It is clear that the theoretical limitations of the architecture of the "900" group became an impediment to the search for a new solution to the problem of the city, precisely because of the presence of architecture as such, with its concepts of space, limit and judgement.

The impracticality of the Futurist intuition, too radical to ever become a system, smoothed the way for a resurgence of literary architecture — in the sense of its being a citation of its own linguistic history — and a tranquillizing response to

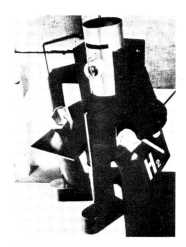

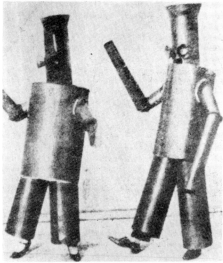

51) Fortunato Depero: costume for "Il Comandante AH/G", 1925.
52) Fortunato Depero: costumes for "Anhiccam del 3000", 1924.
53) Fortunato Depero: craft workshop for Futurist art in Rovereto, 1920

The metaphysical paintings of Giorgio de Chirico and his brother Savinio are a sign not so much of a return to the order of memory, but of the impossibility of living in the latter-day world with its myths of classical history and humanist codes, along with the dissociation from modern life that they imply.

a destructive avant-garde. From that moment the Italian cities chose the dangerous road of stylistic continuity with their ancient centers. The only alternative to this was offered by unbridled private speculation, which led to the creation of something resembling a modern city in suburban districts devoid of any real urban life.

The literary roots of modern Italian architecture have proved hard to eradicate: representation rather than solution of the problems and the tendency towards metaphorical illustration of a cultural task would remain fundamental characteristics of the whole output of this century.

In the political and human destiny of Italian Futurism is concealed an important key to understanding several imprintings of Italian culture in this century. Quite apart from its political transformation from revolutionary movement, aiming at a radical subversion of bourgeois culture, to paladin of the Fascist social order and the academic culture of the regime, Futurism underwent a still more profound internal transformation of its linguistic and design codes. From purely destructive behaviour — "We wish to glorify aggressive movement, feverish insomnia, the running pace, the somersault, the slap and the punch" (Marinetti, "Le Figaro", 1909) — it started on a course that would lead it first to experiment with the applied arts, as exemplified by Giacomo Balla, and then through the experiences of Fortunato Depero and his artisan workshops in Rovereto, to an almost total prefiguration of what would eventually become the language of Italian Rationalism. This type of linguistic transition is highly representative of the history of that generation and still more so of the "continuity in change" of the Rationalist generation that was to follow. A few features typical of Futurism, among them radicalism as an instrument of order and not of revolution, would be directly assimilated, through the language of design, by a modern culture in the making. The fact that Italian Futurism gave birth, in its growth to maturity, to its exact opposite ("Down with intelligence!" Marinetti had cried) and that the "completely full" abstract and dynamic forms of Futurism would generate a primary code of geometric forms that would serve as the basis of Rationalism, prefigures other apparently traumatic transitions through which our modern culture has subsequently passed, succeeding each time in confirming a continuity of development that is much more uniform than would appear from a bare account of the cultural facts.

54) Carlo Carrà: "The Hermaphrodite Idol", 1917.

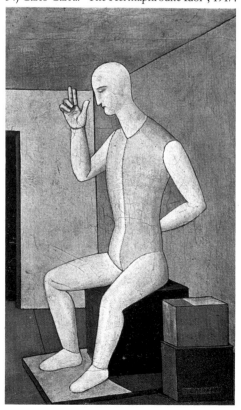

55) Giorgio de Chirico: "The Enigma of the Oracle", 1910.

The Rationalists

IV

In 1925 Ivo Pannaggi produced Casa Zampini, the first Rationalist interior design in Italy, three years earlier than Terragni's Novocomum. Rationalism was quicker off the mark in interior design than in architecture in Italy. It is no accident that Marinetti claimed the interior of Casa Zampini to be a Futurist work; his error is an indirect confirmation that the work, crammed with internationalist quotations and yet standing outside the currents of "900" and "Metaphysics", was not based on any clear theoretical awareness and did not encounter a critical environment in a position to accept and decipher it with any clarity.

It was the works that followed, Gualino offices by Pagano and Levi Montalcini in 1928, interiors by Terragni and Lingeri, along with those by Bottoni at the 4th Monza Triennale in 1929 and Baldessari's stand at the 5th Milan Triennale in 1930, that shed light on what was going on. It was the birth in Italy of modern architecture, viewed not so much as a problem of aesthetics, as the Futurists saw it, but as a working system of analyses and design solutions.

Right from the beginning, Italian Rationalists had one difference from their European colleagues: they were Fascists. Not priests or prophets of Fascism, but open political supporters. This national characteristic, which would not be transformed until much later, through the maturation of individual personalities, into a culture of opposition to the regime, bears witness to several features peculiar to architectural Rationalism, both on an international level and especially in Italy.

The Modern Movement was born in Europe along with the great ideologies of action for the transformation of the world. Secular responses to the Socialist revolution, they adopted its scale of operation and applied it to social problems that in the first decades of the century seemed to require, and in every case did require, revolutionary solutions. Rationalism, Fascism, Nazism and Soviet Socialism were all born in the same climate of history and all proposed, although in widely differing forms, something no other ideology had ever done: the modification of the human race. This modification was the radical answer to problems whose solution could not help but demand extreme measures for the structural alteration of society, starting with its raw material, i.e. its individual human components.

The political difficulties that Rationalism encountered in Germany during the thirties and in Italy during the forties have created some confusion in this connection. In reality there was never any clear logical opposition to the political regimes, but a clash over models within their programmes for reconstruction of the world, and consequently over the instruments to be used — military ones for some, those of planning for others.

Socialism aimed at the creation of a new humanity through the collective use of economic and industrial resources. The reactionary revolution of the major ideologies of the right proposed a new man linked to ethnic tradition, who would be capable of carrying out the unification, by arms, of Europe. The Rationalist technocracy of the Modern Movement proposed a new man able to establish an international culture based on reason and technology. All stressed the urgency of a renewed humanity, more precisely a new human race, as preliminary instrument and as goal of their respective revolutions. All spoke of final revolution, of a definitive turning-point in the history of man.

Of all these ideologies the Modern Movement was the only one that came up with a clear picture of its own model of humanity: above and beyond a social revolution, and by means of it, there could and should be brought about a structural modification of man himself, of his logic and behaviour, whose pattern was already prefigured in the Rationalist scenario. In other words a plan based on changing men through their actions was always understood as a creative transformation of

56-57) Ivo Pannaggi: Casa Zampini, 1925 (reconstruction at the 1977 Venice Biennale by Germano Celant).

Casa Zampini is considered the first Rationalist building in Italy, and it is interesting to note that Marinetti presented it as a Futurist work. In fact the contradiction can be explained: works by Futurists such as Fortunato Depero and Giacomo Balla in those years speak clearly for a process of transformation of the Futurist language into the neo-plastic code that characterized Italian proto-Rationalism.

58-59) Luciano Baldessari: studies and models for "Luminator" dummies for the Barnocchi stand in Barcelona, 1929.

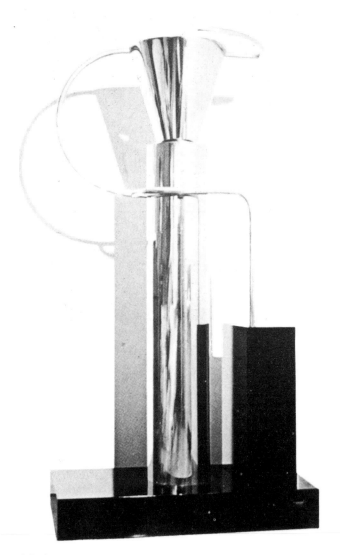

human physical and mental behaviour.

In their political and military prime, Fascism, Nazism and Communism were unable to make use of the revolution independently proposed by the Modern Movement because of its different direction, even though it was not directly opposed to the direction in which they themselves were moving.

The true point of difference lay in the way of looking at history. Fascism and Nazism sought to escape from history, proposing a revolt against the modern world; and Communism rebelled against history and proposed a different modern world. The Modern Movement, conversely, was presented as ahistorical in nature and as a triumph of the modern world.

In Italy this conflict of strategy between Fascism and Rationalism was papered over for around twenty years: Rationalists and Fascists continued to coexist within the same set of plans. In Germany and Russia the contradiction came to the surface earlier, and the two revolutions followed different roads.

Twenty years of coexistence between Fascism and modern architecture in Italy were made possible on the basis of a working hypothesis, a sort of highly simplified but effective separation of functions: Fascism was engaged in the creation of a new society by political means and the Modern Movement in the realization of an architecture appropriate to that society. In this ingenuous symbiosis Fascism did not renounce its role as an instrument for radical change of the human setting, while Rationalism continued to describe itself as new architecture for a new society.

The crisis came later, with the independent maturing of the generation of Rationalist architects, and when, as Pagano put it, they began to look "beyond architecture", i.e. beyond the role of a disciplinary revolution that actually had little or nothing to do with what was going on politically. Taking up a position outside architecture, they resolved to make use of all instruments, even political

60) Albert Speer: architecture of light at the Zeppelin Stadium, Nuremberg, 1937.

61) Military parades on the north-south axis in Berlin.

62) Gymnastic displays at the "Principessa di Piemonte" resort at Rimini, 1940.

At the beginning of the twentieth century, Rationalism represented the idea of a culture capable of transforming humanity. It would have changed the face of the earth, founding a new history of the human race.

63) Mass demonstration in the Piazza Venezia: blackshirts spell out the word "Dux".

64) Vasili Kandinsky: plan for a music room, Berlin, 1922.

Painters began to spread out into space and environment in their work, insisting on the autonomy of painting as a project on a global scale that did not require the categories to which nascent Rationalism would have liked to relegate it, that rejected confinement within the "white walls" of those years.

ones, in the planning of real society, just as it appeared here and now, and not in its transformation into a model external to itself. This acceptance of reality meant accepting dignified development of the world in place of revolutionary change.

But the axiom of designing a new architecture for a new society had become established in Italian architectural culture, almost as a definition of the Modern Movement. Whether the society in question was Fascist, democratic, reformist or specialist, Italian architecture would in each case be put forward, always in vain, as a working instrument of political power, as the constructive action of a social programme. And it would hardly ever succeed.

This troubled infancy left modern Italian architecture with a marked ideological and moral attitude, in the sense of always seeking an element of reformism in the act of planning, one that would be capable of transforming the society of the present into something perhaps better, but at least different.

Refusal or incapacity to actively accept reality as a premise for possible action has remained a characteristic of modern Italian culture as a whole. Apart from a few brief moments of trauma, Italian art has been unable to re-establish a link with its own society; one of the reasons why it has so little knowledge of that society is that it has already marked the latter down for change. The moral act of judgement always precedes and blunts the opportunity to grasp reality.

On the whole, the Modern Movement suffered political and cultural defeat between the two world wars. In Italy it never succeeded in becoming the official style of the regime and was continually obliged to compete with Monumentalism for a far from rich market that was in any case increasingly inflated by the propaganda that took the place of a genuine Fascist reform of society. In Germany the separation between Nazism and the Modern Movement was more profound, and the physical expulsion of the Rationalists from the country cut short any further argument. The model of social austerity proposed by the Modern Movement was also rejected by the working class in charge of Stalin's Russia. A large part

65) Piet Mondrian: "Salon de Madame B", Dresden, 1926 (reconstruction at the 1977 Venice Biennale by Germano Celant).

66) Giuseppe Terragni: chair for the Fascist headquarters in Como, 1935 (reconstruction by Zanotta).

of the Modern Movement emigrated to America, where it was transformed, in the absence of its former reformist bias, into the International Style; only then did it obtain wide recognition and a large world market.

But it was in Europe that what was left of Rationalism underwent its most alienating defeat. The landing of Allied troops and the American invasion of Italy and Germany accomplished the military defeat of an autarchic culture and an industry (which in Germany even had an architect, Albert Speer, at its head) to which an entire class of intellectuals and politicians had attributed a cultural and moral as well as a productive role. In other words industry was seen as a tool for the creation of a society that had nothing to do with that of the present, but was, rather, to be formed by the sons of a revolution. Before the eyes of the old Europeans, American industry was disembarking the "new man" of another, simpler and more brutal but clearly winning ideology, an ideology in which immediate happiness was seen as the only possible foundation for human society, but a real society in which industry was expected to provide health, abundance, surplus and consumer goods.

To a culture accustomed to dealing with history as with a harsh stepmother, America offered the example of a total lack of history, like the absence of original sin. Italian domestic functionalism had to contend with the great ergonomic system of a hyper-organized army. New modes of conduct and new fashions brought about an immediate and profound change in social behaviour.

In general, the intellectual class of Europe preferred to avoid this clash between different plans, instruments and liberties. Once again ideology, this time of the opposite pole, functioned as a lightning conductor. But this was not true of European societies; they discovered the immediate pleasures of consumer civilization, the positive mechanism of a system of production aimed solely at producing itself and its own self-induced needs, without any goal other than that of a happy society.

For the first time since its invasion by the Arabs, Europe had been violated in her historical "hearth", changed by a civilization that differed in its most secret cultural roots. Its historical values and the entire operational framework of its moral culture were reshaped by a surge of new values and new utopias. Democracy brought a new optimism, an openness towards the everyday, but also a compromise with social mediocrity. The Modern Movement was reborn in Italy in an original mélange of realism and rationalism, industrialization and craftsmanship.

67) The Allies landing at Anzio, 1943.

The landing of the Allied troops in Italy caused a profound transformation of Italian culture; alongside democracy, new myths and behaviour patterns were affirmed.

68) Franco Albini: design for a radio for the Wohnbedarf competition.

69) Franco Albini: case structure, 1938.

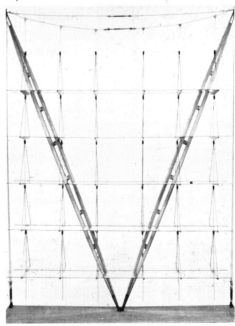

70) Pietro Chiesa: Lamp and stand made fabric and metal, 1933.

The Italian Rationalists proposed "a new architecture for a new society". Nevertheless, in their furniture in particular, they managed to act independently of Functionalism and to attain originality and a certain irony in their work.

71) Gabriele Mucchi: "S 5" stackable chair.

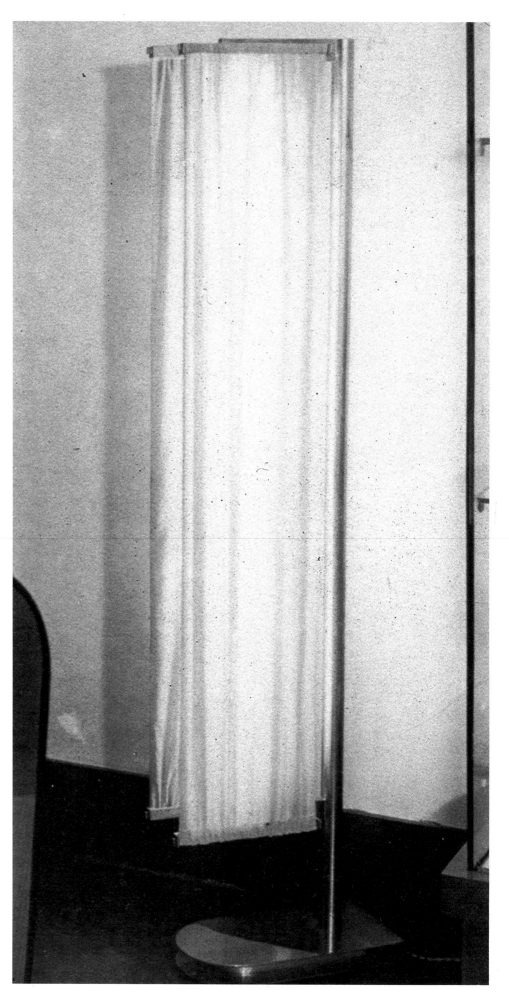

Italian Design in the Fifties

It is difficult to make cultural phenomena fit into the narrow confines of a critical categorization based on decades, given that such categories often contain materials that are unconnected if not diametrically opposed. In the case of the fifties, however, it is possible to define sufficiently homogeneous formal segments that stand out sharply and almost in isolation between the tragic shadows of the forties and the glittering crisis of the following decade. In reality the fifties should be measured from 1948 to 1962, i.e. from the defeat of the Popular Front to the explosion of a new era of social conflict with the events in Turin's Piazza Cadorna. These fourteen years of centrist peace saw the attempt on Togliatti's life, the Scelba law, the Marshall plan, the 20th Congress of the Communist Party of the Soviet Union and the economic boom.

The Italian intellectual class that had emerged from the Resistance, and had to a large extent supported the programme of popular renewal put forward by the parties of the left, underwent a traumatic imprinting in those years which was to have a profound effect on its future. The defeat of April 18, 1948, signified for them the impossibility of playing an active part in the material and cultural reconstruction of the country; driven into opposition, they saw their chance to establish direct contact with the social masses evaporate. Confirmed in their historical separation from the country and from power, Italian intellectuals found themselves a "minority in the right in a country in the wrong."

But this may not have been their worst problem: their first contact with democracy turned out to be a profound disappointment for many intellectuals, just as national unity had disappointed them the century before. A spirit that was perhaps secretly opposed to democracy and motivated by a resentment towards the country and its major political parties often led to a contradictory intellectual stand in which political commitment and elitism were mixed up in a tangle of contradictions fueled by bourgeois intransigence.

The change through which Italy was going in the period immediately following the war tended towards a rediscovery of reality, a reality that had been concealed for too long by Fascism and kept at a distance by the impossibility of political activity over a period of twenty years. "We all feel we are living at a time," wrote Pavese, "in which it is necessary to restore words to the solid and naked clarity they had when man created them for his own use." It is not difficult, as Tafuri was later to point out, to link up what Pavese was saying with what was taking place in all fields of expression: from cinematographic neo-realism to literary and philosophical realism and from the tendency towards both abstraction and realism in art to the psychological functionalism that was shortly to enter the theoretical structure of architecture. But the fifties, which ought to have been the years of realism, were prey to myths and dreams like few previous decades, with a constant search for a formula that would miraculously heal the split between culture and reality and allow the institutional instruments of politics to be supplanted, thereby opening a new channel of action by which the world might be changed. That formula was sought in town-planning, functionalism, programming, sociology and design. Design produced other myths in its turn: mass-production, flexibility, unit assembly, modularity, the synthesis of the arts, and so on. The theme of modern furnishing was one of the favourite subjects of discussion in the urban society of the fifties, just as the cineclub was its intellectual gymnasium. The speed and the numbers in which advanced projects of design began to circulate in the magazines, shops and within the home in the years immediately after the war is striking. Indeed we should ask ourselves what it meant to be a designer in those years and whence came this great unexplored capacity of Italian architects, in a half-destroyed

V

72) BBPR studio: Monument to the victims of the extermination camps, Milan, 1946.

73) Giò Ponti, Alberto Rosselli, Antonio Fornaroli, Giuseppe Valtolina, Guido dell'Orto: Pirelli skyscraper, Milan, 1956-60.

74) Bruno Sardella, Bruno Vallone, Giò Accolti Gil, Alfonso Mormile: reinforced polyester chair with drawing of supports; manufactured by Ionio, Taranto, 1955.

75) Roberto Mango: conical child's chair with black-painted iron frame, Tecno, 1954.

76) Mario Ravegnati, Antonello Vincenzi, Bubi Brunori: armchair made of bent plywood, Darbo, 1951.

77) Gastone Rinaldi: stackable armchair, Rima, 1956.

Starting from the fifties and over the last thirty years the chair has ceased to be a design object and has undergone a process of analysis, taking-apart and re-composition as an ideal architectural model.

country with twenty years of nightmare to put behind it. Undoubtedly industrial design also represented the hope of carrying out, through the instruments of production, the cultural revolution that had been blocked by political institutions and clerical tradition. Design appeared to provide an opportunity to get rid of the bottlenecks represented by the structure of the country and its backwardness, through an operation of planning carried out with a new instrument, industry, capable

78) Osvaldo Borsani: child's chair that can be dismantled, Tecno, 1954.

of acting directly on the real state of the country and changing it.

Industrial design was seen as a great opportunity to give a direction to culture, combining the restoration of the country with the opening up of a new market for quality consumer goods and secular culture, and the aim of progress with the interests of a resurgent Italian industry. It is no coincidence that the first complete manifestation of the new Italian design was the Monument to the Fallen of the extermination camps erected in the Cimitero Monumentale in Milan, designed by the BBPR studio in 1946. Design, anti-Fascism and new culture were joined with the genuine interests of industry, which saw the possibility of creating an effective image on the national and international market with an "Italian line", thus compensating brilliantly for technical weaknesses in the product in order to beat the competition.

But in reality Italian design was not born without traditions in a partly destroyed country; its origins can be found in the linguistic and planning tradition of Italian architecture in the Fascist period and in the experience of Italian architects in the Resistance, in the political radicalism of the thirties ("A new architecture for a new society") and in the impetus towards social renewal from the new culture of the left. On top of all this, design seemed to represent a way of going "beyond architecture" towards new areas of planning and into society itself.

If we look today at the products of Italian design in the fifties, they never, or almost never, appear to be either truly industrial products or authentic expressions of popular culture. The positive feelings they undoubtedly stimulate are of more an expressive than a cultural nature. Much of the design of those years is limited just by its having stubbornly sought to make contact with reality, often continuing to operate on a stylistic projection of itself, with the final result of creating what ought to have been avoided at all costs, a fifties style. But then we see that if this represented a limitation on the level of the culture of design, it formed its great wealth; even if it did not represent a revolution, it came close to it.

This style, rapidly attained and then constantly maintained apart from a few internal modifications, constituted the most appropriate form for a design that was making a deliberate attempt to translate the whole of its world of ideas into an intense, laborious and stubborn manipulation of form, as if trusting in its ability to give unity and meaning, by means of a pleasing shape, to a contradictory and in some ways uncomprehended reality.

Design tended to move towards the essential, towards the reality of the productive, technological and functional necessities of what was thought to be genuine industrial production, even though it was often a question of small-scale runs or semi-industrial products. The style consisted in a radical wearing down of the product, in its reduction to simple but aesthetically pleasing forms, in the identification of structure as the basic feature of the object and in the open display of construction materials. This was still a directly "architectural" manner of tackling industrial design, treating it as the final stage of a more far-reaching project that commenced from town-planning and passed through architecture to arrive at the object and the utensil. In reality, though, this programme often consisted of an attempt to industrialize objects of furnishing, which were seen as components of a larger container, architecture; they reflected the spatial and structural approach of the latter and were understood as the way of putting it to use.

79) Ufficio Tecnico Cova: multipurpose reading-desk, 1950.

Even in its relations with handicrafts, which represented an important post-war discovery of the significance of popular reality and its traditions, design effected a total transfiguration in terms of style, reinterpreting the constructive and to a still greater extent the expressive qualities of the materials: glass, wickerwork, ceramics and wrought iron all found their place within a stylistic panorama of modern furniture, wholly unrecognizable as traditional products. Even the prizes at the Compassi d'Oro, which in the beginning were awarded to products that showed a correct approach to design as part of a serious entrepreneurial policy and a search for advanced projects, often ended up being awarded to examples of pure style such as the Atkinson bottle, the Borsalino hat and the gadget.

Despite the operating limits within which it was obliged to act, the excesses of freedom with which it was confronted and a number of political and cultural misunderstandings through which it had to navigate, the Italian design of those years met with extraordinary popular success. Its influence was widely felt on an international level, and it gave rise to a language whose use overstepped the limits of the individual project to become the first truly popular modern style. Perhaps its ability to represent rather than resolve the problems inherent in modern production made easier its almost uncontested adoption. In this sense the phenomenon of design in the fifties had a larger dimension than the limits of the cultured project with which it began and the number of competent designers operating in the field, who were responsible for only a very small part of the overall social application. It was a phenomenon on a larger scale than the definition of design, which was taken as the starting-point for extended applications in a large number of sectors.

In this paradoxical sense, the revolution that failed in design, architecture and

80) Marco Zanuso: "Lady" armchair made of Nastrocord and Pirelli Sapsa, Arflex, 1951.

New synthetic materials such as foam rubber gave a substantial boost to the design of upholstered furniture, which then became a characteristic of Italian furniture design right up to the seventies.

81) Vases made of coloured ceramics, manufactured by Lavenia, Laverno, 1950.

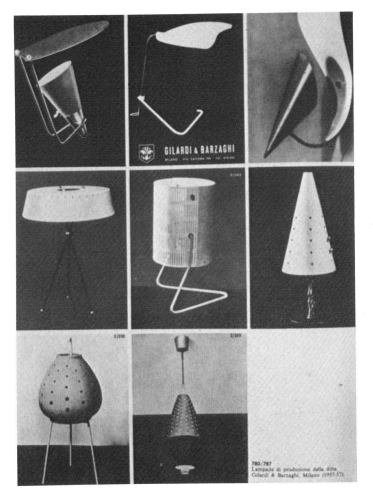

The rediscovery of handicrafts in the fifties meant for some renewed contact with the core of furnishing traditions, for others the possibility of using non-industrial techniques to produce individual objects that formally may have had little to do with the shape of traditional handicrafts.

Furnishings were developed individually in a way that was opposed to the unitary trend characteristic of the sixties. Tables, chairs, ceilings, doors, vases and lights were all designed to be expressive as single objects.

82) Lamps manufactured by Gilardi e Barzaghi, Milan, 1955-57.

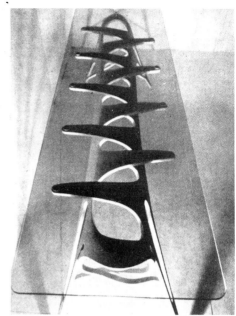

83) Carlo Mollino: glass table with bent plywood frame, 1951.
84) Carlo Mollino: dining table made out of bent plywood, Apelli & Vareso, 1951.

Carlo Mollino is an extreme example of the melting-down and re-composition of all the previous ways of designing; during the fifties he constructed a new style, almost kitsch, with new structural inventions sometimes inspired by anatomy or aeronautics.

85) Carlo Mollino: chair of shaped wood, 1950.　　　86) Carlo Mollino: chair of shaped wood, 1950.

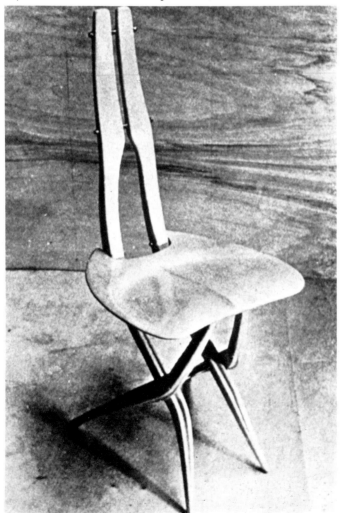

town-planning during those years achieved success as a stylistic code put to liberal and indiscriminate use. In fact there was genuine popular exploitation of a style that drew certain of its linguistic parameters from design, including asymmetry, reduction of forms, aerodynamic contours, the possibility of using simple, new, easily available materials and the adoption of elementary techniques of construction. Even small carpentry shops very quickly learned to turn out bar counters that looked as if they had been designed by Giò Ponti; modest electrical workshops soon learned to make lamps resembling Viganò's; upholsterers spent their time on models of armchairs that imitated those of Zanuso. This kind of indiscriminate and irreverent plundering permitted a renewal of form throughout the middle ranks of Italian society; the new style definitively replaced the gaudiness of Fascism and 19th-century provincialism, allowing a first sketch of modern Italy to take shape in a provisional but complete fashion.

In general this sort of quantitative overflowing was not appreciated in design circles, where it was seen as threatening the commitment to selectivity. In the same way that television altered the language of Italians in those years and introduced them to a new culture of consumption, design represented the first mass utilization of a style in Italy, and perhaps something more, for through pointed table-legs, chair-backs padded with imitation leather and surrealistic ashtrays, industry and society were testifying to a renewal of their own cultural references — a renewal of which the government of the country was not yet aware but which had to some extent already become a sign language in current use, taken out of the hands of its inventors and freely used by hundreds of more banal hands.

Thus was taken the message of optimism that Italian design expressed in almost panic-stricken fashion during the fifties, a message of faith in the country, in industry and in the imagination — a message that differed greatly from much of what would come later. Much of the optimism of those years looked like naïvety later on. The economic boom that began in 1958 represented not only the apotheosis of hopes for reconstruction, but also the start of a true secularization of Italian society and the removal of the primary contradictions of the system in which this was taking place; it caught Italian design unprepared. Industry could no longer

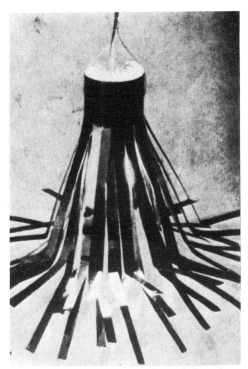

87) Ettore Sottsass Jr.: lamp cut and shaped out of aluminium sheet without welded joints, 1954.

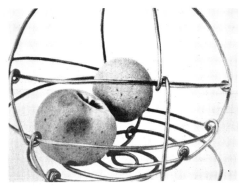

88) Ettore Sottsass Jr.: fruit bowl made of moulded brass tubing, 1952.

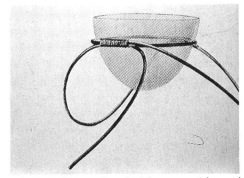

90) Ettore Sottsass Jr.: plexiglass vase with stand made out of moulded brass tubing, 1952.

89) Achille and Piergiacomo Castiglioni: "Colours and Shapes in the House of Today", Villa Comunale dell'Olmo, Como, 1957 (reconstruction, 1977).

Towards the end of the fifties Ettore Sottsass Jr.'s experiments with wire and sheet metal opened up a new vision of what objects might look like.

45

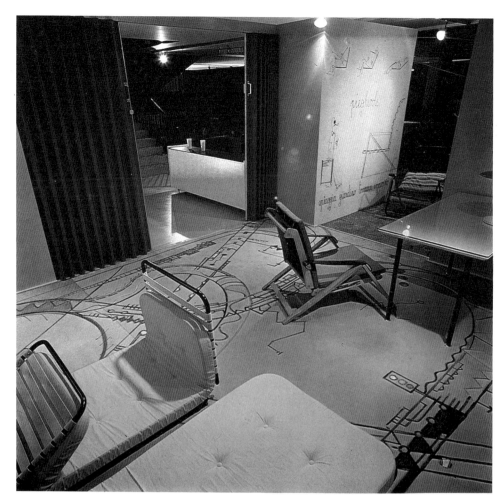

91) Marco Zanuso: elements of an apartment (bedroom for children, living-room, dining-room, terrace) with special applications of foam rubber, 9th Milan Triennale, 1951 (Centrokappa reconstruction, 1977).

92) Alberto Rosselli: kitchen of an apartment for two people, 9th Milan Triennale, 1951 (Centrokappa reconstruction, 1977).

93) Vittorio Gregotti, Lodovico Meneghetti, Giotto Stoppino: I.C.P.M. INA-CASA housing, housing exhibition at the 10th Milan Triennale, 1954 (Centrokappa reconstruction, 1977).

94) Giò Ponti: decorated window, one-room apartment at the 10th Milan Triennale, 1954 (Centrokappa reconstruction, 1977).

be considered merely as a "cultural device" to introduce by stealth the work of a few operatives in the field of aesthetics so as to promote a civilized development of the country. In reality industry was a far more complex phenomenon, endowed with a logic of its own that could only be offset for a balanced development of society by the existence of major political structures. The fifties came to an end for design with a leap in scale: Ponti and Rosselli's Pirelli skyscraper, perhaps the first design project on an urban scale, a true monument to this "Milanese" discipline.

In some ways, as compared with the severe experiments of the Bauhaus and early Rationalism, Italian design immediately after the war had a felicity all its own, as if it were seeking to resolve the world in an unheard-of manner, with a sudden wave of the sign. The critical works of Italian Rationalism carried out since the end of the thirties by important architects like Gardella or Mollino had given rise to a methodology of design that was in some ways already radical, in the sense of its having a high degree of freedom from the strict canons of the Modern Movement.

Carlo Mollino's work has turned out to be crucial to an understanding of Italian design in those years, at least from the linguistic point of view, as the result of complicated cross-breeding and contamination not only of languages but of absolutely original matrices of design. The son of a rich Turinese family, Mollino was always cultivating passions with little apparent connection to his profession;

95) Gae Aulenti: "Sgarsul" rocking-chair, Poltronova, 1962.

he was a stunt flyer and designer of aeroplanes, a racing driver and designer of the bisiluro (rocket-car) and the famous Osca 1100, an expert downhill skier who wrote an introduction to the sport, a photographer and theoretician who contributed a number of fundamental treatises on photographic technique, an inventor, interior decorator, window-dresser, designer of women's shoes, stylist, stage-designer and architect. Mollino brought all these experiences together in his design, within a complicated and in some ways mysterious system of linguistic citations and spatial structures. The trajectory of an aeroplane became the profile of a stair-case, the marks of a slalom in the snow the structure of a table, a photomontage an interior decoration. And vice-versa, in the sense that he took cues for his other research activities from the structures of his architecture. A late Futurist, he combined the gestural culture of his time with a love for movement. He suggested having the Teatro Regio of Turin travel by motor-car; he also utilized the aerodynamic style of the latter for pieces of domestic furniture. As a truly "autobiographical" artist he always used architecture as an instrument and mirror of his private enthusiasms; his sources of inspiration were fashion magazines, the cinema, luxury, sex and dreams. With great professionalism and lack of prudence, he had been the first person in Italy to penetrate deep into the quagmire of kitsch, though this was always offset by the precision and excellence of his design and by a considerable force of expression. He put forward, without misgivings, a Hollywood-style alternative to the architectural moralism of the country.

The end of disciplinary unity in architecture coincided with a total revitalization for Mollino, through external codes linked together by a structural dream which took "inspiration" as the sole useful criterion of composition. The originality of the language, entirely his own invention, was also a positive indication of a period of transition brought about by the profound crisis that enveloped Italian culture as it emerged from the war, and demonstrated extraordinary energy and an absolutely atypical approach to planning. It was this type of unknowing creativity which provoked the first opposition, the first serious proposals for alternatives to the cultural and operational limits of the day. The beginning of the end of so-called fifties Italian design came at the very moment when it began, by taking a critical look at the language and anti-historicism on which it was based, to move away from its stylistic cipher and to create new formal patterns.

At the start of the boom, towards the end of the fifties, came a ripening of criticism and expression on two different planes. This led on the one hand to the presentation of design as a discipline already stabilized in its morphology and method, almost an executive instrument of the ambitions of the forces of the left for a return to government, and on the other to a concentration on the reforging of an active relationship with history. Hence neo-Liberty was at one and the same time a critique of anti-historical Rationalism, a rejection of populism and a pointed avoidance of the stylistic tone of those years. The response to gestural design was to adopt the learned matrices of a historical culture; demagogy was replaced by an openly bourgeois culture, and style by another style. But neo-Liberty was not just an act of polemical strategy, but also a moment of identity for an intellectual and enlightened middle class that was still too fragile to take on the burden of responsibility for government and for renewal of the country.

In other respects the years of the economic miracle saw the evolution of a new way of looking at design, no longer as a positive response to a functional requirement, but as creation of the demand itself, i.e. as active intervention in the modification of behaviour, creating new functions and new freedoms. As early as 1954 Ettore Sottsass Jr. wrote: "When Charles Eames designed his chair, he was not designing a chair, but a way of sitting; that is to say he was not designing for a function, but designing a function." This stand represented one of the first indications of a track that would lead, through pop art, to the creation over the following decade of the premises for the integrated planning work of young avant-garde groups and the radical architecture of 1968. In connection with this date, it is a curious fact that the crucial points in the recent history of Italian culture recur regularly every ten years: 1948, defeat of the Popular Front; 1958, start of the economic miracle; 1968, youth protest; 1978, the Moro case and the end of unity on the left....

96) Vittorio Gregotti, Lodovico Meneghetti, Giotto Stoppino: gaming table of curved plywood, 1955.

97) Vittorio Gregotti, Lodovico Meneghetti, Giotto Stoppino: chair, 1958.

98) Archizoom Associati: "Centre of Eclectic Conspiracy", 14th Milan Triennale, 1968.

Pop Realism

VI

The beginning of the sixties was marked by the birth of pop culture. There is already a large literature on the importance and ambiguity of this movement. Whatever the overall value assigned to this phenomenon, however, the influence it exerted over the field of architecture and design was clearly very great, and in some ways quite different in nature from what is commonly thought.

Pop art is often described as an outburst of subversive and generally vitalistic fantasy, but in fact it presented itself at the beginning of the sixties as a moment of great realism, in the sense that it introduced into a context of highly specialized problems and an increasingly sophisticated linguistic repertoire the now triumphant presence, in major metropolitan areas, of the culture of consumption and the languages of mass communication. Hence the sixties were characterized right from the start by a sudden readiness to question entire systems of aesthetics and the very foundations of disciplines. For a number of years the whole of Europe was swept by a wind of cultural innovation; as students, we saw the first descriptions of English "Archigrams", Japanese "Metabolisms" and the early works of the young Hans Hollein and Walter Pichler, in which we recognized not so much a cultural matrix as hints of a new dimension to the problems of architecture, with which we identified.

When the pop artists of America went on show at the 1964 Venice Biennale, the figurative arts in Italy were still obsessed with sophisticated experiments with the non-representational; what was most striking about the American experience was not so much its aspect of neo-Dada, but that behind the neo-Dadaism of Rauschenberg or Dine could be made out the disruptive arrival of modern objects and street languages and also of a new affective tolerance for the world "as it is today". Reality invaded the field, sweeping away the shadows of the latest languages of abstraction. If Duchamp's Dada in the twenties had introduced the ready-made as a question mark with the power to unhinge the world of culture from that of reality, American neo-Dada saw in the ready-made a confirmation of the intrusive reality of the present and an exclusion of any sort of surrealistic existence.

This was not the first time something of this kind had occurred in the brief history of 20th-century culture: the architectural world of sixty years earlier, confronted by a generation that had emerged from the academic culture of 19th-century eclecticism, was formed out of an industrial situation that had grown up outside the bounds of official culture, equipped with a logic of its own and an original morphology. This was the architecture of the great factories, silos, pylons and machines which the young Le Corbusier busied himself photographing. The violent intrusion of these uncultured shapes into new codes of composition generated the most revolutionary aspect of the new-born Modern Movement, allowing it to gain possession of the real terms of the industrial system in which it was obliged to act. The pylon, a genuine industrial ready-made, would be cited as a form extraneous to architecture in the Modern Movement's code of composition. Yet as far as Rationalism was concerned, pop art represented an important modification of theory, indeed a complete about-face. Whereas at the beginning of the century nascent modern architecture had adopted the profound logic of the industrial machine, assuming a wholly rational man who would realize his creative potential in pro-

Mass communications systems, advertising languages and metropolitan iconography give Pop culture new ready-made possibilities that, unlike the disorientating "objets trouvés" of the Surrealists, are inclined to draw the spectator into the reality of consumption.

99) Advertisement for McDonald's, circa 1960.

100) Robert Venturi, Denise Scott Brown, Steven Izenour: Upper Street, from *Learning from Las Vegas* (MIT Press, 1972).

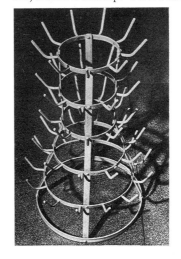

101) Marcel Duchamp: "Porte-bouteilles", 1914.

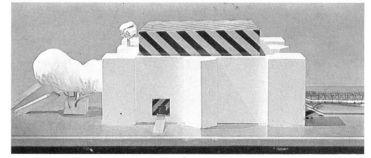

102) Andrea Branzi: "Luna Park in Prato" (graduate thesis, tutor Prof. Domenico Cardini), 1966.
103) Massimo Morozzi: "Cultural centre in the Castello dell'Imperatore in Prato" (graduate thesis, tutor Prof. Domenico Cardini), 1967.

The Faculty of Architecture at Florence gave rise to the first young avant-garde groups, Archizoom and Superstudio, encouraged by an experimental period in teaching (under Leonardo Savioli and Leonardo Ricci) and by a high level of student political debate which not only did not exclude architecture as a political instrument but thoroughly investigated the new Pop scene.

104) First exhibition of "Superarchitecture", Jolly 2 Gallery, Pistoia, 1966 (from the left: Adolfo Natalini, Andrea Branzi, Massimo Morozzi).
105) Archizoom Associati: prototype of bracket furniture, 1966.

These two groups organized exhibitions of Superarchitecture at the Jolly 2 Gallery in Pistoia in 1966 and at the Borough Gallery in Modena in 1977. Pop architecture was the inspiration, and prototypes of some of the articles of furniture displayed were eventually manufactured by Poltronova.

106) Pietro Derossi, Giorgio Ceretti, Riccardo Rosso: "Piper", Turin, 1968.
107) Leonardo Savioli: Course in Interior Decoration, Faculty of Architecture, Florence, 1967.
108) 9999: "Space Electronic", Florence, 1970.

109) Antonio Susini: "Diedron" dance hall, Cremona, 1973.

Another recurrent theme was that of large spaces where the young could gather to hear pop music — an accelerated course of integration into mass culture.

110) Superstudio: "New New York", 1970.

duction, the model proposed by pop culture in the sixties was that of a man total-ly taken up by consumption, who would fulfill his highest potential for cultural creativity in the civilization of prosperity. Thus in fifty years we had moved from a civilization of machines to a civilization of consumers. The frame of values had been turned completely upside down, and mechanisms for the inducement of need had taken over from what had been the Rationalist plan. It was in this change in the culture of planning that the great turning-point of those years was to be found.

The whole of the Modern Movement's culture of design had denied consumption any autonomous value, considering it to be entirely covered by the canons of cor-rect and rational planning. This rationality appeared to correspond to the nature of the whole industrial cycle from machine to factory to market. Now the con-tents of the project had to be completely altered so that the product could absorb all the mechanisms for inducement of consumption, commercial promotion and advertising communication. This meant mass languages instead of the strict canons of Rationalism; spiced-up and contrived designs in place of the logical designs of the Modern Movement.

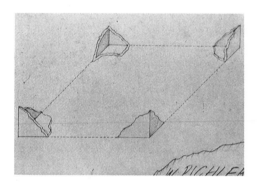

111) Haus-Ruker Co.: project for glasshouse, 1968.

In those same years Robert Venturi began his analysis of architecture in Las Vegas. In *Complexity and Contradiction in Architecture* (1966) and *Learning from Las Vegas* (1972, with Denise Scott Brown and Steven Izenour), Venturi offered the adver-tising imagery of architecture as a model of the modern city. These themes would form the basis of the first operations of renewal carried out by Italian avant-garde groups between 1964 and 1967; a diverse set of cultural and linguistic elements came together in those early projects, ranging from references to the English Ar-chigrams to links with avant-garde politics, pop music and fashion. Despite their profound political and cultural differences, Archizoom Associati, to which I belong-ed, and the Superstudio group mounted two exhibitions, one in Pistoia in 1966 and one in Modena in 1967, both entitled "Superarchitecture". These exhibitions consisted of furnishings and architectural projects, all influenced by pop culture. The topic of a cultural and dimensional updating of the themes of a new culture was made explicit in the stated definition of the exhibition: "Superarchitecture is the architecture of superproduction, of superconsumption, of superinducement to consumption, of the supermarket, of Superman, of super-high-test gasoline. Superarchitecture accepts the logic of production and consumption and makes an effort to demystify it." The highest level of integration corresponded to the greatest degree of demystification of the system; consumption and opposition now coin-cided in a new strategy, which consisted in our becoming fully conscious of the newly operative cultural and political dimension, corresponding to a new general level. Thus it may be significant that the spatial model on which we were work-ing in those days was that of the first great "Pipers" of youth culture and the new pop music. This name derived in Italy from a club that opened in Rome in 1965 facing the Coppedè quarter, which inspired a long series of imitations and increas-ingly sophisticated elaborations. Another "Piper" was set up in Florence in 1965, and my graduate thesis in 1966 was devoted to the idea of creating a large Super-market cum Piper cum Fun-fair. The following year this also became the subject of Leonardo Savioli's course of composition, while in Turin Derossi, Ceretti and Rosso designed and ran a Piper. The last in the series was the S. Space opened by the 9999 group in Florence in 1969 and still functioning today.

The spatial model of the Pipers consisted in a sort of immersion in a continuous flow of images, stroboscopic lights and very loud stereophonic music; the goal was total estrangement of the subject, who gradually lost control of his inhibi-tions in dance, moving towards a sort of psychomotor liberation. This did not mean for us a passive surrender to the consumption of aural and visual stimuli, but a liberation of the full creative potential of the individual. In this sense the political significance of the Pipers was evident as well.

The avant-garde of Italian architecture, unlike those in England, Austria and America, assumed that its own work of cultural revival had a political content. Triumphalism and analysis of the alternative uses of capital allowed pop culture to be used as a "Trojan horse" within the limited and partial setting of bourgeois

112-113) Walter Pichler: conceptual projects, 1966-69.

culture with its fragile reformist equilibrium. The naturalistic and dialectical concept of the market had now been replaced by that of its total artificiality, as the mechanism for the inducement of false needs proved able to substitute for any spontaneous demand of the market. The entire industrial system was developing along wholly artificial channels of consumption, according to a programme that seemed to ensure false but stimulating competition in the social market; in this sense the theme of generational conflict between old and young appeared, at the beginning of the sixties, to stimulate a revival of the consumer market through injections of an ideology that was artificial in the sense that it had no connection with real political conflicts but led to a dynamic differentiation of consumer goods. Archizoom Associati warned: "We should not be deceived by the turbine of consumption and its capacity for absorption, since behind it stands a marble dog-in-the-manger that will neither eat nor move." Imperialism was the hidden factor underlying this worldwide prosperity; it had to be defeated by its own weapons and not by the reformist morality of the bourgeoisie.

A new, more solid and immanent conception of the object was imposed; in place of the myths peculiar to the design of the sixties, based on flexibility, unit assembly and mass-production, the avant-garde proposed unitary objects and spaces that were solid, immobile and aggressive in their almost physical force of communication. In 1967 *Domus* published a range of furniture by Ettore Sottsass Jr. that resembled isolated menhirs standing in empty rooms, amidst the rarefied traces of what had once been traditional domestic functionality. Following the same path, we in Archizoom Associati designed not long afterwards a series of "dream beds", monumental beds with strong hints of kitsch and Eastern Islam. Provocative experiments were begun with a caustic combination of languages, with the intention of forcing a crack in the optimistic view of bourgeois progress. Archizoom Associati wrote in *Domus*: "We want to bring into the house everything that has been left out: contrived banality, intentional vulgarity, urban fittings, biting dogs." While the Milanese editorial staff of *Pianeta Fresco* played on the theme of Ginsberg's pacifistic Hinduism, Archizoom Associati proposed (in "prophetic fashion", as Fernando Pivano was to say years later) the Islamic holy war, abounding with Arab references combined with Tyrolese, Viennese and Hapsburg quotations. In the group's Centres of Eclectic Conspiracy, Zen meditation became an opportunity for theoretical elaboration of an autonomous foundation for culture: a culture that was "hard and secret, to be kept hidden in attics like weapons and good flour, for the day of the Great Celebration".

This new vision of the object also meant using architecture as "obstruction", i.e. as an impediment to the normal running of traditional urban life. The object, closed, hard and artificial, was placed across the routes of everyday affairs, creating an aggressive and ironical barricade and forcing a change in the ordering of the surrounding territory by its very presence as a "different" object, independent of the surrounding political and urban set-up. Aldo Rossi aroused great interest with his Directional Centre for Turin, which expressed in a highly refined and confident manner a similar attitude of aristocratic remoteness from the myths of urban continuity.

Superstudio, which had already devised its "Histograms of Architecture" (genuine elementary diagrams of a conceptual architecture) in 1969, came up immediately afterwards with "The Continuous Monument" which, taken to an extreme, led paradoxically to architecture's autonomy as a system of values from the mediocrity of the building industry. The monument, i.e. the authority of culture as an instrument for bringing order to the chaos of nature and history, crossed the planet as a continuous system, a sort of biblical and inevitable human destiny. Differing in their irony and lightness, Lapo Binazzi's UFOs appeared around Florence in those days in the form of large temporary structures that blocked the circulation of traffic and were inscribed with puns and riddles.

At the same time mistrust of architecture and the instruments of planning was growing; the now open crisis in the Modern Movement came to be seen as a final day of reckoning, symptom of mortal illness in a discipline that, born as the most advanced point of the system, had become its most backward sector. We even began

114) Gianni Pettena: "Wearable chairs", Minneapolis, 1971.

115) Ugo La Pietra: differentiated perception of the urban scene, 1969.

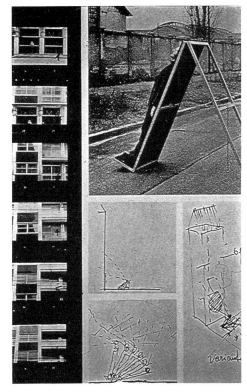

116-118) Ettore Sottsass Jr.: models of furniture made out of laminates, 1967.

119) Ettore Sottsass Jr.: "The Inhabited House", Palazzo Strozzi, Florence, 1964.

Ettore Sottsass Jr. has developed a line of research that undermines the traditional relationships within the house and instead proposes highly figurative objects with autonomous functions that should promote new types of behaviour in the home.

120) Gianni Pettena: adornment of San Giovanni Valdarno, 1969.

121) UFO Group: parade of temporary inflatables, Florence, 1968.

122) Gianni Pettena: ice house, Minneapolis, 1970.

The idea of architecture as an urban barrier together with "happening" - type political protests favoured the political absorption of Italian pop architecture, which took an active part in the youthful protests of those years whilst retaining a creative identity.

123) Archizoom Associati: "Centre for Eclectic Conspiracy", Agliana (Pistoia), 1977.

124) Archizoom Associati: "Centre for Eclectic Conspiracy", 14th Milan Triennale, 1968.

125) Archizoom Associati: "Wardrobe", 1968.

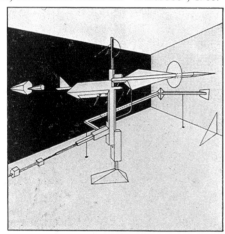

126) Archizoom Associati: "Rosa" record-player, 1969.

127) Archizoom Associati: record player with egg-cup, 1970.

to ask ourselves whether present-day society was still dealing with the problems of managing its own urban and territorial form through architecture, or whether this historical role had not now been taken over by other instruments and other disciplines.

Fifty years in which all the models of town-planning tried out all over the world had failed (Chandigarh, the English New Towns, Dwelling Units, the Swedish and Rationalist districts) began to make one think that the problem lay not so much in the quality of the design as in the very presence of architecture as such, with its spaces for observing and its metaphorical messages getting in the way of any radical refoundation of human settlements. The role of depicting history always assumed by architecture lost a great deal of its credibility in a system that possessed thousands of images and no unified form. The inability to induce its own consumption in a convincing manner, except through ridiculously monumental pretensions, produced a permanent weakness in architecture, almost an "impossibility of [its] living in the modern world".

The "death of architecture" became an open subject of theoretical debate in those years, but what was really going on underneath this was an impassioned search for new ways of using dwelling space, for it was understood that the architecture of the future would not emerge from an abstract act of design but from a different form of use. Engels had already argued, in his essay on the housing question, that the problem of a different city did not arise for the worker; if anything his problem was the ownership of the present city. This meant that there was no such thing as a workers' metropolis, only workers' opposition to the one already in existence.

Talking about the death of architecture confirmed on the one hand architecture's autonomy from politics and, on the other, suggested the possibility of a kind of planning free from traditional professional contraints.

In this way avant-garde architecture regained a sense of reality: by accepting the

128) Archizoom Associati: "Naufragio di rose" dream-bed, 1967.

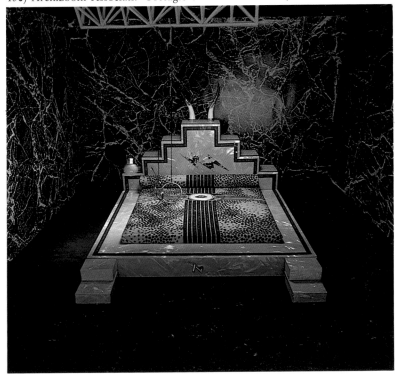

129) Archizoom Associati: furniture project, 1969.

Intervention took an aggressive, even vulgar form; neo-kitsch edged in, destroying all logical links.

130) Archizoom Associati: "Presagio di rose" dream bed, 1967.

131) Archizoom Associati: "Rosa d'Arabia" dream bed, 1967.

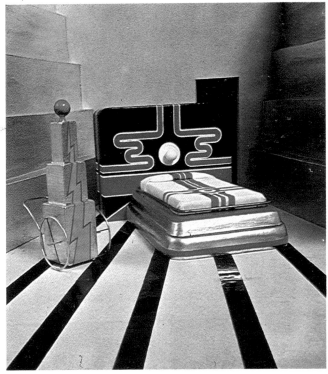

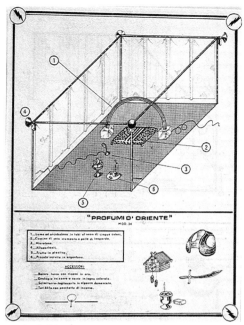

132) Archizoom Associati: "Gazebo's inc. Export-Import", *Pianeta Fresco* no. 1, 1967.

conditions of a discontinuous reality without postulating an alternative, it accepted that it had to work on a continuum of the present, refraining from making strategic projections into the future. The performance art of the UFO group and the purely theoretical designs of Superstudio, Archizoom, Pettena and the 9999 bore no hint of a further process of realization. It had been discovered that doing architecture did not just mean making houses, or constructing useful things in general, but signified expressing oneself, communicating, arguing and freely creating one's own cultural habitat, according to the instinctive right that every individual has to create his own environment, but from which the division of labour in society had totally alienated him. Doing architecture became an activity of free expression, just as making love means not just producing children but communicating through sex.

In contrast to the unwitting utopia of modern architecture and town-planning, which proposed an impossible order for the world, avant-garde architecture turned the process on its head: it assumed utopia as the given basis of the work and developed it realistically. Once the process was completed, nothing was left out; everything was accomplished in an act that was perfectly executed in itself, as pure creative energy transformed, without loss, into constructive energy. The utopia was not the end but the reality of the situation; there was no allegory in it, just purely natural phenomena. Paraphrasing Flaubert, we were able to say: "l'architecture c'est moi."

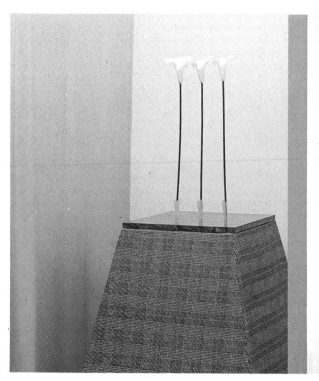

133) Archizoom Associati: "San Remo" palm lamp, Design Center, 1971.
134) Plastic gazebo lilies, 1969.
135) UFO Group: "Dollaro" lamps, 1969.
136) UFO Group: "Paramount" lamp, 1970.

Irony played a prime role in those years, allowing linguistic and projective experiments which professionalism would not have permitted before. Afro-Oriental "Gazebos" become a game for imaginative domestic micro-architecture, destined for individual meditation as a refuge from participation in the System.

137) Archizoom Associati: "Gazebos and Empty Rooms", exhibition at the Mana Art Market in Rome, 1969.

138) Archizoom Associati: "Wind Town", 1969.

Radical Architecture

VII

The term "radical architecture" was coined to describe a particular kind of research by avant-garde groups, but its use was soon extended to cover all the eccentric phenomena of the seventies. The term was borrowed from American radical culture but was used in Italy (first by Germano Celant) to indicate a new form of radicalism as an instrument of struggle and of cultural research. In fact it denoted a special use of the concept of utopia that was typical of the work of both Archizoom Associati and the Superstudio towards the end of the sixties. In opposition to the purely formal utopias of the Archigrams and Japanese Metabolisms, which clung to the old idea of a Machine Civilization by proposing a mechanical architecture and metropolis, the Italian groups conceived of a critical utopia, in so far as their use of a utopian system was purely cognitive and represented a level of clarity beyond that of reality itself. This was an instrumental, scientific utopia, one that did not put forward a different world from the present one, but rather presented the existing one at a more advanced level of cognition.

Superstudio's "Twelve Imaginary Cities" were actually a radical version of many characteristics of the present-day metropolis, each of which, developed in isolation, led to a world of absolute madness. This was a back-to-front utopia, then, literary in nature but intended as an explanation of what already exists and its perverse logic of extremes. In this climate of research, Archizoom Associati initiated, in 1969, a scientific analysis on the problem of housing and the metropolis that led to the project for the No-stop City. This study was carried out using traditional means of architectural representation, and, as in all languages, the main problem turned out to be that of maximizing clarity; in this sense utopia represented the maximum degree of communicative clarity simply because it took the form of a scientific hypothesis, i.e. abstract, theoretical and conjectural.

Operating in scientific terms also meant first ridding the research of all the qualitative parameters that typify the current concepts of design, architecture and town-planning.

This factor seemed very important to us: if we wanted to come up with a valid scientific picture of the city and the objects it contained, in order to understand the real manner in which they functioned outside ideology and history, we had to treat the urban artefact as a chemical datum, as if it were a crystal. In this way it would be possible to investigate the laws that determined its formation, independently of the history of individual crystals and of aesthetic or functional value judgements.

The most important development to which we wished draw attention was the profound change that the very concept of a city had undergone. For some time the modern metropolis had ceased to be a place and had become a condition; it was this state of being that was uniformly circulated throughout society by consumer goods. Living in a city no longer means inhabiting a fixed place or urban street, but rather adopting a certain mode of behaviour, comprising language, clothing

Our first projects were imaginary, ironic interventions. They were ideological models in the sense that they were meant to serve as pointers for architectural design, placing it in conflict with existing buildings and with geography.

139) Archizoom Associati: "Skyscraper with Rubber-Plant Leaves", 1969.
140) Archizoom Associati: "Parallel Quarters in Berlin", 1969.
141) Archizoom Associati: "Roof-Garden", 1969.
142) Archizoom Associati: "Condominium for Historic Centre", 1969.

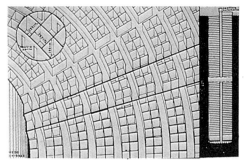

143) Superstudio: "First City: City 2000t." (from "Twelve Imaginary Cities"), 1971.

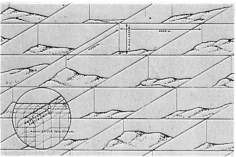

144) Superstudio: "Second City: Winding Temporal City", 1971.

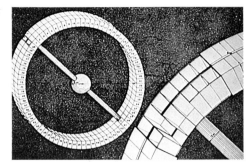

145) Superstudio: "Fourth City: Spaceship City", 1971.

146) Superstudio: "Third City: New York of Brains", 1971.

147) Superstudio: "Fifth City: City of Hemispheres", 1971.

148) Superstudio: "Sixth City: Barnum Jr.'s Magnificent and Fabulous City", 1971.

149) Superstudio: "Seventh City: Continuous Production Strip City", 1971.

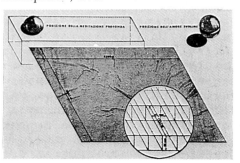

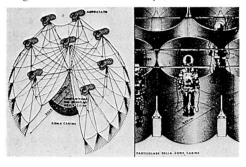

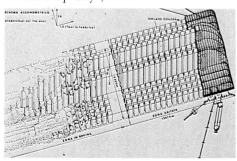

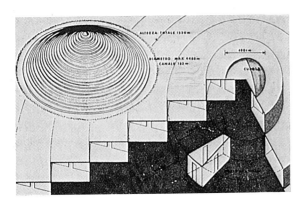

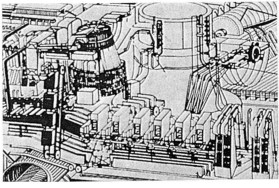

150) Superstudio: "Eighth City: Tiered Conical City", 1971.

151) Superstudio: "Ninth City: La Ville Machine Habitée", 1971.

The "Twelve Ideal Cities" along with the "No-stop City" represent the most complete analysis of urban morphology and ideology to be carried out by the Italian radical designers. Superstudio chose to use a literary idiom of a slightly enigmatic nature to illustrate the extreme consequences of the contradictions and illogicalness of the bourgeois metropolis.

153) Superstudio: "Eleventh City: The City of Magnificent Houses", 1971.

154) Superstudio: "Twelfth City: City of the Book", 1971.

152) Superstudio: "Tenth City: The City of Order", 1971.

"No-stop City" is the outcome of a scientific and deliberately non-ideological analysis of the urban product. The application of factory and supermarket typologies to residential buildings (artificial light and air-conditioning) means that architecture becomes no more than a mere form of land exploitation.

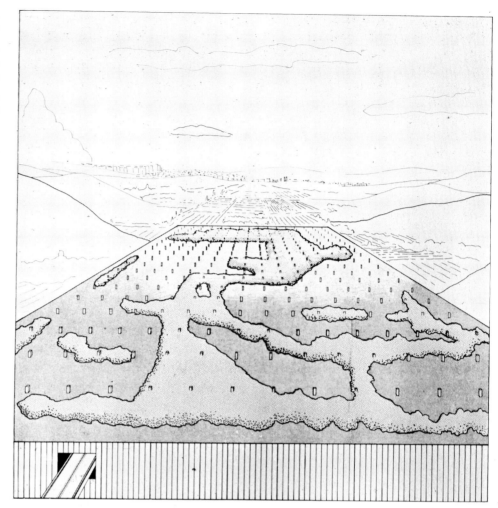

155-158) Archizoom Associati: No-stop City, homogeneous quarters, 1970.

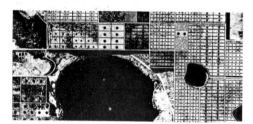

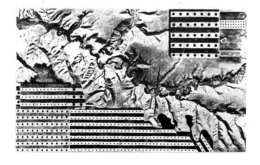

and both printed and electronically transmitted information; the city stretches as far as the reach of these media.

There no longer exists a culture outside the urban phenomenon, or the kind of social integration that it represents, since there is no longer a countryside linked to a genuine alternative culture. There is no place left that is not in some way tied to the city and its patterns of consumption. The growth of mass-production and the social distribution of merchandise have created a new "mobile urban condition", possessing all the characteristics once thought to be confined to the city, that can be exported outside any metropolitan area. The ideological sway of industrial products over the individual is total: merchandise distributes the metropolis throughout the territory. Every day industry produces cubic kilometres of city in the form of mass-produced articles, and every day many of these molecular metropolises enter into circulation, are consumed and are turned into rubbish within the old immobile cities of stone. By operating, with varying degrees of success, on this merchandise, design has become the fundamental planning instrument used to bring about a real modification in the quality of life and of the territory.

We were fully aware that the traditional hierarchies that saw town-planning as a means of introducing order into the territory had been overturned. The progressive abandonment of the traditional limits of design, now seen as a form of territorial planning, fostered an understanding of the new reality of the metropolis, which could now be defined as a market for consumer goods, and of an architecture caught up in the new dimensions of design but still unable to come up with a renewed image of itself, i.e. a credible role of its own.

Somehow we had to go beyond architecture, but only in the sense of looking for the formative process of urban structure outside its streets and squares, i.e. on the other side of the traditional city's facades, those scenes from the grand performance put on by the city. Each corner of the city, each street or square, each square metre of asphalt turned out to be different from the others, for its location was different with respect to urban points of reference. Every city seems to possess its own intrinsic quality, which sums up its merits and its defects; and until now study of the city has been limited to a survey of these histories, in the absence of any general laws to which they can be referred. Notwithstanding profound changes in life-style and the availability of technology, even the new urban developments still present themselves as a series of scenic events based on a sort of memory buried within the city, the memory of the "village".

In fact the "village" is one of those never-lived experiences that Jung would call myth and that keep the man of the great metropolises company, helping him to deal with phenomena of gigantic proportions by clinging to the viewpoint of little things and little houses. It is as if the metropolis were the logical development of an ancient pre-existence that comes down to us directly, magnified and confused but not lacking in the structural features that constitute its profound nature.

The present ideology of the city derives from the 18th-century view of it as natural object, in harmony not only with the surrounding landscape but also with the logic of nature itself, in the sense that its architecture was built in accordance with the laws that regulate the whole world of nature. The city was seen as the civilized intermediary between man and nature and between man and his society. Thus it realized that not impossible harmony between public and private, nature and technology; these different factors were accepted as components that could not be separated from one another. The result in fact is never unity but the co-existence of contrasting kinds of logic. Hence the city becomes the natural environment in which merchandise freely circulates and acquires value; urban chaos produces an effective integration of the individual into the system and develops patterns of consumption in a dynamic manner. The traditional model of the city turns out to be obsolete in this sense as well, since it corresponds to a naturalistic level of organization of the market and of consumer goods; the introduction of electronic

The youthful generation declared themselves a "different" or "alternative" culture, completely separated. "Meditation centres" became places for cultural conspiracy with an internal linguistic tension that became ever more rarified and acidic until it began to outline, instead of the principles of beat pacifism, those of the Holy Islamic war.

159) Archizoom Associati: No-stop City, homogeneous quarters, 1970.

160-162) Archizoom Associati: No-stop City, internal landscapes, 1970.

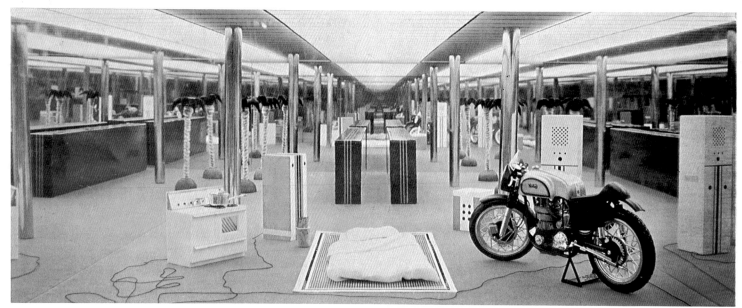

media and all the mechanisms for artificially encouraging consumption guarantees a deep penetration, as Marshall McLuhan put it, not only of the social body but of the territory. It was indispensable to get over the very idea of a limit to urban space, of its specific history and particular form. We now sought to understand the city not as a cultural unit but as a utilitarian structure, a homogeneous collection of facilities and functions for living over which is superimposed a mesh of scenic events, of spatial incidents acting as if they assigned to such functions a uniform cultural significance. The street, which divides up and serves this solid mass of buildings with their facilities and functions, has also become the dynamic backdrop against which the faces of individual buildings display their architectural language, thus acting as a formal check on individual architectural organisms.

We sought to overturn this relationship by defining the city as "a toilet every hundred metres", seeing urban space not as a group of architectural masses but as a hollow space filled with furniture. We tried to sidestep architecture, seen as an obstacle, a local accident, to track down the (non-ideological) features of a true urban theory. At a certain point we realized that the most complete expressions of the logic of the industrial system were the factory and the supermarket. Factory and supermarket are optimal and potentially unlimited urban structures, where manufacturing functions and market information are freely organized on a continuous plane, rendered uniform by a system of artificial ventilation and lighting

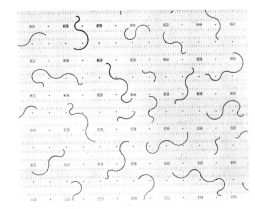

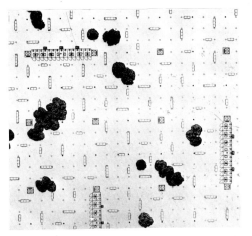

The interiors of "No-stop City" consist of ample tops equipped with artificial lighting and micro-conditioning. Here it should be possible to enact ways of living that are open and continuous and thus suitable for new forms of communal existence or for dividing up into "residential lots" to be hired out. Architecture therefore no longer represents society but contains it.

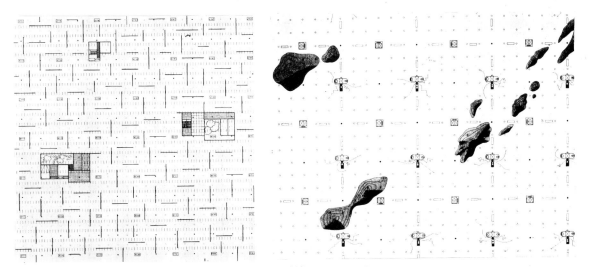

163-168) Archizoom Associati: No-stop City, residential diagrams, 1970.

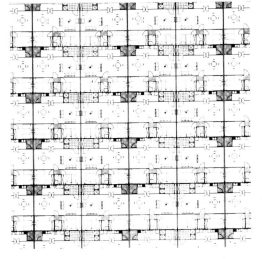

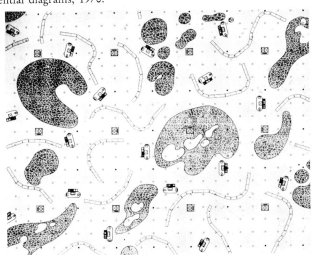

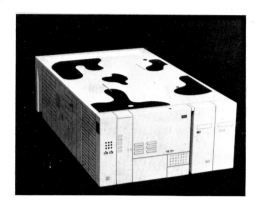

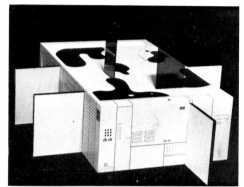

169-170) Archizoom Associati: No-stop City, habitable cupboard, 1970.

without any interference or interaction. These organisms have no external image, in so far as their facade does not constitute the linguistic structure of the building but is simply the surface of contact between two situations at different levels of development, just as the boundary of a piece of farmland does not represent the nature of its crop but just the transition between two different types of cultivation.

The No-stop City applied the principle of spatial organization to be found in the factory and supermarket, to which a scientific value was attributed because of its lack of architecture and its affinity with an extreme industrial logic, to housing as well. This resulted in a completely revolutionary urban end-product. The generalized use of artificial ventilation and illumination, which we inferred from our study of the anti-naturalistic aspects of the present-day metropolis, made it possible to remove one of the main impediments to the functioning of architecture in the city. The metropolis, and all other traditional types of settlement, are in fact based on a respect for certain standards of natural lighting and ventilation. The whole history of architecture revolves around styles or modes of composition; over the centuries languages and techniques of construction have changed, but whatever the style or period, the buildings themselves, all over the world, have been limited to some 20 to 25 metres in depth so that light and air could penetrate to their interiors. This is a structural law of architecture and the historical city alike, one that has brought about a continual fashioning of architectural blocks riddled with inner courts, facades and gaps.

By introducing the principle of artificial lighting and ventilation on an urban scale, the No-stop City avoided the continual fragmentation of real property typical of traditional urban morphology: the city became a continuous residential structure, devoid of gaps and therefore of architectural images. By the installation of a regular grid of lifts, the great levels, theoretically infinite, whose boundaries were

In the No-stop City homes are organized as residential parking lots in which the user rents temporary space. The home ceases to be a fixed place and becomes space available for social mobility.

171) Archizoom Associati: "The Neutral Surface", habitable cupboard, 1972.

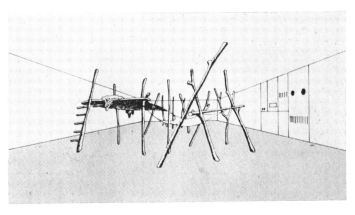

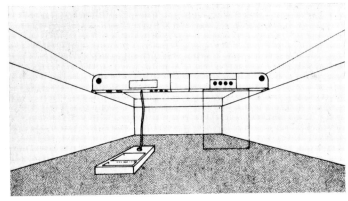

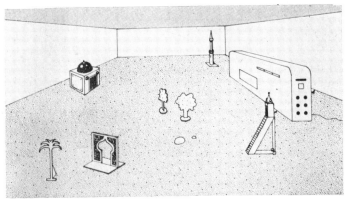

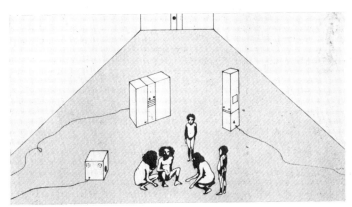

172-175) Archizoom Associati: residential car park, 1971.

176) Archizoom Associati: "The Neutral Surface", habitable cupboard, 1972.

of no interest whatsoever, could be laid out freely in accordance with differences in function or new forms of social aggregation.

The No-stop City, as the apex of industrial integration, also boasted the advantages of a freedom from the problems of architectural form, which allowed it to become a neutral and utilitarian structure. Traffic, whose territorial organization was separated from urban form, could be handled in an optimal fashion: the No-stop City guaranteed a "car under the house" and the highest possible concentration of population. Problems of energy and waste were provided with a theoretical solution.

Nature, outside the urban pattern, could regain its complete autonomy. The individual would no longer see it contaminated by architectural elements, which always tend to intrude a cultural significance; instead it would remain a neutral field, devoid of values and open to a wholly physical and undistorted awareness. It this sense the No-stop City was a mental project, a sort of theoretical diagram of an amoral city, a city "without qualities", as Hilberseimer would have described it; but it represented an important radical analysis of architecture and design, in which we took to its extreme consequences just that rational planning whose demise we were predicting, demonstrating its political inability to follow that guiding thread which united its most radical experiments: "an architecture that is no longer architecture" in the words of Hannes Meyer, or the "dead houses" of Adolf Loos. Jumping over the intermediate category of urban organization represented by architecture, the No-stop City struck a direct channel between the metropolis and its furnishings. The city became a collection of beds, tables, chairs and cupboards; domestic furniture and urban fittings were made one.

We answered all the utopias of quality with the only feasible utopia: that of quantity, the only one which by adopting the perverse logic of the system was also capable of bringing it to the point of crisis or at least of total transformation. In those years Mario Tronti had expressed his opposition to all improbable social utopias by coining the workers' slogan, "More money, less work." We went on to claim that the greatest inventions of modern architecture had been quantitative inventions; perfect examples are the skyscraper and the housing unit, which subvert the equilibrium of the bourgeois city by undermining its form. This revolution did not succeed only because of the limited application of these two models.

By carrying out a ruthless quantitative accumulation of levels on a traditional parcel of urban land, the skyscraper has totally destroyed the traditional relationship between plan and elevation. The skyscraper still has four facades only because it is located on a very small plot of land: potentially it could extend in all four horizontal directions as impartially as it does vertically. It is still architecture just because of its exceptional ventilation and illumination. In practice it is a segment of the No-stop City.

The housing unit is an example of a different kind of operation: here a city has been taken, with all its traditional components, and stood on end. In practice town-planning has been eliminated by its assimilation within an architectural megastructure. The result is that the difference between the individual building and the city has vanished; there are no longer different architectural forms corresponding to different urban functions. Shops, theatres and schools no longer possess a form of their own, but have become homogeneous parts of a single story of amenities indistinguishable from those used for apartments.

The nihilistic logic of the maximun quantity was the only logic of the system in which we were living; instead of denying this logic, we decided to make use of its inner workings to achieve a demystification of all its ideals of quality, and at the same time to carry out scientific research into the real nature of the metropolis, avoiding the cultural battles over putting it onto "a human scale".

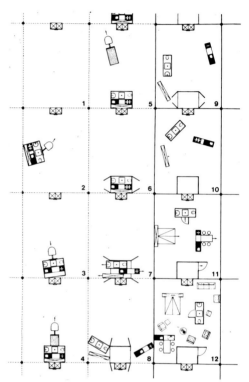

177) Archizoom Associati: residential parking lot, 1970.

178) Archizoom Associati: No-stop City, assembly scheme for a homogeneous quarter, 1971.

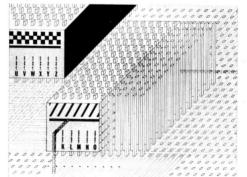

The Joyful Science

VIII

The debate over the death of architecture, which was carried on by supreme theoreticians like Manfredo Tafuri as well as by radical groups, bore several interesting implications for research in the field of design. There is nothing strange in the fact that, while talking about the death of architecture, everybody was engaged up to the hilt in producing new hypotheses of design, for this death was an assertion of a conceptual kind that carried research beyond the bounds of traditional composition towards new urban forms and towards a new way of looking at the history of architecture. Architecture was no longer seen as a perennial institution but as a fragile cultural activity, circumscribed, and often at odds with history.

Criticism of the Modern Movement was also and above all expressed by taking Rationalism to an extreme, with the intention of exposing the underlying contradictions of the movement, along with the fragile nature of its apparent unity of research. It was no coincidence that Archizoom Associati wrote at the time:

"Superonda" was a curved piece cut from a polyurethane block and then covered in mock leather to be used as a bed, divan or chaise longue.

179-180) Archizoom Associati: lights for the Yamajiwa competition, Tokyo, 1968.
181) Achille and Pier Giacomo Castiglioni: "Mezzadro" seat, Zanotta, 1957.
182) Archizoom Associati: "Superonda" sectional couch, Poltronova, 1966.

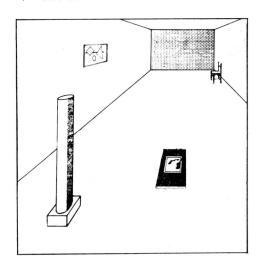

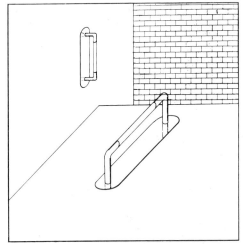

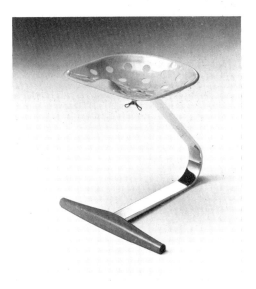

183) De Pas, D'Urbino, Lomazzi: inflatable armchair, Zanotta, 1969.

"The ultimate aim of modern architecture is the elimination of architecture itself." And the No-stop City was nothing but the furthest outpost of Rationalism, reached by pushing all the data of the project to the point of paradox, almost in hyper-realistic fashion; the elimination of any striving for quality led towards an architecture that was all function, to the point of its being swallowed up by the latter.

But more careful analysis of the crisis in modern architecture revealed that it was the result of two active processes, one negative and concerning the discipline and its foundations, the other positive and regarding the figure of the architect and the change it was undergoing in industrial society. The two processes seemed to be concomitant and interdependent; the growing emphasis on the professional skills and techniques of the architect started with the gradual decline of architecture as a disciplinary institution, and at all events with the crisis in its historical code.

In effect, the Modern Movement had postulated a profound change in the role of the architect, making him increasingly indispensable: he was involved at all levels, from plan to structure, to territory, to design, right up to co-ordination of production, the social role of industry and eventually the planning of society as a whole. The dramatic history of Albert Speer no longer looked, from this point of view, like the abnormal case of an architect acting outside his sphere of competence, but on the contrary seemed an exemplary parable of the first true modern architect: the technocratic architect who uses his instruments to adjust the delicate machinery

184) Ettore Sottsass Jr.: "Grey room", Poltronova, 1969.

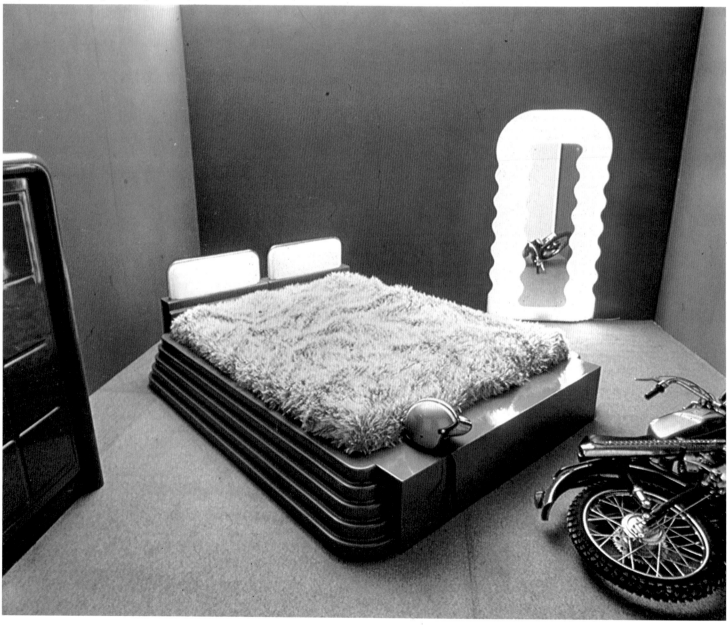

185-186) Gaetano Pesce: "UP" series, C&B Italia, 1969.

187) Gatti, Paolini, Teodoro: "Sacco" armchair, 1969.

Products of this sort brought about a change in the way furniture is conceived and built: "Sacco" by Paolini, Gatti and Teodoro was made of a large leather bag filled with polystyrene balls and could thus fit any way of sitting; the pneumatic armchair by De Pas, D'Urbino and Lomazzi represented the most advanced attack on consumer excess in furnishing objects. Likewise Achille Castiglioni's armchair-kneeler contributed to the subject of change in the way objects are used. Objects by Ugo La Pietra speak for the designer's effort to find alternative uses for electronics and mechanics, in his view to be seen as cultural rather than technical instruments.

188) Archizoom Associati: "Safari" sectional couch, Poltronova, 1967.

189) Archizoom Associati: "NEPP" chair, 1968.

of society, as a manager who takes some logical mechanism and analytical processes from modern architecture but disdains the tools of the discipline.

The architect's ability to make use of this rational logic, as if it were free energy made up of a feeling for construction and figurative skill, has made him ready to tackle any problem, so that he has become an invaluable figure in a society devastated by the division of labour, where each member follows the biased logic of his own specialization. Thus we come across architects in government, technical management, scientific research, marketing, planning, politics, sociology, teaching, fashion, ecology and in general all activities that require, apart from specialization, an overall vision of a plan of intervention.

So the project as a potential unification of human technologies became the social model of technological programming; the architect changed from a constructor of artefacts to a co-ordinator of human and technical resources. This historic transformation of the architect into "roving technocrat" has left a profound mark on the whole story of modern architecture, to the extent that the Modern Movement itself can be seen today as the framework for this conflict between technocracy and disciplinary constraints; in other words, the conflict between architect and architecture.

The fact of feeling themselves to be architects even in places that are apparently remote from the ones delegated by the discipline in the past, actually constitutes a new and characteristic feature of modern architecture; hence industrial design should be seen as part of a much broader phenomenon and collaboration with industry set against a much more complex background than that of merely designing the shape of mass-produced articles. Technological research in fact, as far as its creative application in the sector of furnishings is concerned, has led to the presence of architects within the industry becoming almost indispensable.

Towards the end of the sixties and throughout the seventies, radical groups played a major role in an important internal transformation of industrially produced furniture. Their readiness to tackle technological problems not as immutable truths but as the data of an open-ended problem facilitated a substantial renewal, even

190) Ugo La Pietra: wind machine, 1968.

191) Ugo La Pietra: audio-visual helmet, 14th Milan Triennale, 1968.

192) Superstudio: "Bazaar" couch, Giovanetti, 1968.

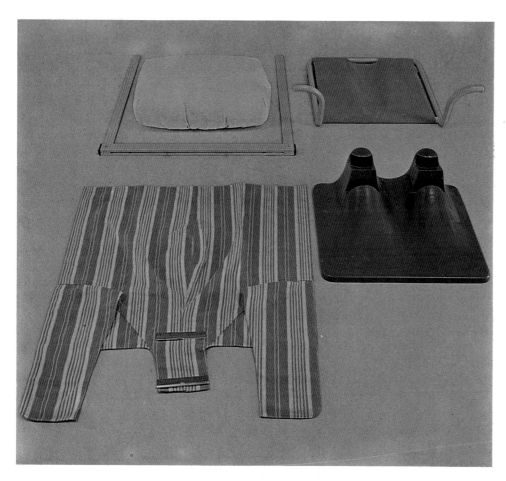

193-194) Archizoom Associati: "AEO" seating system, Cassina, 1975.

In these products, for the first time the structural components are made with separate and specific technologies. The object achieves its unity only when it is assembled.

195) Superstudio: architectural histograms, 1969.

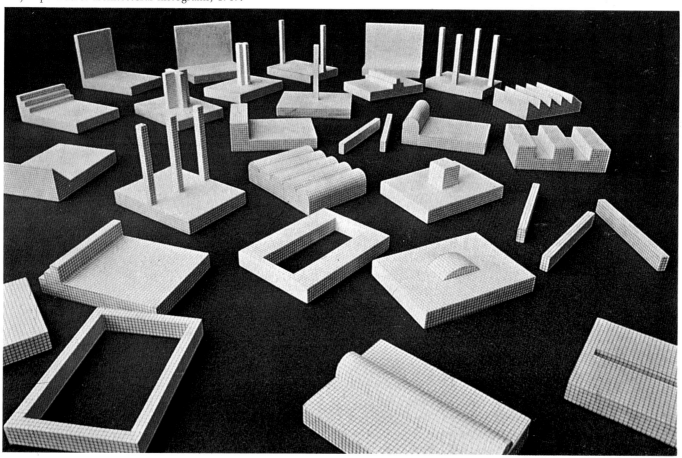

196-197) Archizoom Associati: "Mies" flexible chair, Poltronova, 1969.

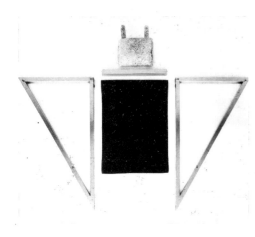

This strange elastic chair made of a sheet of rubber held between two slats was a comfortable counter-proposal to the over-upholstered furniture of the times.

in conceptual terms, of the idea of the industrial product.

Since the war, the guiding principle common to designers and manufacturers of furniture alike had been the idea of the definitive product, i.e. the object that fulfilled a particular function once and for all. The idea that mass consumption would lead to a shift in the market towards a limited and closed number of definitive objects, acceptable to all and suitable for any setting, had pushed design research in the direction of extremely unitary and technically advanced objects, made out of a single material (plastic, wood or metal) and produced in a single colour. A good example of this approach, both for the success it met with and for its wide distribution, was Joe Colombo's plastic chair for children, which brought together all the most advanced features of this kind of utopia. At best it represented the idea of the object cum tool, of the product made, apparently, in a single moulding operation, of a single material and single colour — the ideal product for a stereotyped society of consumers.

The unity of form actually referred to a unity on a larger scale: the cultural unity of the market, which was a constant assumption for the design of the sixties. A uniformity of design, then, mirrored the uniformity of consumer society. This myth was rapidly blown by the growth, from 1968 onwards, of widespread political and, to a greater extent, cultural conflict; the result was a progressive and relentless dismembering of the social body, until the current situation was reached where many minor markets are linked to semantic groups, as Charles Jencks would call them, which cut across social classes diagonally, giving rise to "families" distinguished from one another by mode of conduct, tradition, religion or fashion. We shall return later to this phenomenon, which has been given the name "post-industrial".

In direct correspondence to this kind of cultural and social rupture came the loss of formal and technical unity in the product; it was re-examined in the light of a new view of design, analyzed into its structural components, each of which was shaped in accordance with an appropriate technology, modified in function according to the possible uses permitted by new patterns of social behaviour, stripped of all material consistency and often transformed into a hollow image of itself.

The new objects, often produced in close collaboration with the research centres of the most progressive furniture manufacturers, took their place in the home without any pretense to be part of a more far-reaching formal design aimed at bringing new order to furnishings; on the contrary they pointed, by their autonomy, to a rupture with the surrounding environment in terms of both behaviour and style. It was aptly said that an age without bearings had begun, and out of this open system came a new tolerance that did not merely envisage a creative attitude on the part of the customer but often set out to stimulate such an attitude through the eccentric appearance of the product. The new range of commodities, then, no longer claimed to be offering a definitive product but openly admitted its partiality and made its presence felt on the basis of a new functionality and uncommon cultural value. Designs no longer presupposed any kind of uniformity, but on the contrary made a continual cultural selection of their customers.

In this way the internal technical transformation of the product proposed a reining back of design, a diminution of the planned part of the house, which became, in its most important area, freely available to intervention by the user. Thus a strategy of total planning was replaced, by a point-by-point strategy in which vitality was injected into the space at a few centres of radiation.

In 1973 Dario Bartolini of the Archizoom group designed this motor car composed of a minimal carrier that could be lengthened by additions to the hydraulic suspension, allowing a container to be added.

198-201) Dario Bartolini: sectional automobile with variable wheelbase (graduate thesis, tutor Prof. Pier Luigi Spadolini), 1973.

Mass Creativity

IX

202) Henry Matisse: "Dancers", 1910 (reproduction on a 1:1 scale handmade by Studio Alchymia in 1980).

In 1972 Emilio Ambasz organized the show "Italy: The New Domestic Landscape" at the Museum of Modern Art in New York. Archizoom Associati and other radical groups designed an environment for this exhibition in which there was an empty room with a little girl's voice describing a bright, colourful domestic scene. We wanted the visitors themselves to imagine what this environment might really be like, rather than come up with the answers ourselves. "Living is easy" was the slogan devised to encourage this.

203) Archizoom Associati: "Empty Room", New York Museum of Modern Art, 1972.

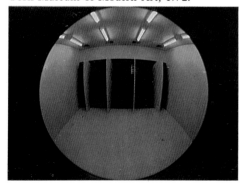

During those years the concept of space had been gradually replaced by that of void, seen as a sort of neutral expanse open to individual and collective modification. Inside the great fitted-out levels of the No-stop City, the house was turned into a "cavity with fittings" in which the individual was free to use his creativity in arranging his own habitat. The house became a great gymnasium in which the best possible conditions for technical comfort were guaranteed, but where there was no pre-established pattern of distribution.

The theory that the void provided the greatest degree of flexibility and liberty was a sort of *tabula rasa* our generation had made, or was trying to make, of all previous experiences, in an attempt to build a new foundation for design and architecture by putting them to a different, alternative use. In 1967 Ettore Sottsass Jr. had written an article entitled "How to save beauty from the dust and the piranhas", which described the houses of the beat poets as places free of objects and books, i.e. empty parking places for a life that was to be re-invented from scratch.

In 1972 a major exhibition of Italian design entitled "Italy: The New Domestic Landscape" was held at the Museum of Modern Art in New York. The radical Italian groups, Archizoom, Superstudio, Strum and Ugo La Pietra, were invited, along with Zanuso, Bellini, Aulenti, Sottsass, Rosselli and Joe Colombo, to create their own environments. Archizoom Associati took the theme as an opportunity to make a genuine declaration of intent: they set up an empty grey aseptic room in which a voice described a luminous and brightly coloured domestic setting. In place of a complicated technology for living that suggested unlikely futures for the home, the group preferred the public to imagine, at the prompting of a vague narration, its own house. Our slogan at the time was "Living is easy", and by this we wished to convey the effort we were making to get away from the constraints of the formal avant-garde, which all over Europe continued to churn out machines for living; the slogan conjured up the right to live freely in the space of one's own home, unfettered by all the patterns of behaviour imposed by traditional culture.

It was in this sense that we spoke of a movement for the liberation of man from culture, meaning by culture all those already existing moral, aesthetic and religious values that condition man by limiting his freedom of action and of judgement. "One culture less" was the direction in which the vanguard of architecture should be moving, in the sense that its eventual aim ought not to be the proposal of a new framework of cultural or behavioural values for society, but rather its liberation from character structures, in the Reichian sense, allowing expression of its own creative potential.

Cutting down on culture or, as we said at the time, the technical destruction of culture, seemed to be the intention behind every single one of our actions, which were aimed at eating away the values of traditional design from the inside, not as a mere act of cultural provocation, but as a step towards a liberated society. In this sense the work of the avant-garde was indirectly political, since it tended to modify individual and collective attitudes towards revolution by paring away all the traditional structures of culture and morality. Reality is devoid of values in so far as it is generated by an economic system without any goal; by attributing values and meaning to reality and to history, culture, aesthetics and morality prevent man from acting freely in their regard.

The reduction of reality to solely quantitative parameters was the direction in which the avant-garde was moving: it must be recognized that "the sea has no meaning", as Alain Robbe-Grillet had written. To do this we wished to change the social use of culture itself. Morton Feldman has drawn a highly significant parallel be-

An important point of research for Global Tools was the work that Riccardo Dalisi undertook in the Traiano district of Naples. The result was a series of structures, objects and living spaces that Dalisi called "poor technology", which partially confirmed the theories of the creative potential of the general public.

tween the composers Luigi Nono and John Cage: Nono, realizing that society did not work, wanted art to change it; Cage, seeing that art did not work, wanted it to be changed by society. Nono put forward art as a model for society and Cage envisaged a modification in the social use of art, handing it over to society as a free psychomotor activity, already totally dismantled from the technical point of view and completely in keeping with individual creativity and the bustle of life. Hence the regaining of all one's own creative faculties as a natural right was for us the new social use of culture; the production of models of behaviour by culture is a feature of the organization of production in society. Hence to deny culture meant to reject work. We realized that all culture is repressive because the social distinction on which it is based is repressive: the functional separation between the producers and the consumers of culture. If all men are equal, only an improper distinction exists between consumer and artist, based on the social division of labour. Cultural atrophy, we claimed, was an extremely serious form of social alienation, which prevented the production and consumption of one's own creative activity as a manifestation of spontaneous communication.

Just as spontaneous creativity was the myth towards which our action was directed, so the liberation of man from labour was the utopia towards which were working not only the avant-garde of the sixties, but also the historical avant-garde movements and indeed all conflicting social forces in general during the 20th century. In fact it looked to us as if the destiny of the industrial system was to lead, by different and incompatible roads, towards the same kind of final solution: the abolition of labour. To the worker, indeed, the rejection of work seemed to be the utopia that formed the basis of his economic and hence social growth; the businessman's response to this refusal appeared to be the automation of assembly lines. By getting rid of human labour, capitalism was laying the foundations for a society transformed into pure consumer force. And in an industrial society, consumption is a creative activity in that it is a producer of values and models.

The society of leisure or, as the technicians called it, of the death of work, was the final stage of the entire process; but it was certainly not a solution for all the political and social problems of our age. We merely saw it as a necessary outlet for the conflict over work, a qualitative leap in the evolution of the industrial system and its still largely anthropomorphic mechanisms of production, still tied to manual technology. But the leisure society was also a society in which a new mass-production for the intellect was beginning.

What is called leisure or free time today is based on the need to re-establish a temporary psychophysical equilibrium that allows recovery of one's own possibilities for production. Present-day culture serves to concentrate in a product, or a book, an accelerated process of meditation, a function proportional to the time available for consumption. The need to get across a message in a fraction of the time lies at the bottom of the whole technical evolution of modern culture. The quantitative reduction in working hours and the proportional increase in free time, and therefore in the time devoted to the cultivation of one's own creativity, would have thrown today's cultural organization into confusion, causing it to break down. The slow pace of cultural consumption and production would have removed the premises of the synthetic game on which the whole of the message of art is based, laying bare its own morphological complexity without the need for it to be packaged in an obligatory communication, as a pure manifestation of natural human communication.

The historic appointment with a mass-production of the intellect had to be made once the structures and technology that make culture into a product for specialist, not utilizable by the masses, had been undermined and dismantled. It seemed ab-

208) Riccardo Dalisi: experiments with poor technology, Naples, 1973.

"The Planet as a Festival" by Ettore Sottsass Jr. predicted the use of the earth's sub-equatorial areas for endless dancing and enjoyment, with architecture contributing enormous palaces and fairgrounds; it was the illustration of a myth of a society with endless free time and was often referred to by radical groups of those years.

surd that years of study and a very strict social selection were required in order to make music, architecture, poetry, painting, sculpture, dance or any other physical activity: every possible technique of cultural reduction adopted by the avant-garde had to act as a minus sign that led to a decreasing of the distance between the operator and his own action, between meaning and physical dimension, putting a stop to the continual critical excision to which our actions are subjected by morality and culture.

It was against the general background of these conceptual and operative problems that the idea was born, in 1973, of founding a counter-school of architecture and design that we called Global Tools. The school set out to bring together all the groups and individuals in Italy who represented the most advanced realms of radical architecture, under a unified programme of research. Rather than uniform contents, our goal was to channel the energies of the avant-garde in the direction described above, energies which were already staggering towards an uncertain maturity after the years of the great creative compression triggered by 1968.

In other words, Global Tools was put forward as a general strategic programme for a core of highly diversified creative forces, each of which had its own theoretical bias. Despite this, an organization that would represent, even formally, a unified front aimed in general terms at the promotion of public and private creativity would have made it possible to give a positive meaning to many group experiences that were now drifting towards different goals and in directions that were often already fixed or taken for granted. We worked on this idea for three years without a break, carrying along the entire younger generation of Italian architects and even some critics and artists. We set up a co-operative as a legal instrument for managing this type of organization; we prepared a large number of work programmes based on the themes of the body, and construction, communication, survival and theory, we managed to obtain some private financial backing. In November 1974 we met in Florence and officially founded this counter-school of architecture and design, making the announcement in the January 1975 issue of *Casabella*. We talked of a non-school rather than a counter-school, the first attempt to provide a yellow pages for culture, a handbook of temporary and private workshops in the cities, agencies of social diffusion for all creative activities linked to the use of techniques of construction and all the sub-architectural systems employed in shaping the environment. The working structure derived from the idea of a secretariat that would bring into contact people and groups working in the direction defined as liberation of man from culture. In this way levels of seasonal availability would be set up as a gymnastics of recovery, as an expedition into an unexplored stratum of the human and creative resources of a city. This meant founding a school to get rid of school, teaching in order to learn, organizing to ensure discontinuity, coming together to get across the personal, giving ourselves a history in order to remain a pure phenomenon.

Perhaps the closest parallel, in this sense, was the experiment that Riccardo Dalisi had been carrying out for some years in Naples; his research derived from a general theory that he had christened "poor technology". This started out from the supposition that, by taking away from technology the logical code of its internal relationships even temporarily, the door was opened wide for constructive energies; going over the safety limits of techniques permitted entire strata of the population excluded until then from the *ars aedificandi* free access to constructive (and creative) processes. In effect architectural culture has been invigorated by the identification between building structure and mental logic ever since the 18th century. Structural correctness and incorrectness has always been the secular ideology that has split the world of constructed things; in fact the only constructive energy accepted up to now has been science, while ignorance has never been recognized as potential energy of the opposite sign—like Heaven and Hell, which imply each

209-210) Ettore Sottsass Jr.: "The Planet as Festival", 1972.

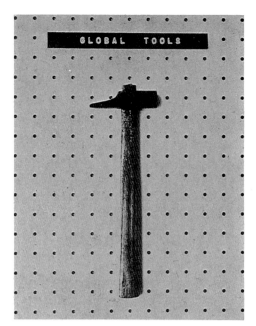

211) Cover of the internal bulletins of Global Tools, published in Milan by Giorgio Ferrari's gallery "L'uomo e l'arte", 1973.

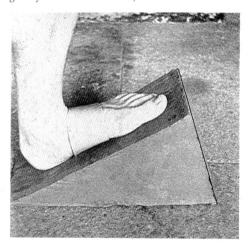

212-213) Global Tools: seminar on the body, 1975.

other's existence and only make sense as a pair.

Riccardo Dalisi carried out experiments in the spontaneous teaching of groups, giving the street urchins of Naples the chance to manipulate the structures that make up objects and environments. In a way his work was not just another attempt to work out a method of teaching based on spontaneity but a probing of unexplored depths of energy. Dalisi's experiment was not social or didactic, but scientific, in that it aimed to try out the liberation of collective creativity "in the field", without pushing it in the direction of a new aesthetic language. The use of poor and half-wild children from the Traiano district in Naples should in fact be understood as an attempt to find subjects as little polluted by culture as possible, so that their creative reaction would be the closest to a state of total spontaneity. In this sense the discoveries of poor technology were models of understanding for a potential public retrieval of the productive processes of culture; with its total unburdening of meanings and goal-oriented patterns, it was an experiment in communication outside the canonical codes of cultured languages.

But complex theoretical problems were beginning to crop up. The discovery and listing of simple manual techniques carried out by the American neo-encyclopaedists (the *Whole Earth Catalog*, the *Dome Book*, etc.), on which Global Tools was based, was born out of the urge to reappropriate and control techniques that guaranteed a minimum of survival and at the same time new qualities; but it still looked to us, or at least to the most observant of us, like a theft of information, a narrowing of the possibilities promised by an alternative use of capital. In some ways these "poor" techniques even looked like a dangerous revival of the virtue of poverty. If this was what had happened, then the work of Global Tools would have amounted to no more than the creation of a new pattern of consumption, reductive, punitive and reformed, but essentially fated to offer society a new strategy of poverty, as an ideology that promoted the virtue of renunciation, highly relevant to the growing energy and cultural crises that assailed the western world in those very years. In other words we did not want to tread the same path as the Bauhaus, which revived and regenerated the destructive force of the historical avant-garde as analytical and rational energy, transforming it into a new language and a new design intended to propose a model for man that was suitable to industrial production. The solution to this contradiction seemed to be a rejection of systematization, in which Global Tools was presented as both organization and discontinuity, as liberated design and as rejection of cultural productivity. The myth of social creativity, of liberation from labour, towards which the avant-garde movements were working as vectors for reducing the "character armour" of the present, also led to an elitist range of operations stripped of values in their intentions but in fact the ever more widespread and official language of a cultural category that seemed to be already settled. We saw that instead of being deserted, the avant-garde became more crowded every day; its languages were spreading more and more widely and at the same time losing any real innovative content.

In fact the contradictions of the system in which we live were being directly reflected in our work, stripping it of that partiality out of which it had emerged and which was its *raison d'être*. After about three years of schemes and discussions, Global Tools broke up in a painless and irresolute manner like a boat that

Global Tools was an avant-garde co-operative, a counter-school of architecture and design encouraging creativity in free laboratories by they intended to open in Milan, Rome, Florence, Naples and Padua.

The first and only study seminar that Global Tools organized was dedicated to "The Body" (the others were to have been "Construction", "Survival", "Communication" and "Theory"). By constraining certain movements and expressions of the human body, others were supposed to be freer to develop. Radical architecture, supposedly dedicated to liberation, thus ended up studying inhibition, even if this was supposed to develop hidden resources.

had lost its sail. In any case, the general conditions of society around us were changing; the energy crisis was giving way to an increasingly tangible social and political crisis. The unity of the left, on which the whole of progressive post-war culture had been based, was being replaced by more and more serious conflict. Left-wing opposition to Communism, which brought together Socialists, Radicals, extra-parliamentarians and even armed extremists, led to a profound change throughout the political world in which the cultural avant-garde had worked. Terrorism was increasing, with its rhetoric and anti-Communism, making a clean sweep of any critical stand as sophisticated and basically defenceless as ours was. Faith in the unified direction of the changes under way collapsed in the face of an ambiguity made up of many different factions and the vigorous growth of a new right-wing culture that we watched spring up out of the bosom of the "logical left", a sign of a decadence of ideas and of a moralism that became more and more closed from fear of seeing what was really going on.

In 1975 Alessandro Mendini's editorship of *Casabella* also came to an end. The magazine had been a point of reference and meeting-place for all the radical groups, including Global Tools, over the previous four years. Mendini was succeeded by Maldonado, who edited the magazine with varying success until 1981, when Vittorio Gregotti took over the position. In the same year our group, Archizoom Associati, broke up, and many of its members moved to Milan; Superstudio became part of the university and began a long and silent period of didactic research. The UFO group was dismembered, and only Lapo Binazzi kept up a resistance as solitary as it was tenacious by opening up shop in the centre of Florence. The majority of the other groups disappeared; everyone was to follow his own road as best he could. In 1976 Ugo la Pietra made a last appeal to his fellow travellers from the pages of *Domus*, in an article entitled: "Where has radical architecture gone?" Alessandro Mendini answered him (somewhat tardily) at the Bologna conference in 1978 that accompanied the exhibition "Absence/Presence", by announcing the official death of the movement.

214-215) Enzo Mari: "Proposal for Self-Design", Simon International, 1974.

Other efforts made to involve users in design included Enzo Mari's simple build-it-yourself systems.

216) Cover of *Casabella* no. 377 (May 1973) on the occasion of the foundation of the Global Tools co-operative.

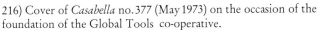

217) Silhouette of the founders of Global Tools, 1973.

Dress Design

X

218) Mario Terzic: "Visit to the Renaissance: Classic Dress in Pure Silk", *IN* no. 8, 1972.

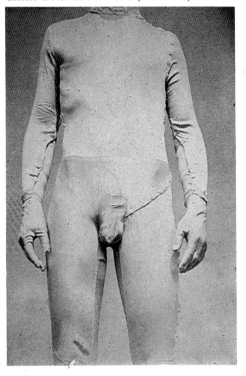

219-221) Archizoom Associati: "Dressing Design: Nearest Habitat System", 1971.

The first "Nearest Habitat System" designs consisted in very slight bodystockings over which decorated overalls could be worn.

If radical architecture was dead, the energy it had stirred up was still alive and kicking. Global Tools' work on theory and planning had been preceded and accompanied, from 1970 to 1973, by a highly interesting series of new research experiences, conducted by individuals as well as groups. Following the channel cleared by the pop acceptance of phenomena from mass culture, and ready to explore new frontiers of design opened up by the so-called death of architecture, Archizoom Associati initiated projects in "dress design". Tackling the design of clothing meant moving outside the limits of the discipline and beginning to concern ourselves with mass communications and new forms of consumption.

By that time, fashion had ceased to be a model of dress proposed by a few opinion makers and supinely accepted by the masses; it had become a free circulation of symbols and citations that seemed to arise spontaneously from an increasingly broad spectrum of society. The uniqueness of fashion and its rigid seasonal patterns had been replaced by the simultaneous presence of more than one fashion. Potentially, there were as many fashions as there were people who wished to create their own self-image. The myth of being in fashion seemed to collapse: everyone could be; the place of the old *maisons de haute couture* was taken by the "diffuse design" of a new manner of dressing.

We saw the new definition of the metropolis as arising out of the consumer market and not the traditionally accepted areas of town-planning. Dress design signified a branch of urban design where it was possible to experiment with the new dimension of a collective culture as a specific requirement of the project. Our entry into the world of fashion was partly the result of an attempt to find a new intermediary between the necessities of production and the stimulation of consumption, or between industrial design and peculiarities of taste. It was not a question of looking for clues or predictions of taste, and still less of translating current fashion into

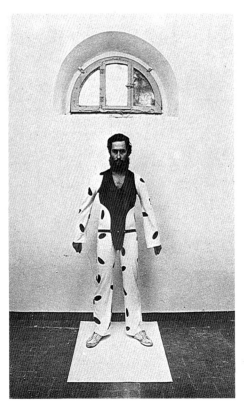

222) Nanni Strada: ethnological collection, 1971.

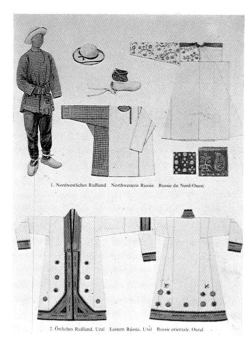

223) Max Tilke: *Folk Costumes* (Zwemmer, London).

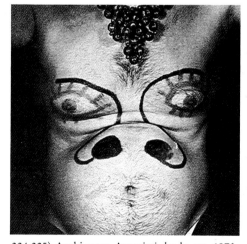

224-225) Archizoom Associati: body art, 1972.

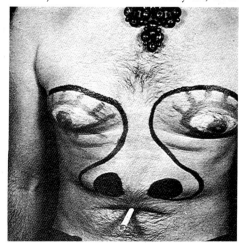

The experiments of Nanni Strada, based on studies by Max Tilke, resolved the problem of separating dress from fashion by rational constructive methods.

design, but rather one of adapting to a different cultural pattern that affected the organization of production as well as design. We were not interested in definitions of fashion based on surplus (economy, sociology, politics, history) or on scarcity (psychology, marketing, caprice); we also avoided interpreting the phenomenon in a merely eulogistic way, as a linguistic sector that in some mysterious, mediumistic fashion anticipates the marks of history and culture; or alternatively as a sector that records the same events with a delay of ten years. Instead we looked on fashion as material culture, a creative field with its own independent foundation and endowed with its own strong artistic intuition; at the same time we saw it as a theoretical model for a new kind of production, given the name post-industrial by theoreticians in that the all-embracing logic of mass-production, which represses changes in taste as an unpredictable and irrational variable, was giving way to a search for flexibility. It was no longer society that must resemble the factory in every way, but the factory that had to try to adapt to society.

From this axiom, which we call fashion but which signifies a different pattern of development and role for industry, design can derive a different strategy of research, aimed not so much at an optimal solution for the problems of production, but at a symbolic attachment between man and his household articles.

This was not an experiment without precedent: exchanges between the two cultures have formed part of the history of the Modern Movement. In his 1911

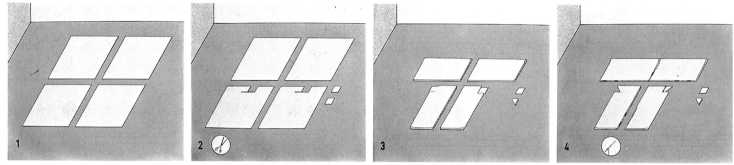

226) Archizoom Associati: assembly sequence of a 4-piece garment from the film *Dressing Is Easy* (Abet Print, produced by Politecne Cinematografica), 1972.

The film Dressing Is Easy *was a cartoon showing how to make do-it-yourself clothes with square pieces of cloth (and no waste) and simple sewing lines.*

essay "Architektur", Adolf Loos wrote: "Many will have been perplexed... as to the parallel that I draw between architecture and tailoring." The radical change that he introduced into the very concept of design, as Benedetto Gravagnuolo has pointed out in his book on Loos, was based on considerations that did not belong to the realm of building, but to that of inhabiting.

In general, architects who have shown an interest in the design of articles of clothing have used methods already proven in the field of classical design: they have designed "objects" that have a rigid shape of their own; by wearing them, the individual subjugates his own "shape" to that of the clothing, i.e. to a geometrical and rational form. Our experiment took a different path: we were not operating as stylists looking for a new line or the clothing of the future, or any kind of "different" dress; instead we were investigating a different way of using clothing.

The system of dress that we exhibited at Moda-Mare-Capri in 1973 was an open structure made up of two basic articles of clothing: a scanty costume, elastic and coloured, that could substitute for underwear while remaining a complete article of clothing in itself, the minimum basis of urban dress, and a coloured and very loose overall to be worn over the costume cum underwear or over other clothes.

The problem of planning industrial production in a market as "spontaneous" as that of fashion was a new and fascinating one. Production, with its myths of infinite runs and uniformity of the consumer market, had to deal with a highly advanced culture of consumption, where each consumer tended to be different from the others and to re-invent the product through an original mechanism of combination and assembly. Design was obliged to concentrate not on the production of fashionable clothing, but on basic clothes out of which fashion could be

227-229) Archizoom Associati: examples and details of the system "Dressing Is Easy", 1972.

The system could supply over 60 different models of skirts, overalls, blousons, trousers, etc. The seams were decorative as well as functional.

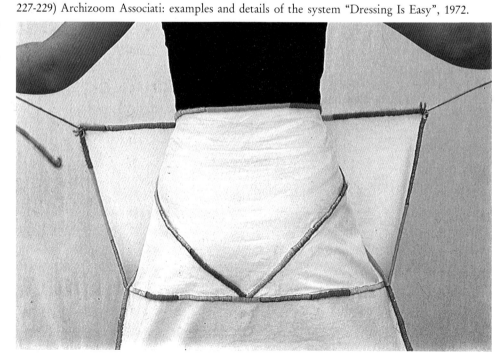

230) Andrea Branzi: component system of hats, *Domus Moda* no. 1, 1981 (from the exhibition "Hats and Shoes by 12 Designers" devised by Alessandro Mendini and Patrizia Scarzella, mounted by *Domus* and Borsalino).

created, in an artisan process controlled by the consumer himself. The goal, then, was a product that would stimulate but not exhaust the creativity of its user.

A good example of a modern industrial process of this kind is furnished by the functional and cultural use to which blue jeans have been put over the last thirty years. Born as a functional article designed for large-scale industrial production and devoid of any really expressive features, but practical and robust, blue jeans became the "neutral base" out of which developed the most advanced fashions of the post-war years. Existentialists, Teddy boys, Rockers, Beatniks and Hippies, and the youth movements of the sixties in general, each used blue jeans in a different way, that is to say in the context of different and often contrasting modes of behaviour and cultural patterns.

The clothing industry, forced to follow in the wake of these giddy changes of style, was obliged to reproduce by machine what had been thought up according to an exclusively decorative logic. Not possessing a design culture of its own, i.e. not basing its product on the best utilization of machines and materials, the clothing industry behaved like a gigantic tailor's workshop, reproducing a hand-crafted product on an industrial scale. In the film *How Gogol's Overcoat Is Made*, exhibited at the 15th Milan Triennale (1973), the production situation in the clothing industry was analyzed, showing among other things how at the end of the assembly line of a major manufacturer there was a mock client who tried on the clothes. Hence the whole cycle of the tailor's workshop was reproduced in a large factory, still concluding in a client who actually put the product on. Anthropomorphism, waste, regression to the artisan level: this is what happens when the logic of pro-

231) Enzo Mari: lady's hat, *Domus Moda* no. 1, 1981.

In 1981 the magazine Domus *dedicated two issues to fashion and illustrated the advanced work of a few designers. Others were asked to design specific objects, such as these hats co-ordinated by Patrizia Scarzella.*

duction and the logic of consumption come into conflict.

With a view to making logical and progressive use of textile technology, outside the narrow limits of the current range of commodities produced by the clothing industry, Nanni Strada had for many years been carrying out advanced research based on an analysis of the way clothes are put together. Starting out from Tilke's ethnological studies of dress, where clothing was examined for the first time in terms of its structure and its use of textile materials, Nanni Strada postulated new habits of dress linked to the internal structures of the clothes themselves. In 1971 he had put together a completely revolutionary ethnological collection, based on quantitative exploitation of the most modern technology for producing tubular knitwear, spot assembly of seams through a welding process, elimination of linings and above all abolition of anthropometric sizes by means of a rational system of ties and pleats. The decorative effect of the product arose out of its inner structure; in his presentation of the project in *Domus*, Tommaso Trini wrote: "Although the structure of this fashion design is fundamentally technological, and intends to stay that way, it does take into account the process of communication in which it cannot avoid becoming involved and handles it by proposing an iconic structure (its images) which, apart perhaps from the choice of colour, is closely tied to production. Thus the visual details are evidence of how the clothing was manufactured." The very term "ethnological collection" tended to underline the revival of a skillful way of doing things — very different from the folk-fashion of those years — in which the solid method of basing construction on the materials and the structures of the clothing was drawn from ancient popular traditions. At the

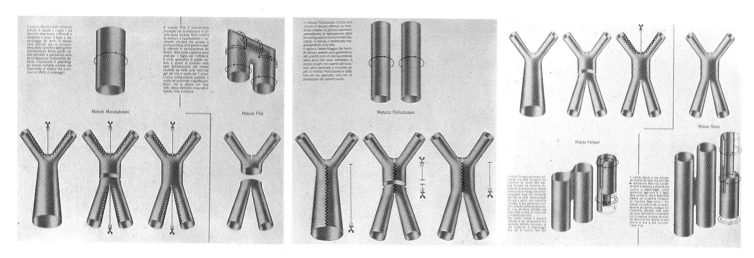

232-236) Nanni Strada: *The Cloak and the Skin* (directed by Davide Mosconi, script by Tommaso Trini, production Bossi S.p.A. and Bloch S.p.A.), 1973.

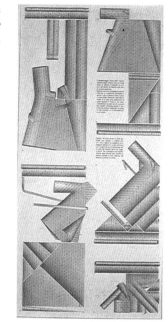

The "Cloak" is made of layers of quilted cloth cut along straight lines, the seams being simply placed edge to edge and overstitched.

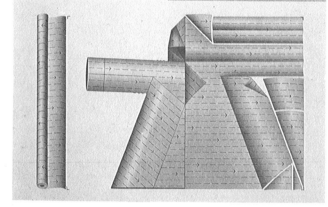

237) Nanni Strada: image of the "Cloak", 1973.

238) Nanni Strada: image of the "Skin", 1973.

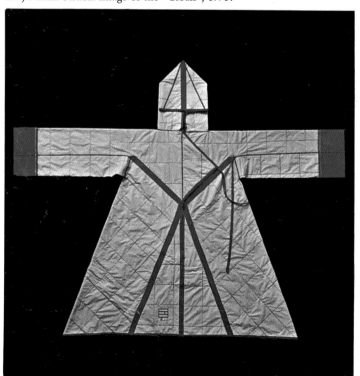

same time these were resolved in the form of a distinctive visual image.

In 1973 Nanni Strada made a film with Clino Castelli called *The Cloak and the Skin*, in which he presented two combined systems, i.e. two different levels of clothing, outer and inner. The outer one was formed by a "mantle" whose structure was determined by the mechanics of its single-piece construction, and the inner one was made out of elastic knitted material, exploiting the technology of tubular knitwear to the maximum, so as to obtain the first complete one-piece body-stocking produced in a single manufacturing operation. Thus the skin was a continuous elastic sheath that could be compressed into one hand and would stretch to three or four times its length, taking shape only when worn.

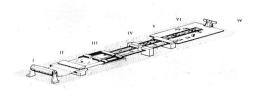

The film analyzed current production methods for elastic sheaths, starting with the Pilot method normally used in the manufacture of tights; this involves the creation of cylinders linked together to form a C which can be used, after cutting, as the upper or lower part of the suit, without any seam appearing in the separate parts. Then came the polytubular method based on different combinations of two elastic cylinders that can make up the tunic or the entire article of clothing, but still sewn vertically along the lines of junction of the two cylinders. Next was the Pantysol method which allowed the production of tubular structures in the form of a Y. These can be used as whole tunics, tights or bodices, but cannot be made into a complete overall without seams; that is, they cannot be produced in a single operation. The method developed by Nanni Strada and Clino Castelli was based on an extension of the Pantysol method, permitting fabrication of an H-shaped tubular structure in which the cut for the neckline corresponds to the crotch of the tights.

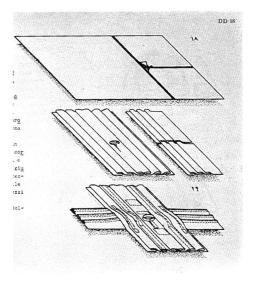

In a move towards rational analysis of the techniques of making clothing, as constituent structures of the product, Archizoom Associati produced a do-it-yourself system. This system, called "Dressing Is Easy", was based on the use of simple techniques of assembly, stitching and cutting (always rectilinear). The first logical step in using the raw material involved taking a square of cloth as the basic element. By making a series of folds in this piece of material, almost in the manner of origami, it was possible to use all of it without waste, and also to avoid all the different sizes normally associated with anthropometry. By renouncing the traditional methods of tailoring, it became possible to make the best use of new and simple technologies and elementary systems of production, deriving the very criteria of design directly from these. Here it was essential to view the fabric as a continuous strip of constant width, and not an indefinite area out of which sections could be cut in a haphazard manner. This fundamental awareness of the realities of production taken as the basis of design was subsequently applied by Dario and Lucia Bartolini in their entry for the 1975 competition for the national costume of Libya. Their design, which was rooted in an elementary organization of textile machines, allowed highly expressive results to be obtained from an extremely simple technological base and mode of production.

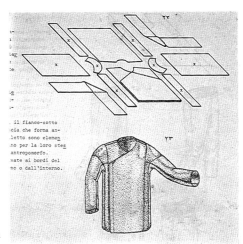

239) Dario and Lucia Bartolini: "Libyan National Dress", 1975.

This group of studies and proposals was made the subject of numerous publications, including the monographic issue of the review *IN* that we produced in 1974, in which many exponents of so-called international radical architecture tried their hand at clothing design and the critical analysis of its social function; among them were Ettore Sottsass Jr., Ugo La Pietra, Ugo Nespolo, Superstudio and Mario Terzic. Working professionally in the field of dress design, Dario Bartolini produced, in 1977, a basic study of alternative techniques in the manufacture of clothing for the Centro Design Montefibre. It was entitled "This Too Is Clothing" and was followed by a series of studies of elastic structures and of the standardization of anthropometric sizes based on a different system of measurement, with highly original and methodologically rigorous results. Nanni Strada also continued to do work of a high standard, seeing dress design as a problem of inculcating logic into the formal and technical production of articles of clothing.

In 1981 *Domus*, edited by Sandro Mendini, devoted two special issues to fashion, in which various contributors made a cultural analysis both of current production and of alternative and more advanced designs for clothing. The previous year, the revived Milan Triennale had devoted a special section to the phenomenon of

This project made use of simple techniques that combined mass-production with the features of handmade garments and local traditions.

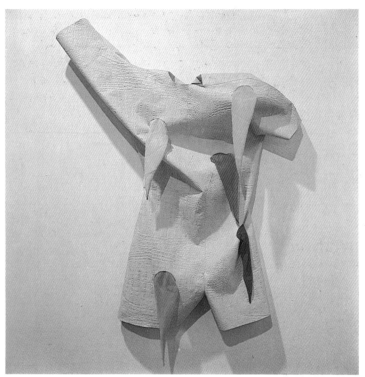

240) Cinzia Ruggeri: "Statue of Liberty" overalls.

241) Cinzia Ruggeri: garment made from a fabric with liquid crystals, 1982.

242) Cinzia Ruggeri: kinetic solution for dress.

Cinzia Ruggeri's dress designs make use of new expressive technologies: the liquid crystals take on different tones of colour according to environmental conditions and body temperature. The kinetic effect is achieved by means of chromatic sequences and a band of polarized light.
The "Statue of Liberty" garment includes micro-ventilators inserted into the dress so that the sleeves puff out.

243) Cinzia Ruggeri: evening dress with insertion of Leds.

fashion, by this time one of the major structures of modern society, whose influence on metropolitan culture was an actively beneficial one for both environment and individual. The presence of many high quality fashion designers, including Missoni, Versace, Krizia and Ferrè, made Milan one of the capitals of the fashion world during the seventies; the unfailingly high standard of their products was an indirect confirmation of the quality of design culture in the city. Throughout the decade Fiorucci, one of the most progressive and well-informed cultural milieus in Milan, served as a point of reference for the vanguard of design.

Design "Primario"

XI

The seventies were marked by a painful series of "crises"; in place of the critical optimism of the previous decade, we witnessed not only a gradual falling off of creative energy in the cultural debate, a direct consequence of the energy and economic crisis, but also a questioning of all the design assumptions on which we had been working. The conceptual stage through which the arts were passing was at one and the same time a political reaction to the commercialization of culture, an internal analysis of aesthetic action and, even more, a silence after so many political proclamations.

As early as 1970 Superstudio had responded to an invitation to contribute to an issue of *Design Quarterly* devoted to "Conceptual Architecture" in the following words: "In their attempt to communicate theories, designs and construction, the architectural reviews may be setting up a bogus form of communication by means of semantic redundancies, reaching the point of publishing (nothing but) themselves. Hence it becomes an act of clarification to attempt a logical extrapolation of the process and to propose an object that is identical with the very act of its being made public. We propose a HIDDEN ARCHITECTURE as conceptual architecture: an architecture that is only an image of itself and of our unexploitable aphasia." This proposal, which sets out all the limits that "drawing-board architecture" was to demonstrate only a few years later, was in fact suggesting a black-out of design and of communication.

While organizing the International Section of Design at the 15th Milan Triennale in collaboration with Ettore Sottsass Jr., we decided to present, instead of objects, an anthology of films concerned with the criticism of ideas in design and architecture. We marshalled the available creative resources of Europe, America, Japan and Australia, receiving more than 140 films, which we copied onto videotape. The result was a cross-section of current critical thought in the world of design and architecture, a unique exposure of the grey matter inside the temple of the "good industrial product".

The reflections of those years, unfortunately carried out in the shadow of increasingly obscure contradictions, were turned towards the search for a "safe place" for the arts, a proper foundation for intellectual action and the specific meaning of aesthetic thought. In some ways this was a genuine refounding of cultural debate, with a search for new frontiers of design, and in other ways it was a reinstatement, after a period in mothballs, of old means of expression; the most mature results of this attitude were to come, in fact, at the beginning of the eighties with the trans-avant-garde and "painting-painting", and with the return to historical design in architecture. In some respects Italian post-modernism, so different from the international movement discussed by Charles Jencks, bore a similarity to the reaction against the Futurist movement that had taken place fifty years earlier in "900" and "Metafisica", with their attempt to put back together again a frame that would encompass both art and design. But in midstream, i.e. at the height of the conceptual obsession, all of us were committed to the great quest for ties of logic outside specific forms and for conceptual values that would throw light on the roots of our own design work. Very small aims again, but ones that showed great potential for changing the environment by getting a hold on and vertically extending channels of original analysis.

The economic crisis augured an increasingly poverty-stricken horizon, i.e. a landscape devoid of all superfluous values. The reduction in the material possibilities for using design to enrich the environment by means of acts of formal saturation led to a search for new qualities connected with a conceptually more sophisticated usage of simple technology, i.e. technology already available but requiring further

244) Romanesque cathedral: interior of the Abbey of Saint-Martin-de-Canigou.

The Romanesque cathedral represents an experience that is connected with the bodily perception of space (light, sound, perfume, colours), whereas the Renaissance, transferring the concept of space to the universe of ideas, modified its relationship with the human body, reducing it merely to a basis for perfect proportions.

development through basic research work. This was a "cool" kind of work, but one that left room for user to reflect on use and on the independent development of the message. That myth of previous years, public creativity, survived only as the potential for a "deep echo" of the new instruments, and as part of an exchange of views, though at a high level, in a society of intellectuals. In reality it was the end of the dream of quantitative, or mass, communication and a return to the quest for a new culture — a new quality, certainly, but one that no longer belonged to the utopia of the "great machine" and of mass-production for the intellect.

The breaking down of traditional limits of design that had been going on throughout the radical phase and the new climate of conceptual culture led, towards the middle of the seventies, to the maturation of a group of theoretical and design experiments that we called "design primario". This was not the first time we had needed to find a name for a series of new experiences with design; it had already happened with radical design and dress design. The critical emphasis that we placed on a general comprehension of our research activities and on the need to communicate them in a clear form have always led us to take care over the educational packaging of our work, not so much to invent new labels as to round off the research at the informational level. Le Corbusier would not have been what he was without the effort he made to communicate his ideas regularly and clearly.

The starting point for primary design was this: industrial design, as part of the Modern Movement, and indeed the whole ideology of design, is based on the conviction that the fundamental quality of a setting or an object lies in the correctness of its structure, i.e. in the balanced harmony of form, structure and functional requirements; from this equilibrium derives, in a direct and almost mechanical manner, the expressiveness of the product, its social value, and in the case of architecture its fitness for habitation, i.e. the quality of its domestic space. The origins of this conviction lie far back in time: in the Renaissance, in Christian morality and in the spirit of the industrial revolution. "Design primario" stood aside from this tradition, shifting attention onto other structural qualities, which we called "soft"; to the way of thinking of both the Modern Movement and classical architecture, these were generally wholly secondary, and included colour, light, microclimate, decoration and even odours and background music. These are all experiences of space that are not directly assimilable to the constituent qualities of an environment or an object, but are linked instead with the physical perception of space, i.e. with its "bodily" consumption. In this way new attention was paid to the user's real sensitivity of perception, bound up more closely with the direct consump-

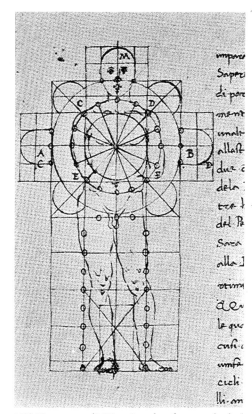

245) Francesco di Giorgio: plan for a cathedral based on human proportions.

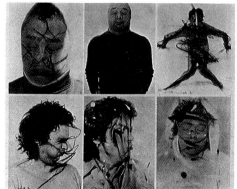

246) Arnulf Reiner: "Face Farces", 1968, Vienna.

247) Clinio Trini Castelli: "Gretel's Soft Diagram", 1977.

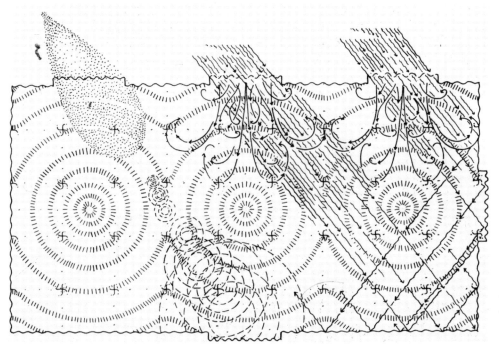

Wittgenstein's analysis of the "void", as perceived in the house he designed in 1926 for his sister Margarethe Stonborough, confirmed the presence of a complex system of "soft" structures that fill space and make it culturally active.

tion of soft structures than with the grasping of an architectural composition and its sophisticated allegories of form.

Our bodies are capable of actively processing the data that they receive from our surroundings, transforming them into experience and culture. We know today, and the whole experience of body art has confirmed this, that our perception of the environment is an essentially physical process, i.e. carried out to a large extent by our bodies, which are not crude instruments for picking up sensations and stimuli to which only the intelligence of the mind is able to lend order and meaning; our bodies, on the contrary, are active instruments of cultural elaboration, capable of acting within a systematic complex of sensory cues, processing and evaluating them independently of their allegorical or ideological significance.

248) Centro Design Montefibre: general diagram of the Fisiolight, 1976.

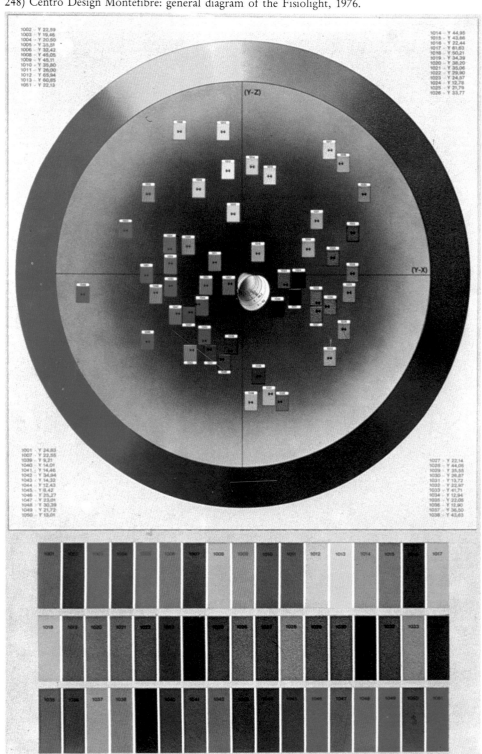

The space in which we live is no longer a space of perspective, in the sense that there is no longer any distance between us and reality, no critical gap, no bulwark of theory in which to set the ready-made filters of a solely mental judgement. The distance between us and others, between us and politics, between us and the market, has completely vanished, and our experience takes place by direct contact, through the pressure on our skin, the active surface of a sensory circuit that immediately organizes it as historical experience.

The city itself is an integrated space, in which we move like fish in the sea, no longer needing to represent that sea in allegories of form, as it is no longer an external setting for our experience but a dense ambient made up of a ceaseless flow of bodily experiences. Information itself, as Marshall McLuhan pointed out, is absorbed directly through the pores of our skin, just as environmental qualities are consumed by the body. To some extent this type of experience harks back to a conception of architectural space predating the Renaissance. The Romanesque cathedral, for example, cannot be perceived in isolation from several factors that are apparently subsidiary but in reality fundamental to the perception of its significance: these include the sudden change in temperature between interior and exterior, the nature of the acoustics, the highly unusual lighting that filters through panes of stained glass and even the smell of the unventilated building, heightened by candles and incense. The whole of this complex of soft structures forms an integral part of the definition of this type of monument, not only in its everyday experience but also in the monumental entity's complexity of expression. This sort of directly physical experience of architectural space was completely abandoned in the revolution of the Renaissance, which shifted the relations with the human body from the direct sphere of the senses to that of proportions; architec-

249) Centro Design Montefibre: model of room with a curtain producing a warm effect, 1976.

250) Centro Design Montefibre: model of room with a curtain producing a cold effect, 1976.

251) Centro Design Montefibre: model of room with a curtain producing a neutral effect, 1976.

ture moved towards an exclusively ideological definition, whose perception is based on a philosophical concept, that is to say a form of thought that is physically realized in space.

In 1977, against a background of research into primary design, Clino Castelli published in *Data* an analysis of the famous building designed by Ludwig Wittgenstein in 1926 for his sister Margarethe Stonborough. His analysis was conducted on the basis of the symbols, materials and structures of the building, and was concluded by a new critical hypothesis, represented by "Gretel's soft diagram". This diagram rendered the real "fullness" of that conceptually empty space visible by revealing all the "soft" structures that were interacting in it. In Castelli's words: "The 'soft' environmental diagram of the drawing-room of the Palais Stonborough visualizes parameters connected with subjective perceptions and with their use. The hidden aspects of environmental organization, such as the conditions of heating, sound, lighting and colour, are no less important in determining the environment's quality than those of space and composition, which belong to the traditional canons of architecture. In the diagram we find distribution of heating by panels in the flooring, vibrantly coloured surfaces, diffusion of artificial light sources, the murmur of the forced exchange of air on the threshold of the two French windows and the natural light that filters through them. The way space is organized to reduce relationships to their elements, such as the tension between symmetry and asymmetry, the waves of sound made by the steps of a visitor as he makes his way toward Gretel's apartment and the aura of her perfume that drifts through the leaves of the steel door."

Shifting our attention to the recovery and control of these physical parameters of space, we tried to take a step towards a new definition of the real quality of the environment in places for living and working, away from the abstractions to which much of modern architecture has fallen prey. The quality, for instance, of a building's air-conditioning, or its insulation from noise, constitutes a condition of the use of space that is not merely technical but genuinely cultural, simply because modifying any one of these structures profoundly alters the expressive value of the ambient. When Ettore Sottsass Jr. and I mounted an exhibit entitled "Italian New Renaissance" in Rotterdam in 1980, we decided to introduce as the sole element of "window dressing" (apart from Brian Eno's background music, *Music for Airports*) a strong smell of mint, which was intended to fill the space around my prototypes and embroideries as a critical comment on the setting.

But to design colours, lights and decorations, instruments different from the traditional architectural ones of pencil, square and compass were required. To register and control this kind of parameter, other working instruments were indispensable. "Design primario" was also concerned with the invention of new instruments, which had to be worked out in advance and to contain preselected information; in other words they had to be open structures within which individual designers or users could proceed further.

An example of this kind of preplanning is the research that we carried out in 1976 into "controlled-light curtains", i.e. a system in which decorated and coloured curtains would not alter the physical and colorimetric characteristics of sunlight. This system, called "Fisiolight", could be used as a perfectly neutral decorative filter or, alternatively, produce a predominance of warm or cold light according to the different demands on the product. With Fisiolight the curtain ceased to be the mere supplement to decoration that it had always been considered (in 1724 the manager of the royal dye-works of Gobelins wrote in a treatise: "Curtains ought generally to be the same colour as the chairs, and their borders the colour of the paint") and became an active filter, capable of exerting a qualitative control over the natural lighting of the ambient, without losing any of its decorative function. Natural daylight is an important physical factor for settings like schools or hospitals and can be conserved intact even through the filter of a decorative curtain which, while toning down the intensity of the rays of light, preserves the colorimetric characteristics of sunlight in their entirety. Thus in Nordic countries, where the light of day is particularly rich in violet components, it was possible to correct for this presence by a filter that enriched the spectrum of warm red and yellow

252) Centro Design Montefibre: Fisiolight controlled-light glasses, 1976.

light. In conditions where sunlight was excessive, it was possible to adjust the filtered light to add blue-green components, to create a more restful environment.

This system of natural ergonomy of daylight was based on an original and practical procedure: an initial range of colours was identified, forty-seven in all, arranged in various shades; these colours were then marked as points within a simplified projection of the chromatic solid. Having chosen the design or pattern to be reproduced on the curtain, one had to identify its colours from the colour chart and then join the corresponding points by a broken line, producing a polygonal and irregular geometric figure. By calculating the barycentre of this figure one obtained the actual chromatic effect of the curtain; if the barycentre fell around the axis of the greys, i.e. in the centre of the circle, this meant that the chromatic effect and illumination of the curtain was neutral, in that it did not affect the quality of the sunlight. If the barycentre fell in the blue-green or red-yellow sector, it meant that the chromatic effect of the filter was cold or warm, respectively. In order to modify the chromatic effect of the curtain, it was sufficient to shift the barycentre of the figure by altering its corners, i.e. the colours selected for reproduction of the pattern, until it fell within the chosen chromatic area. Thus, by the sophisticated use of simple techniques, such as printing on fabric and an innovative exploitation of the principles of colorimetry, it was possible to begin controlling a sophisticated "soft" structure that is of great importance in an environment for which the sole quality proposed has too often been that of architectural composition.

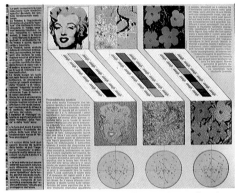

253) Centro Design Montefibre: scheme for chromatic transformation of images in the Fisiolight code, 1976.

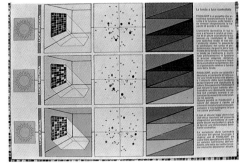

254) Centro Design Montefibre: checking of chromatic polygons against different dominant colours, 1976.

255) Centro Design Montefibre: Fisiolight, pattern producing a warm effect.

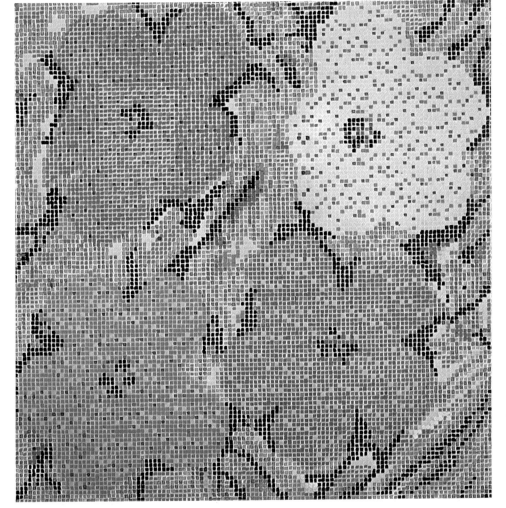

The Fisiolight system for curtains and blinds designed by Centro Design Montefibre consisted of a particular balance of colour components in decoration. Those in the red-yellow range were called "warm", those in the blue-green range were "cold", and those in the achromatic range were called "neutral".

Colour Design

XII Control over the quality of colour is one of the central problems of modern environmental culture: the development of the chemical industry, of plastic materials and paints, has meant that the vast majority of the objects in our surroundings and in everyday use are artificially coloured; this colour no longer has any connection with the nature of the materials used in construction, but is applied onto them, laid or painted on, mixed with plastic polymers or glued onto backing. Hence the colour of our surroundings, both at home and in the city, is the product of design. This means that colour today is not just a specific feature of the human habitat, but a sort of mediation between man and the physical world. Even before we become aware of the form or function of an object, we perceive its chromatic identity; hence the combination of colours in the surroundings has come to represent a specific level of use of the ambient itself. The quality, degree of definition, coordination and expressive content of colour are instruments that permit us a direct influence over the quality of the environment and of life. This is true not only in the realm of individual domestic objects, but also in urban and territorial structures, which are formed out of the sum total of metropolitan merchandise.

Part of the problem is that colour has become the object of an autonomous design

256) Faber Birren in Milan for the first seminars on "Colour design in industry", 1977.

257) Centro Design Montefibre: scheme of the perception of shapes and colours by the human eye, 1976.

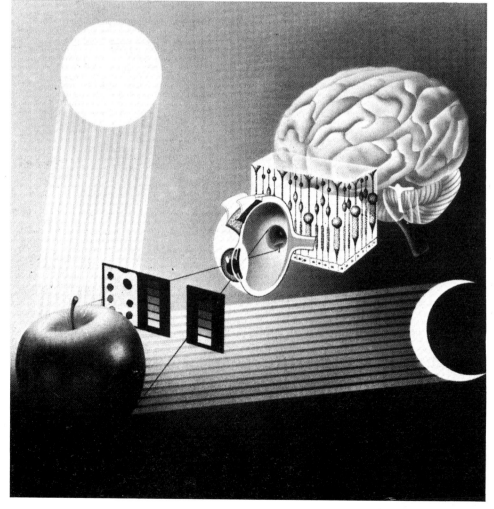

The colour that surrounds us at home or in public is always the outcome of design. It thus tends to be a means of mediation between man and the world around him. White light variously reflected off matter gives rise to the nervous stimuli of vision when it falls on the retina.

process. Until now colour has been the final attribute of the industrial product: the designer, after having worked on its form and function, selected its colour as the finishing touch to a structure that already possessed all its fundamental qualities. A little marketing combined with a little good taste, and a colour was chosen that remained outside the general criteria of design. Apart from later testing on the market, and the overall quality of the product, there was an almost total lack of control over the effects induced by colour on both use and acceptance.

The refusal to acknowledge that colour has a cultural autonomy of its own, i.e. to recognize it as an expressive structure requiring serious thought in its design, often means falling back on confused and unpredictable data provided by the so-called psychology of colour. Starting out as it does from an analysis of colours already on the market, the latter is not usually in a position to come up with reliable criteria for chromatic design. A sociology of colour certainly exists, but it confines itself to revealing some of the permanent characteristics of a few industrial markets and is of more help in the avoidance of mistakes that in supplying any real indications for design.

It is a well-known fact that islands of acceptability for particular chromatic groupings exist in countries which are clearly under the influence of a collective conditioning with respect to certain colours; everyone has heard of the use of violet and electric green in England, colours that are nowhere to be found on the domestic market of the continent. Equally one might point to the special affinity for green in Islamic countries, where it is considered a sacred colour. In Germany, too, the colours used for fabrics in the home have been drawn for many years from a single chromatic family, subject to continual refinement, which may be described as edible colours, the colours of the national cuisine: wurst, sauerkraut, beer, mustard, cucumber. These possess a homogeneity of expression, but above all a proven acceptability, being in fact the colours of foodstuffs.

Much more important are the design indications supplied by the information channels of the so-called international culture of colour. This is based on the presence of fixed colours and chromatic areas in vast geographical markets such as Europe and America. They are used in the arts as well as in industry and make up a genuine social language, quite apart from forming a limited and reliable reference catalogue of colours that registers the changes of taste in matters of colour that take place in society. The existence of such a catalogue, which is modified and extended in response to technical and cultural developments, is one of the characteristic results of the growth of technology and information in our time. No situation, problem or market can be considered in isolation, without immediately acquiring a global currency. In this situation minority cultures, i.e. those linked to ethnic, religious or national groups, find it difficult to maintain their own borders intact and are subject to constant pressure from the international flood of industrial goods, information and urbanization. This constant circulation of information produces what has been called the international culture of colour. It is made up of an unstable equilibrium of chromatic families, continually modified and driven forward by cultural, social and technical developments.

Among the institutions involved in the circulation of this type of information, one can point to *House and Garden*, an American magazine that publishes an annual portfolio containing the 36-38 colours present on the American market in the sector of furnishings and consumer goods, together with a graph depicting fluctuations in the popularity of different colours on the market since 1946. There are also the ICA, the International Colour Authority, created by a group of textile manufacturers with the aim of providing forecasts of sales twenty months in advance in the sectors of women's and men's clothing and of fabrics for home decoration, and Mafia, a French group of consultants who have produced seasonal portfolios of colours and their combinations for the clothing industry since 1968, eighteen months in advance of sale.

We initiated *Colordinamo* in 1975. Unlike the above publications, which are intended primarily to provide select marketing information or forecasts of fashion trends in clothing or interior decoration, the *Colordinamo* annuals present 40 colours chosen on the basis of a single theme, supplemented by technical and cultural

In 1977 the colour terminal of I.V.I. run by Centro Design Montefibre was inaugurated in Milan. This was called the Centre for Creative Colorimetry and introduced for the first time in Italy the Munsell Code, the most important international system for identifying colour, as well as Graficolor, an electronic system of screen simulation of colours. Within this sphere, in collaboration with the Colordinamo *group, Milan witnessed the first international seminars on "Colour design in industry".*

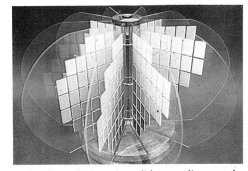

258) The colorimetric solid according to the Munsell system of color notation.

259) IVI Colorterminal, Centre for Creative Colorimetry, Milan, 1978.

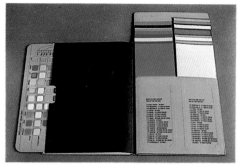

260) *Colordinamo*: interior of the folder containing the colour file, sample cards, and manual.

261) *Colordinamo*: "colour isolator" for dark, medium and light colours.

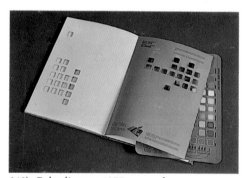

262) *Colordinamo 1977*: manual.

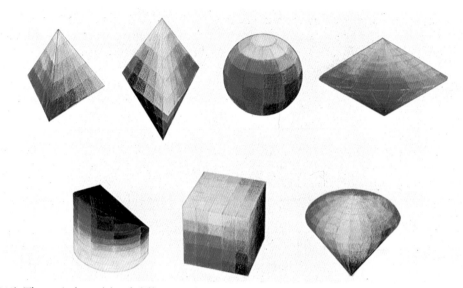

263) Theoretical models of different colorimetric solids. From top left: A. Heinrich Lambert (1728-1777), B. Tobias Mayer (1745), C. Philipp Otto Rünge (1777-1810), D. Wilhelm Ostwald (1853-1932), E. Prase (1910), F. Charpentier (1885), Hickethier (1952), G. Richter DIN 6164 (1962).

264) Poster of the *Colordinamo* operation, 1975.

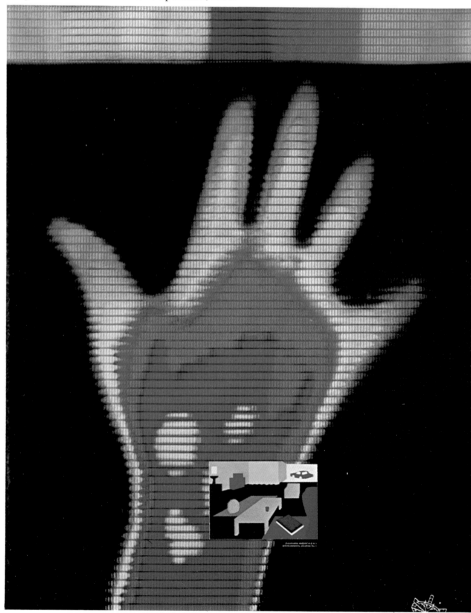

The Centro Design Montefibre each year published in Colordinamo *a selection of 40 colours articulated around a given subject, backed up by technical and cultural information and by work instruments necessary for the design of colour.*

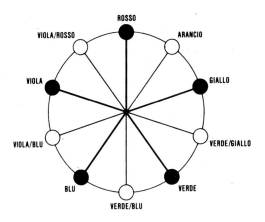

information and by working instruments suitable for design. The editions of *Colordinamo* did not contain colour forecasts in the strict sense, i.e. selected on the basis of market predictions, but rather colours on grand monographic themes, chosen for their cultural relevance and not for their consumer demand. They were aimed at designers, manufacturers of textiles for the home, interior decorators and the furniture and domestic appliance industries — areas where long periods of time are devoted to design and which therefore need up-to-date but wide-ranging information rather than cues for seasonal cycles of production.

In 1977 the first seminars on industrial colour design were held at the Museum of Science and Technology in Milan. Along with prominent European experts, the participants include Lanclos and Faber Birren, the foremost theoretician in the field. In addition, *Colordinamo* introduced the Munsell colour codes and colorimetry to Italy.

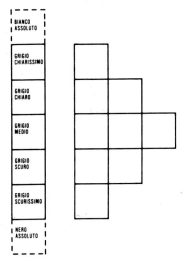

The *Colordinamo* manuals encompassed a sufficiently broad and internally homogeneous chromatic family, but one which formed an intermediate phase between the great international colour codes, like that of Munsell, and the chromatic portfolio on which the designer bases his choices. *Colordinamo*'s first monograph, in 1975, was on the theme of "The colours of energy". It analyzed chromatic series deriving from modern thermography, i.e. from spectographic surveys transmitted by means of television that interpret anatomical or geographical reality not on the basis of natural colours but on that of the different thermal and energetic states within the material. In this way images are obtained in which groups of warm colours are set alongside groups of cold colours in a sequence that is no longer naturalistic but is connected with the fundamental state of the material. In addition, colours such as these, which are reproduced by means of television, represent a further electronic elaboration of the original orographic data, transmuted into modern technical code. Those were the years in which colour television made its advent in Italy, and this event brought about a profound change not only in the chromatic culture of the country, but in the amount of colour used in the environment.

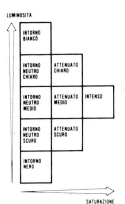

Today the instrument through which we receive chromatic information is very important; one has only to think of the profound influence of the colour Polaroid on American hyper-realist painting, or of xerographic copies on the work of Andy Warhol. What we in fact receive is always the colour of the colour; that is, the natural datum is always actively reworked by the instrument or medium that transmits it, whether this is a colour photograph, a pair of sunglasses, television or the press. The manipulation of the primary chromatic data effected by instruments of communication is no less important than a cultural manipulation. The individual always receives colour after it has been altered, transmitted, packaged; his chromatic culture always starts out from this elaboration and is conditioned thereby. New technical instuments permit an expansion of our chromatic perception of reality. By means of thermographs, for example, it has become possible to reveal the "deep" colours of things: the different chromatic qualities that can be represented by sensitive media correspond to different strata of energy in the environment.

Colordinamo 1976 dealt with "Pre-synthetic colours", i.e. the textile colours used in dye-works prior to the discovery of the chemical synthesis of aniline in the 19th century. These colours were extracted from natural raw materials such as spices and vegetables, or from animals or minerals, and were applied to the textiles by traditional methods. The interest in this kind of colouring was of a historical and semantic nature; their pre-industrial character gives them an aspect that is foreign to and remote from our chromatic world. Among pre-chemical colours, linked as they were to the spice trade with the Orient in the 14th and 15th centuries, there is a high degree of homogeneity, generated by the nature of the ingredients

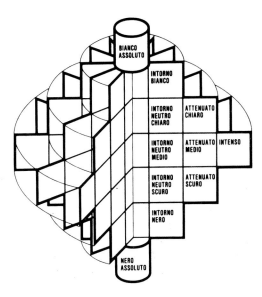

265) *Colordinamo*: simplified representation of the achromatic colours.

266) *Colordinamo*: simplified representation of the relations between the chromatic families.

267) *Colordinamo*: simplified representation of the relations between the various tonalities of a chromatic family.

268) *Colordinamo*: the colour solid dissected to show a family.

Colordinamo 1975 *followed two themes: thermography, in which contrasting colours underline hot and cold zones; and cathode colours as seen in colour television and from which thermography derives — a key to the chromatic culture of to-day's society.*

Colordinamo 1976: *"Pre-synthetic colours", the colours that existed before the introduction of aniline in the 19th century, were obtained from natural materials such as spices and vegetables or were of animal or mineral origin. These colours formed a harmonious group both historically and structurally and expressed a chromatic universe with their range of shades which to-day has totally disappeared.*

269) Centro Design Montefibre, with the aid of Alessandro De Gregori: "The colours of energy", *Colordinamo 1975*.

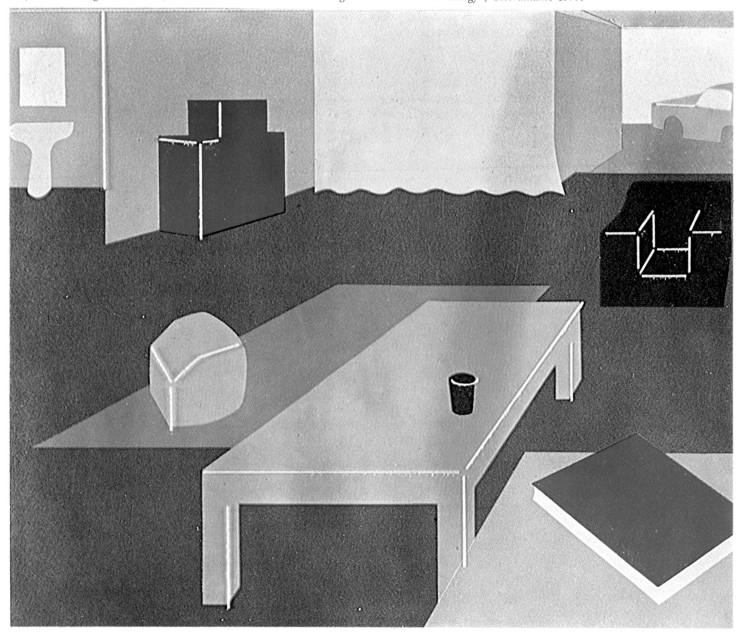

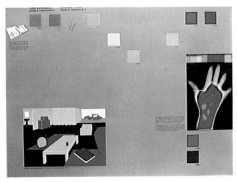
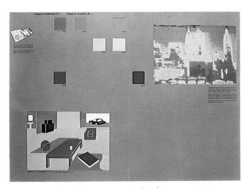

272-275) Pre-synthetic colour: copper acetate, Buddhist monks at prayer, indigo, orpiment, *Colordinamo 1976* (consultation by Prof. Franco Brunello).

270-271) "The colours of energy", housing and thermographic diagrams, *Colordinamo 1975*.

276) Andrea Branzi and Centro Design Montefibre: Piaggio colour system, 1979.

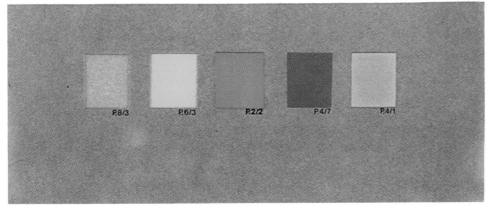

Colordinamo 1977: *An analysis of colour on the international markets over a fairly long period of time reveals that there is a limited number of colours that undergo little or no change and that act as reference points for other colours that come and go. Pinning down these standard colours has been of great consequence because it has meant that decisions regarding colour for household goods can set out from a sure basis.*

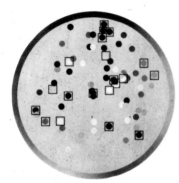

277) "Permanent colours", general colorimetric diagram, *Colordinamo 1977*.

employed in dyeing processes. The extent to which soft, neutral or intermediate colours were present demonstrates how in the pre-industrial mercantile world colour was always of secondary importance with respect to the merchandise itself, and was never used as a substitute for the latter. Indeed the development of colour chemistry and of industrial manufacture has not only led to a broadening of the chromatic range available but has introduced a different way of using colours in relation to the products to which they are applied. If for almost a thousand years prior to the 19th century the range of colour dyes was extremely limited, the huge range of different dyes available today and their high degree of saturation have led to emphasis being laid on all those aspects that in some way accentuate the attractiveness of the product and hence its commercial viability. This has favoured the increase in the use of the intense, highly differentiated colours on which modern design is based. The international culture of colour starts out from the technical premise that, today at least, the possibilities for creating tints and tones are practically unlimited, and although there was once a time when the dyeing industry could not develop further without profound historical changes in the market, brought about by such events as the discovery of America, it now operates with perfect autonomy.

The rapid metabolism to which the international colour market is subject concerns only a part of this range; there exists a central core of colours that tend to remain constant or to undergo very slow change. Generally these are colours that could be called permanent, used either in the manufacture of long-lasting goods or in architecture itself; they are made up of the "heads" of families, i.e. colours that characterize a chromatic area which may be modified on the fringes but remains permanent in time and is identified by one or two fixed colours. It was to this theme of "Permanent colours" that *Colordinamo 1977* was devoted. Precisely because of their durability, the permanent colours typify our physical surroundings by providing their fundamental chromatic characteristics. Other colours move into or out of the market, and therefore the environment, embodying a particular moment of cultural innovation, but this happens against a background of a chromatic array stable enough to provide meaning and reference for all the other colours. The slow mutation in permanent colours represents the line of structural evolution for the whole of chromatic culture and forms a measure of progress in the cultural development of society. Analysis of this evolution constitutes the fundamental instrument in the chromatic design of the environment.

The *Colordinamo* manuals, distributed throughout Europe to pathfinders in the sector, are the first sign of a reawakening of interest in chromatic design. Until recently the colours utilized in design production were fundamentally graphic in nature, i.e. highly simplified and used to distinguish between the supporting structure of the product, always black or chromium-plated, and its functional parts, always marked by strong colours, i.e. by colours that stand out clearly in the surroundings. A great innovation with respect to this tradition appeared in 1970, with Ettore Sottsass Jr.'s design of a system of office furnishings for Olivetti, Synthesis 45, where colour was tackled for the first time as a problem of interior landscape, in which different products were coloured with a view to their eventual combination in modern open-plan offices. There was, for example, a precocious chromatic quality to the plastic laminates manufactured by Abet Print, which introduced a remarkable degree of refinement in the use of colour in its production range for kitchens, offices and home furnishings. Today there is not one furniture manufacturer in Italy that does not seek to follow a controlled policy of improving definition in all the finishing materials of its products. Moreover, all the major automobile and engineering industries, from Piaggio to Lancia, from Fiat to Alfa Romeo, have accepted colour design as an essential part of industrial design, which must be subjected to programmed control as a specialized phase of automobile design.

The Active Surface

XIII

If there was any one significant and really new feature of the cultural nucleus of the seventies, it was perhaps the fact that for the first time the suspicion was growing that modern architecture, in the form it had gradually assumed since the beginning of the century, would remain unchanged in its most important aspects for some centuries to come. In contrast to what was believed in the sixties, it seems that a consensus has been reached over the last fifty years that is destined to remain unchallenged for many centuries — a change similar to the one brought about by Brunelleschi and Alberti in the 15th century, which determined and shaped a frame of operation that survived unaltered, apart from various manners and variants, until the last century. Unless the near future brings a series of profound social changes, for the moment hard to envisage, the linguistic and compositional framework of the Modern Movement has entered a phase of extreme stability that shows little sign of altering, not so much because it has reached a level of lasting beauty as because it finds itself in a situation of neutral stall, an unsteady equilibrium in the midst of a disciplinary crisis that does not seem at all open to dramatic solutions.

If we look at the trend of cultural debate over the last twenty years, we see that it has followed a very clear pattern in this connection: from a rediscovery of the social implications of the Modern Movement at the beginning of the sixties, it moved to a critical examination of its social limits in 1968 and then to official adoption of these limits, accepted precisely because they were limits, i.e. constraints, linguistic institutions in which variants of style could be worked out. What is being created, then, is not a society "without architecture", as the radical avant-garde had postulated, nor a society "all architecture", as envisaged by the prophets of the Modern Movement. What seems to be taking shape instead is a society where architecture is present but not active, where it is accepted as one factor in the equilibrium of a historical and hereditary context that is not being questioned but dispassionately used as a repertory of possible means of operation.

Under these circumstances, the culture of design has gone through several significant shifts in direction; on one hand, by liberating itself from the myth of progress, it has concentrated on a nostalgic return to a pre-modern order, going back to the recycling of historical styles, and on the other it has aimed at new environmental qualities that are not linked to the "structural form" of buildings and objects, tackling new problems and fields of research so as to bring its own design instruments up to date. Space as void is now defined by its "active boundary", the expressive effect of the sum total of its surfaces, which act as radiant panels in the realm of material communications. Thus, the project of primary design is also aimed at perfecting the whole range of components that make up the environment and our world of objects. The great formal inventions left to us by modern design are subject today to a probing analysis of their material, a re-examination of all their intrinsic possibilities for development.

The devising of new materials is part of a vast tradition of modern technology; design, already at the stage of historical formation, has contributed greatly to this kind of research, approaching the problem on the level of a search for new possibilities of use and expressivity. There were seven workshops in the Bauhaus: one each for working with stone, wood, metal, terracotta, glass, pigments and fabrics. In them the student learned craftsmanship to go along with his theoretical lessons on stuctural analysis and formal composition. The technology was still that of

The first true experiments in textile design took place in the Bauhaus in the laboratory directed by Anni Albers, combining yarns with opposite qualities to produce fabrics with a communicative power generated by internal contrasts.

278) Anni Albers: fabric of cotton and rayon fibres.

279) Anni Albers: fabric of wool and rayon fibres.

280) Anni Albers: fabric of cotton and cellophane fibres.

281) E. Dieckmann: composition of heterogeneous materials.

282) "Stratitex", stages in the gluing of textile laminate onto chipboard panels.

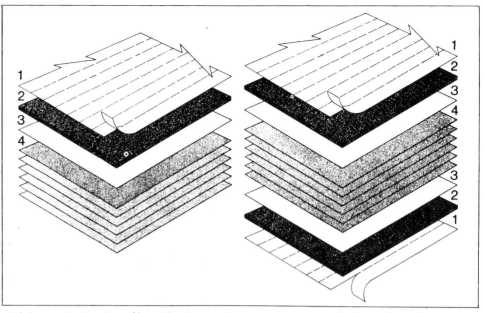

283) Centro Design Montefibre, Abet Laminati: Stratitex, 1975. 1 - self-adhesive liner (for restoring textile surfaces); 2 - pre-compressed textile layer; 3 - thermosetting adhesive layer; 4 - layers of thermosetting backing.

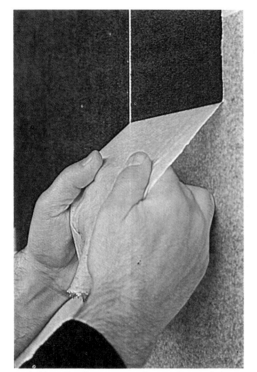

284) "Stratitex", process of restoring and drawing textile surfaces.

"Stratitex" used the technology of sandwiching with a special layer of fibre on a surface covered with an adhesive liner, which, after passing through a special press is then removed.

the craft tradition, but the approach was already a new one and concentrated on the search for a new identity for the material on a linguistic as well as a constructive level. Unusual combinations of materials were tried out in the design of utilitarian objects: leather and steel, glass and wood, glass and steel, etc. New relations were sought between dissimilar materials, and discontinuity was planned in order to create expressive new surroundings. Contradiction, trauma, shock and surprise were the new methods of experimentation. Typical of these were Kurt Schwitters's famous Dada compositions, made out of collages of different kinds of debris. In these compositions chance materials are made to "speak" through the complex web of interactions between the materials within the frame. The Bauhaus's research went further, seeking to design a material that possessed these expressive qualities internally, that would communicate thanks to its own intrinsic nature and not through the conjunction of suggestive external relationships, as in the case of Schwitters's works.

Anni Albers, who taught weaving at the Bauhaus, took up this line of research and made the first modern experiments on materials to have been carried out in the field of textile design. These included fibres made out of combinations of paper and cellophane, wool and rayon, cotton and rayon, cotton and cellophane, etc. The research method was still the same as Schwitters used (internal shock), but the expressiveness of the product derived from an intimate blending of different materials in the yarn. The yarn was then woven to produce a new fabric with original features of communication, set up by the different expressive potentials of its constituents. For the first time the possibility was glimpsed, through these alchemical experiments with fabrics, of obtaining a new artificial material whose useful characteristics (durability, maintenance, softness, etc.) could be controlled along with its expressivity by means of a careful mixture of its basic constituents.

A traditional definition of textile design would emphasize the design of decorative patterns or colours, which industry draws on extensively since it allows them to renew textile products that are centuries old in technical terms by simple changes of styling. Yet textile design is also concerned with the manufacture of advanced textile products made out of new materials; these are designed on the basis of new technology and exploit the inherent characteristics of chemical and artificial fibres. Chemical fibres have long been utilized as a substitute for natural ones: imitation wood, imitation cotton, imitation linen, etc. The use of these fibres has often been limited to applications proper to traditional materials, despite their great innovative potential. It has been the common fate of many new materials when first discovered to imitate rather than to introduce change. It suffices to think of plastics, used

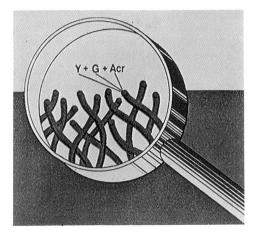

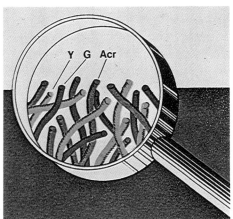

286) Meraklon Fibermatching 25 system, 1976. The product is the same colour as the preceding one but has been made using "base colours" of the Fibermatching 25 method; the fundamental chromatic components are subdivided into individual fibres and can therefore be altered at will.

285) Centro Design Montefibre: Meraklon Fibermatching 25 system, 1976. "Finalized" product made out of coloured fibres; the dyes are introduced into the polymers and their proportions can therefore no longer be modified.

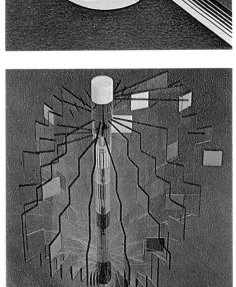

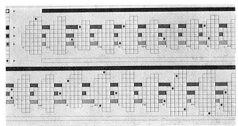

288) Overall view of the sections of the chromatic solid, with reference to the three basic chromatic shades (greys) and to black and white.

287) Meraklon Fibermatching 25 system, 1976. Model of the chromatic solid used for the Fibermatching 25 system.

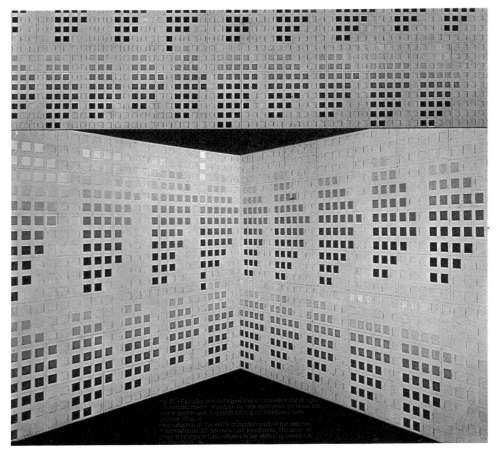

289) Planar reproductions of the entire chromatic solid of the system.

The new Louis Vuitton fabric is composed of lengths of Kevlar covered in spiral polyester. The design of materials creates new possibilities. This new technical knowledge allows a new range of planning and a wider exploitation of the thermal and expressive qualities of materials.

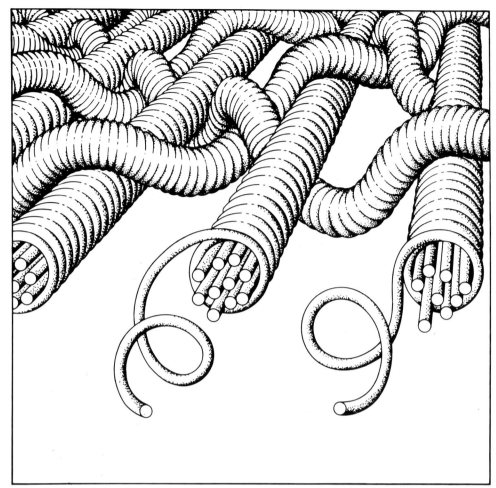

291) Clinio Trini Castelli, Massimo Morozzi - C.D.M.: studies for a new super-fabric Louis Vuitton, 1976.

290) Clinio Trini Castelli: "The Enigma of the Clock", Eurodomus, 1971.

292) Clinio Trini Castelli: "Glowing Chair" with "Green Print Lumiphos 14-580", plastic photoluminescent laminate, 1972.

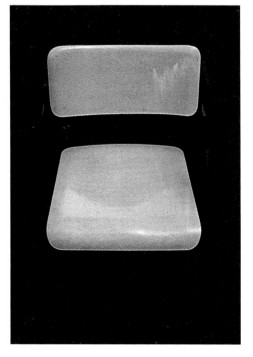

for a long time as a substitute for wood and only later revealed as an autonomous sector of technology and construction in a position to yield highly innovative products. In any case chemical fibres are to be found in widely differing fields of application, where they perform specialized tasks. For instance, they are used in reinforced concrete, where they assist the transmission of forces within the structure, in tires and in filter pads used in processes for settling backfill.

Following this trend towards innovative technological applications for chemical fibres, we began a programme of research in 1976 into modern techniques for producing planar surfaces. This centred on an original combination of different construction processes to obtain, by the sandwich technique, a final result that united the properties of different materials. Specifically this involved superimposing resin-bonded laminate technology on the technique of producing knitted textiles, resulting in a completely new end product: a kind of laminate with a textile surface, known as Stratitex. This product combined the techniques of textile finishings with the ease of application of ordinary laminates. While fabric is normally fixed onto a backing by the traditional methods of upholstery, the Stratitex process produced a rigid textile in a single manufacturing operation which could then be handled in the same way as a laminate; at the same time it offered all the advantages of textile panelling: acoustic and thermal insulation and a velvety finish. Exploitation of all the innovative technical possibilities of resin-bonded laminates has been a feature of much of the research into primary design, and in the case of Stratitex this permitted an extension of textile design. Right at the beginning of the seventies Clino Castelli had carried out some highly interesting research into a combination of sandwich and laminate technology. In collaboration with Abet Print, he had designed the first fluorescent and electro-luminescent laminates and had contributed to the growing use of laminates as a specialized chromatic element in interior decoration. In 1979 it became possible to produce, once again for Abet

Print and alongside a large number of prototypes of new surface finishes, the first three-dimensional laminate, called Reli-tech, that coupled decoration and plastic relief in a single process of lamination, resulting in a product with great force of expression. The need to design new materials to act as boundaries to space and as communicating surfaces, independently of and separate from the form of objects, meant getting involved in new industrial processes and paying attention to all those expressive as well as innovative components that could be guaranteed by design.

Generally speaking, the designer has traditionally carried out his profession in collaboration with the consumer goods industry; primary design was starting to work with the manufacturers of raw materials, retracing the cycles of production back to the industrial phase where work is no longer carried out on a finished product, but on the preparation of semi-finished materials, with a view to facilitating their further elaboration on the part of processing industries and other designers. In this way design came to be defined as a "service". In a modern conception of the market, the production of raw materials is no longer confined merely to their supply to the processing industries, but is evolving towards the status of a service industry; in other words, it is moving towards a policy that sees the major structures for the production of raw materials as a centre of co-ordination and information for industry as a whole, a new policy of service as value added and as a guide to all phases of the industrial market. Design is included among these services, as an activity of basic research and a source of select information for industrial processing and professionals. In this new kind of relationship, the work of the designer is no longer confined to a single industry, but is aimed at an entire processing market and makes use of instruments of information and pre-elaboration.

In this way the power of the "diffuse design" of modern industrial society is effectively demonstrated as it diversifies into design decisions through different phases and at co-ordinated times and places. A typical example of this process was the "Meraklon Fibermatching 25" project for bulk-dyed polypropylene fibre that we carried out between 1975 and 1977 as chief consultants to the Centro Design Montefibre. Polypropylene fibre is spun from isostatic polypropylene (Moplen) by a process of melting. Its principal application is in knitted textiles for flooring and wall coverings; it is the lightest fibre in existence, and its thermal conductivity is lower than that of wool. This fibre does not absorb or react with stains, and it is also resistant to attack by micro-organisms and moulds. But these characteristics render the fibres impervious to normal dyeing processes; colour cannot be applied to them, and as a consequence they have to be "dyed in bulk", i.e. produced ready-coloured. This is done by adding a certain quantity of granules of a strong dye to the polymer. This shortens the production cycle, with major benefits to the ecosystem, and also means that after extrusion the colour of the fibre is especially stable and resistant to all the outside agents that usually attack the chromatic stability

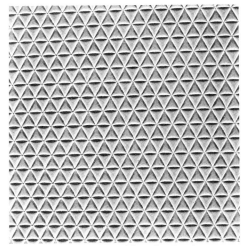

293) Massimo Morozzi: fabric for Cassina, 1980.

294-295) Denis Santachiara: luminous wallpaper, 1980.

of products dyed in the normal way. Yet dyeing a fibre in bulk presents a major problem from the commercial point of view.

The way in which colour is fixed at an early stage by bulk dyeing makes it difficult to plan the production and subsequent processing of textiles, especially where the demand for new colours on the market is a factor. To overcome this problem in an empirical fashion, the producers of Meraklon had accumulated over time a range of commercial colours (approximately 40) which had originally been produced at the request of customers; an attempt was made to drop some of these and replace them by new ones every year. Apart from being extremely costly on an industrial scale because of the number of colours and the need to change them, this method did not satisfy customers who had to work with fibres in already "fashionable" colours, so that it became difficult for them to make their final product stand out from those of other manufacturers. To avoid this obstacle, they resorted to a mixing process, uniting different quantities of coloured fibres in order to obtain new shades. The result was that they got "dirty" products in which the initial colour was contaminated by other "fashionable" colours not suitable for blending. The operation that we undertook was to impose a "rational" production of coloured fibre, based on the selection of well-defined "basic" colours, and not just those that happened to be in fashion. The range of colours was cut down from 40 to 25 (plus black and white), distributed as evenly as possible across the colour spectrum.

"Fibermatching" was based on the principle of assuming each fibre to be a particle of primary colour which, when mixed together in the right proportion and observed from a conventional distance, looked like a solid colour; by means of a chromatic rectifier of very broad range (600 colours) it was possible for each manufacturer or designer to choose a colour, or design a mix or shade, and use the reference scheme to blend differently coloured fibres so as to obtain a result that was not only identical with the colour sample, but perfectly "solid". This system constituted a step forward in the production of the raw material in view of the greater suitability for application that resulted from a strengthening of its expressive potential even before processing; in this manner the possibilities for the development of a technology were grasped in a logical and co-ordinated fashion. The upshot would be that the next few tens of millions of square metres of textile panelling that would enter the environment in which we live would no longer exhibit the formal limits of the previous technology.

296-298) Andrea Branzi: "Reli-tech", Abet Laminati, 1978.

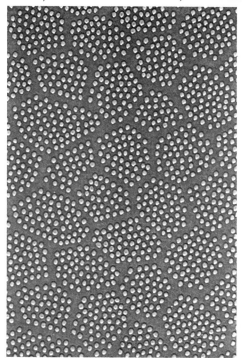

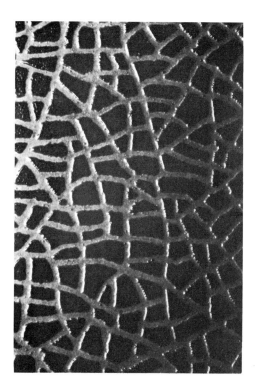

Decorative Design

XIV

Industrial design and the Modern Movement have always been nagged by the "question of decoration", a complex question that has never really been cleared up and over which a battle has been fought in the name of that cleanness of form that is indispensable to the civilized development of industrial society. In some ways this bias against decoration seems characteristic of Rationalism's search for purity of form and function. For a long time the slogan "ornament and crime", coined by Adolf Loos in 1908, closed the door on any possibility of a revival of decorative design. But in reality the problem of decoration has never been clearly either resolved or totally eliminated from modern design. There were highly complex motives, and not just stylistic ones, for the ardour with which this question was tackled at the beginning of the century: it meant getting rid of the encrustation of symbols and decorations which industrial civilization continued to churn out in hollow imitation of a vanished craftsmanship. What was needed was to stress the diversity and autonomy of the machine-made product and its shapes from hand-crafted models. Design brought about a reduction of forms to simple figures — planes, spheres and cylinders — that would fit into the machines that had to reproduce them; this neo-plastic language appeared to coincide with the "rational" nature of production mechanisms and any feature at odds with this language seemed alien, unnatural and therefore immoral.

The real state of affairs was somewhat different: it is possible to show that the Modern Movement's battle against decoration was directed at a certain type of ornament, while a different code of decoration was adopted in its own design, such as the way planes and masses were used as a means of communication. Like other modern architects of his time, even Adolf Loos, whose crusade against ornament was an attempt to get rid of what had become a mechanical and empty habit, used the "natural decoration" of construction and facing materials: stone, marble, wood and leather. The difference for Loos, then, lay in a choice between artificial and natural decoration; materials "speak", but Loos made them sing through his use of refined techniques of processing and enhancement. Typical of this was his selec-

Decorattivo is published annually by Centro Design Montefibre for the relevant industries and, in general, for the designers, decorators and artists of the sector. Past themes have included: "Paquebot", "Drapery", "The nineteenth century", "Amorphous shapes", "Ties", "Stripes and checks".

299) Centro Design Montefibre: analysis of the function of decoration in the use of objects, 1976.

300) Centro Design Montefibre, Adela Coat Turin: *Decorattivo 1975.*

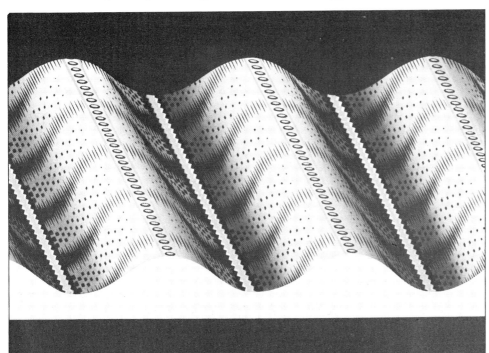

301) Romolo and Mauro Lenzi: "3101" child's chair, expanded polyurethane, GI.MO, 1970.

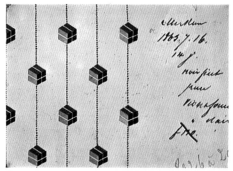

302) Studies of textile decoration, Paris, 1863.

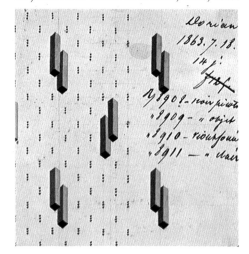

tion of "sick" marble, in other words stone that was heavily veined, cut into thin slabs and mounted mirror-fashion, i.e. in a rhythmic repetition of the pattern of veining, so as to create genuinely decorative surfaces that served to enhance the expressive quality of his interiors.

As a result of the growth of the building industry, modern architecture itself has often limited design to the choice of a repetitive and decorative pattern for the external fixtures of the great walls of the metropolis. As Christopher Alexander has pointed out, the difference between one skyscraper and the next depends more on the patterns of their windows than on any other architectural mark. The metropolis takes on the appearance of an uninterrupted succession of decorative textures, of rhythmic two-dimensional patterns that make up a sort of rabbit warren of languages in which advertising signs and commercial hoardings are the only projections into the environment.

Even the design project has had to take a hard look at its own historical code; born out of the need for a correct interpretation of the construction possibilities of new materials, which meant transforming them into simple shapes to facilitate their use by industry, it now has to deal with construction materials that have suddenly done away with this "necessity" and demand completely new criteria of design. By eliminating the notorious problems caused by shrinkage during cooling, designers can now use the rigid polyurethane foams in large sections, that is to say in shapes that are anything but geometric, as well as in hybrid structures and integrated technologies. The case of the chair in the style of Louis XIV with plastic legs, such a source of merriment to all orthodox designers, now turns out to be perhaps the most correct use of this technology and of modern moulding machines.

Consequently, many of the methodological presuppositions on which design is based have shown themselves to be of more use in setting limits to the formal choices open to the designer than in taking advantage of all the expressive and constructive possibilities of mechanized production. The profound logic on which industrial production is based today can no longer be called rational, except by distorting the meaning of the word: the logic with which the machine is built and by which it works is rational, but its advanced level of technology now permits an enormous range of formal variation, including decoration. This means that the "state of necessity" from which design derived its rigid forms in the past has been completely eliminated, leaving it to deal with its outmoded codes of composition on an exclusively decorative and moral basis.

Fifty years of technical progress have made it clear, by the way in which manufacturing machinery has evolved, that the rational quality of industry is actually subsidiary to the quantitative growth of production, i.e. to the acceleration of industrial cycles. In fact acceleration is the one factor that has really affected daily life.

We have inherited an extremely narrow concept of decoration, one that is ac-

303) Centro Design Montefibre, Adela Coat Turin: *Decorattivo 1*, 1976, internal section of tire, radio-isotope containers, composition of biscuits and two printed cotton fabrics from circa 1850.

304) *Decorattivo 1*: gymnastic display in China, jacquard silk fabric for ties from 1935 and printed silk from 1867.

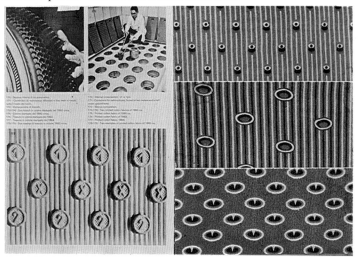

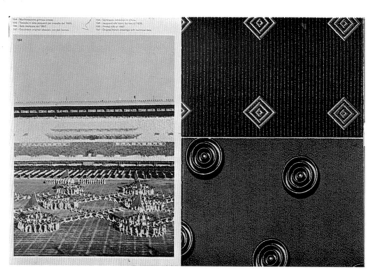

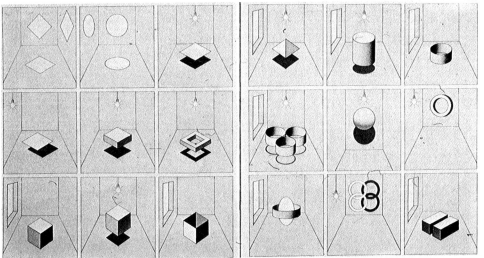

305-306) *Decorattivo 1*: analysis of the three-dimensional language of the "cravatteria" system, 1976.

The manuals entitled Decorattivo *contained stimulating and creative graphic material: documents concerning modern textiles and those of the 1800's, descriptions of the industrial and scientific world, structural analyses of decorative linguistic systems.*

In the large ateliers of the latter half of the 19th century, research on textile decoration focused on the changing role of graphic design and produced advanced results comparable to the work of painters of that period.

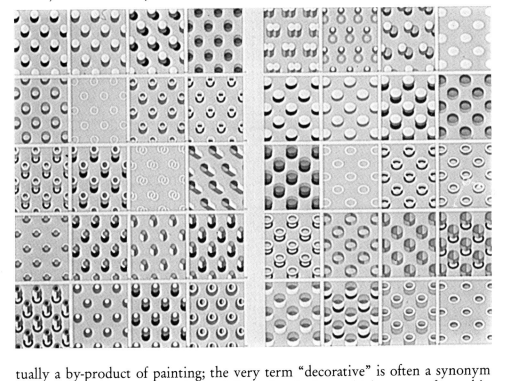

307) Centro Design Montefibre, Adela Coat Turin, Sauro Mainardi, Fabrizio Sabini: *Decorattivo 2*, 1977, structural analysis of Scottish tartans.

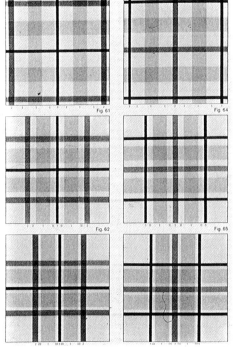

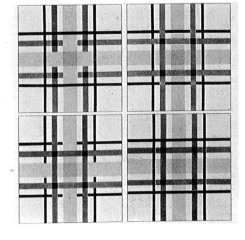

tually a by-product of painting; the very term "decorative" is often a synonym for the vulgarization of graphic and figurative devices, which are transformed in the repetitive processes of decoration into signs devoid of any cultural value. But this constricted view of ornament needs revising today; decorative thought has a modernity of its own and in some ways represents an extremely advanced type of aesthetic production even where experimental painting is concerned.

Nowadays decoration ought to be seen as a system of information in its own right: cultural information about the product and information on its use as well as linguistic and visual information.

Ornamentation represents the layout of a practically infinite system of signs, extending uniformly on the unbounded plane formed by its backing. The decorated surface is nothing but a segment of a universe that is analogous to it. In this "quantitative" utopia resides its great relevance to the present day, as well as its kinship with all the repetitive processes typical of modern industrial civilization. On this hypothesis, decorative design possesses certain totally original features; unlike a painting, which always presupposes the existence of a limit formed by the edge of the frame and in which the pictorial message is set as a unit, the decorative surface assumes its limits to be infinite and contains in the smallest of its parts the total information carried by the system as a whole, since each part contains the single symbol that will be repeated over the whole area covered by the decora-

308) Mario Bellini: ornamental design for laminate, Abet Laminati, 1982.

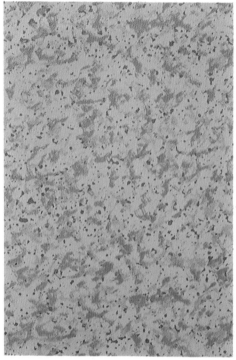

309) Andrea Branzi: studies of photographic decoration, 1976.

310) Nathalie du Pasquier: chintzed cotton printed in eight colours, Memphis, 1982.

311) Andrea Branzi, Alessandro Mendini: architectural decoration, Giulianova, 1978.

tion. Decoration is cultural information about the product because it affects its cultural identity, in other words its historical references in general, quite apart from the form of the product itself. It is information about use since the cultural identity of the product not only determines the function to which the consumer will put it, but also the way it will affect his behaviour. It is linguistic information simply because it communicates by means of a system of abstract signs, the symbols and implications of a social culture. Finally it is visual information because it determines the use of the product, independent of the latter's function.

Taking these reflections as our starting point, we initiated, around 1974, a programme of research into decoration, with particular reference to textiles. Having interested a number of manufacturing companies in experimenting with new types of ornamentation, we started to publish a yearbook on decoration and its history in 1975 to which we gave the name *Decorattivo*. These publications possessed two fundamental characteristics: the first concerned the nature of the material published and the second the principles underlying its selection. *Decorattivo* presented a selection of original documents, just as they had been unearthed in archives, museums and collections, without any further graphic treatment; hence they were offered to designers as material to be interpreted and developed according to their own technical and cultural requirements. *Decorattivo* was essentially a sort of working handbook, a compendium of graphic information chosen to provide a basis and stimulus for the creative work of other professionals. The illustrations of fabrics were accompanied by topical images, to provoke a stimulating comparison between decorative tradition and the cultural imagery of the modern world. Many of the designs published in *Decorattivo* had in fact been produced during the last century and were taken from fabrics for clothing; unlike fabrics used for the home,

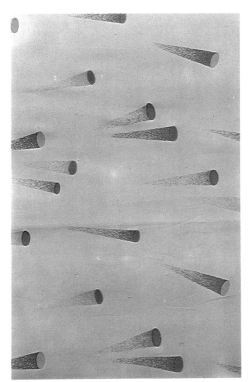

312) Daniela Puppa: decoration on silk, Studio Alchymia, 1980.

313) Paola Navone: graphic ornaments processed by Graficolor for the 16th Milan Triennale, 1979.

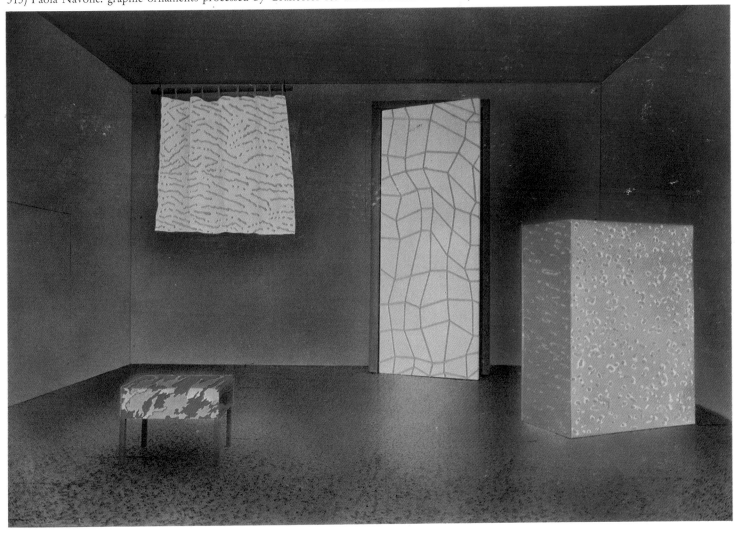

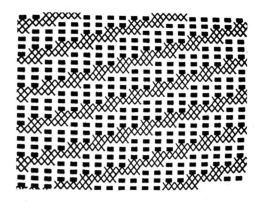

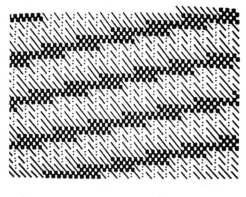

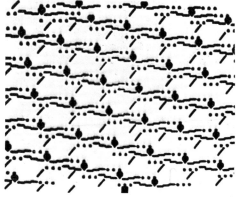

314) Denis Santachiara: decorations devised on a computer, 1980.

where decoration has always been considered secondary in importance to the shape of the room and the objects contained therein and where the themes of decoration have always been limited, the design of fabrics for clothing possesses a long and rich tradition. In any case, decorative culture has to be viewed as a unitary phenomenon, varying in the merchandise to which it is applied and the fashions to which it is subject, but profoundly linked at heart through a semantic continuity.

The second feature of the *Decorattivo* handbooks concerned the criteria behind the choice of material for illustration. Themes were selected not on the basis of seasonal market forecasts but rather on the basis of constancy over historical periods. The first edition of *Decorattivo* dealt with "amorphous" decorations, i.e. textures without organization, and with "tie designs", i.e. geometric decorations that conveyed a strong impression of three-dimensionality. These two veins of decoration are to be found in Europe in periods separated from each other by over a century. These graphic traditions have taken on different meanings in different periods of history, but they have remained essentially unchanged as patterns of decoration.

The topic of the 1977 edition of *Decorattivo* was that of stripes and checks, without doubt one of the most constant themes in decorative culture; they appeared simultaneously with the invention of weaving, one of the oldest of all human activities. Lines and squares are the primary structures of decoration and can be found in the cheapest as well as in the most sophisticated of products. They emerge out of the very structure of the textile, its warp and woof, and have become a highly spontaneous but rational scheme of organization in decorative communication.

The surprisingly up-to-date character of even ancient patterns of decoration is worthy of some comment. We know very little about "decorative culture": excluded from the history of art, it has always been thought of as a mere chapter in the history of customs and ethnography. Even today we have no critical yardstick capable of throwing light on the origin of decorative symbols and patterns, an origin that remains mysterious and often extraordinary despite the fact that we come across them every day. At times even the source of their communicative force remains unclear. A sort of cultural racism has meant that not a single name has come down to us from the many generations of anonymous fabric designers, and only an erroneous criterion of selection has made us familiar with what are thought to be nobler applications in the richest fabrics or most cultivated circles. No-one, for instance, has explored that submerged continent formed by the millions of tiny motifs of decoration used for everyday clothing in the last century and at the begining of this one, and yet here one finds an anticipation by about fifty years of all the avant-garde movements in painting in the 20th century. The reason for this anticipation as far as the official history of painting is concerned is that, with the great progress made in printing on fabrics over the last century, the textile industry was transformed into a huge experimental workshop for decoration. The ateliers were crammed with designers who spent their lives devising new graphic patterns for decoration. This enormous effort of fundamental research, carried out on quantitative principles alien to the pictorial culture of the time, constituted a kind of separate history that led to the gradual and often unconscious scientific discovery of a use of the sign that would be achieved by painting only after a gap of many years. Abstractionism, expressionism, the Fauve experiments and Surrealist composition were already themes in textile decoration during the latter part of the 19th century.

New attention from the critics and publication of the decorative manuals resulted in a strong re-awakening of interest in this kind of design: between 1977 and 1980 a series of experiments created new applications for decoration. Ettore Sottsass Jr. designed a series of laminates with new decorative patterns for Abet Print; these were subsequently mounted on the first prototypes produced by Alchymia. Paola Navone's contibution to the 16th Milan Triennale in 1979 was a room entirely covered with decoration, in which the surfaces of objects and walls became the backing for an uninterrupted series of "textures" projected onto them from slides electronically processed by Colorterminal's Graficolor. At the same time "Progetto Decoro" was set up, a programme of research into environmental decoration with financial backing from a number of major Italian industries and coordinated by Alessandro Mendini and Paola Navone.

315) Paolo Portoghesi: decorative design for laminate, Abet Laminati, 1982.

316) Alessandro Mendini, Paola Navone, Studio Alchymia: "The Modified Surface", decorative research for a group of industries, 1981.

317) Massimo Morozzi: decorative design for laminate, Abet Laminati, 1982.

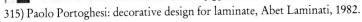

Banal Design

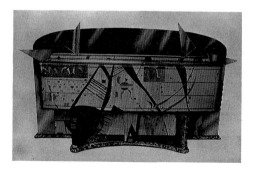

XV After fifty years of ostracism from cultural developments in design, decoration suddenly re-emerged as a characteristic feature of the most advanced research during the latter half of the seventies. It could even be said that the use of decoration gradually took on a highly complex and wholly original ideological connotation. Under the impetus of a continuous series of critical hypotheses that accompanied the theoretical evolution of radical architecture — from the discovery of mass-production for the intellect to primary design, the rediscovery of the fifties and indeed the rehabilitation of decoration by *Decorattivo* — a new nucleus of criticism began to form towards the end of the decade. This acted as a magnet, attracting a group of young designers who, under the theoretical leadership of Alessandro Mendini, were to create what has been called "banal design". To some extent the idea of banal design derived from the same social hypotheses that had been behind the avant-garde groups' search, from 1970 onwards, for a way of cutting cultural structures down to size, based on their faith in a mythical advent of mass intellectual production. Only now this advent was not seen as a utopia of liberation, but as an everyday reality. The nature of its ties to the social spread of empty and decorative stylistic features, drawn from the latest languages of a cultured production, was now realized, along with the way these had become tranquillizing symptoms of a mass-consumption devoid of moral or cultural stresses. For the first time, the crisis of cultured design in an industrial society was presented not as a battle to be fought, but as evidence of a transfer of design itself out of the hands of a few specialists into the more numerous hands of ordinary intellectuals and technicians: surveyors, the lower middle-class and uncommitted proletarians.

As Mendini put it: "We postulated the existence of a proletariat that has turned out not to exist; in its place is a lower middle-class; we envisaged some sort of conjunction between highly cultured design and the lumpen proletariat, but we got mass-design because the intellectual is disappearing; direct design by the masses themselves has turned out to be yet another mirage, and instead we have indirect design and the petit bourgeois designer. The avant-garde as a generalized phenomenon... is a phenomenon that we call 'banal' because in one sense quality is 'banality'." The intermediate range of cultured forms is boundless, and banal design proposes a use for it, as the only possible adaptation to the post-industrial universe that surrounds us — a chaotic universe born out of a supra-national order lacking history or destiny, a discontinuous world created out of what has turned out to be impracticable planning and a mediaeval culture that is the outcome of progress being turned on its head.

As the only true linguistic code of contemporary as opposed to modern architecture, it is the banal that forms the great back-drop to the urban periphery, understood not only as a town-planning term for new and untidy settlements, but as an existential condition of present-day society that has grown up on the values of television, do-it-yourself and cars on the installment plan. In the words of Franco Raggi: "To the utopian state in which planning plays a central role, these areas

Operations of redesign consisted of touching-up found objects or famous products of design to illustrate the impossibility of designing something new in respect to what has already been designed.

318) Alessandro Mendini: redesign of a chair by Joe Colombo, 1978.
319) Alessandro Mendini: redesign of a chair by Giò Ponti, 1978.
320) Alessandro Mendini: redesign of a sideboard from the forties with decorations by Kandinsky, 1978.

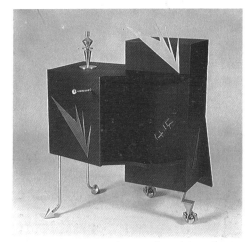

322) Alessandro Mendini, Studio Alchymia: "Infinite Furniture", 1981.

323) Prospero Rasulo: "Elements of Architecture" (oil on canvas), "Forum Design", 1980.

324) Studio Alchymia: interior of the "Forum Design" exhibition, Linz, 1980.

321) Alessandro Mendini: "Poltronova di Proust" (Proust's new armchair), Studio Alchymia, 1978.

of the planet contrast an organized chaos: fragmentation instead of unity, the particular instead of the general, details instead of the whole and the individual instead of the collective. The utopian idea of architecture giving form to society is replaced in reality by an architecture that adapts itself to the organized forms of that society." Thus the "banal" turns out to be the realistic and pitiless face of a world to which neither architecture, and thereby design, nor industry has given the "dignity of the modern" except as a tarting up of the traditional and as a definitive and implacable alienation of man from every possible tradition.

All the critical research into design that had accompanied the radical experience of the seventies went into a collapse that hit rock bottom with the advocates of banal design; here a delight in playing with uncultured codes was combined with a cold certainty that the surfaces of objects formed the insuperable limit of design as a field of action. According to Alessandro Mendini, these objects are like fish,

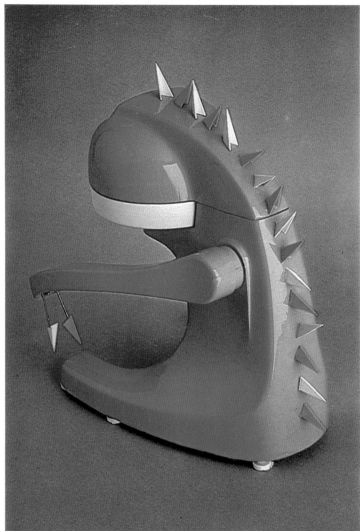

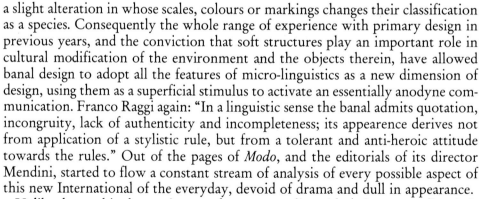

325-327) Alessandro Mendini, Franco Raggi, Daniela Puppa, Paola Navone: objects in common use at the exhibition "The Banal Object", Venice Biennale, 1980.

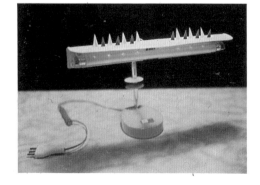

a slight alteration in whose scales, colours or markings changes their classification as a species. Consequently the whole range of experience with primary design in previous years, and the conviction that soft structures play an important role in cultural modification of the environment and the objects therein, have allowed banal design to adopt all the features of micro-linguistics as a new dimension of design, using them as a superficial stimulus to activate an essentially anodyne communication. Franco Raggi again: "In a linguistic sense the banal admits quotation, incongruity, lack of authenticity and incompleteness; its appearence derives not from application of a stylistic rule, but from a tolerant and anti-heroic attitude towards the rules." Out of the pages of *Modo*, and the editorials of its director Mendini, started to flow a constant stream of analysis of every possible aspect of this new International of the everyday, devoid of drama and dull in appearance.

Unlike the neo-kitsch experiments of ten years earlier with their stress on linguistic excesses, the banal tends towards a levelling and stereotyping of values. While the former is the simulation of a potential revolution carried out by the uncultured classes, those who consume rather than produce culture and whose economic rise has shattered all the social and political equilibria on which cultural patterns are based, the banal stands on the contrary for the attainment of a state of calm, a sort of sheltered cove in which the serene imitation of what were once cultured codes occurs without strain, as if it were a collection of flotsam and jetsam floating on the water. One leads to the other, but while the former is filled with heroic tension, the latter is frozen in its own realm of dreams; while the former is artisan-based, the latter is the product of a late industrial empire. While neo-kitsch is proletarian, the banal is petit-bourgeois and as conservative as the former is revolutionary.

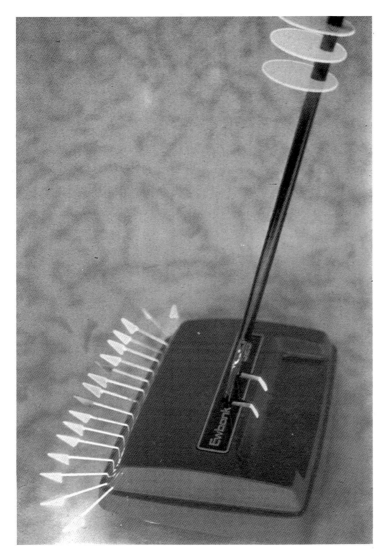 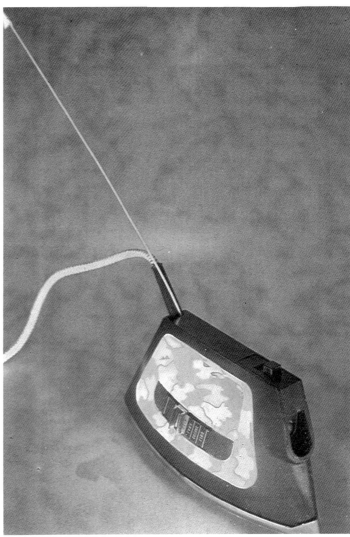

328-329) Alessandro Mendini, Franco Raggi, Daniela Puppa, Paola Navone: objects in common use at the exhibition "The Banal Object", Venice Biennale, 1980.

In 1968 we said: "There is no workers' metropolis, just a struggle for possession of the existing city"; hence the alternative culture expressed by the working class is in reality based on the models of their bosses' culture, which are employed in a distorted fashion, stripped of all their tension. They are satisfied by merely having gained possession. What Franz Fanon said in the fifties about the revolutionaries of the Third World is true: they emerged out of an attempt to imitate the white colonialists and not to assert the rights of an improbable "négritude", a concept for which not one shot has ever been fired. So it is imitation, and not design, that has turned out to be a historical force capable of changing the world. On it is based the logic of today's industry, society and culture.

The banal is the logical result of a mode of production that has overcome any imbalance between values, messages and objects, within a social unity that refers to nothing but itself in an elliptical circuit with no prospect of development: this is the "uniform society" of which Pasolini despaired. This circular nature and the absence of growth were effectively portrayed in the exhibition entitled "The Banal Object" at the 1980 Venice Biennale, where a range of specimens of this kind of output were subjected to linguistic analysis; a series of coloured vectors were set around the edges of the objects to emphasize the banality of their form, spruced up by everything from light to wood and set inside a sort of cold storage that brought out the sour nature of imitative decoration, the sadness of the standardized, proletarianized man who is at the same time the owner of his own system of objects, inhabiting peripheries on an unmistakably human scale.

In his analysis and use of the banal code, Mendini also carried out a series of redesigns, i.e. alterations to existing objects, "as bursts of design in explanation of banality", as they have been described by Barbara Radice, who interprets them

In the exhibition "The Banal Object" at the 1980 Venice Biennale everyday objects were on show to demonstrate their significance in our visual code: their shapes and outlines were emphasized in colour to accentuate their banality.

330) Alessandro Mendini, Studio Alchymia: "Labourer's Room", Galleria d'Arte Moderna in Bologna, 1981.

331) Alessandro Mendini, Paola Navone, Daniela Puppa, Franco Raggi: "Room of the Century", Palazzo dei Diamanti in Ferrara, 1978.

332) Alessandro Mendini, Paola Navone, Daniela Puppa, Franco Raggi: "Banal Room", S.I.C.O.F., Milan, 1979.

in the following way: "The explanatory bursts of design are generally aimed in two directions, corresponding to two kinds of redesign. The reworking of famous designs like the chairs by Rietveld, Breuer, Ponti, Colombo, Thonet and Mackintosh and the redesign of everyday objects like the Proust armchair or the objects for the 'Forum Design' exhibition in Linz or put on show at the Venice Biennale. In both cases redesign is a way of emphasizing the banality of the alteration and of the object altered when contrasted with different situations of an aulic type". Redesign emerges out of an attempt to demonstrate that from today and "for at least ten years into the future, one can do nothing but redesign."

In fact redesigning something is presented as an action that enhances but does not modify reality. So it is curious that banal design arrives at a formulation that bears some resemblance to the one made by the post-modern towards the end of the modern culture of architecture's period of development. At the 1980 Venice Biennale a direct confrontation took place between these two theoretical hypotheses in two concurrent and adjacent exhibitions, "The Banal Object" and "The Presence of the Past", organized by Paolo Portoghesi on the theme of post-modernism.

These two initiatives were marked by profound differences, but both derived from a common fundamental realization, that of the impracticability of the modern moralistic and methodological project, to which Mendini gave a last farewell ("Goodbye design") and which Paolo Portoghesi wished to supplant by an act of cultural liberation ("The end of prohibitionism"). Both claimed that the historical period marked by the culture of the Modern Movement had come to an end, but whereas banal design postulated the advent of an era which would see the collapse of any possibility of putting design back together again as a culture, and in which it would survive only as free circulation of superficial signs, the latter proposed a return to the orderly world of historical tradition, styles and the academy.

In one sense the theoretical path followed by banal design came very close to the one put forward by Charles Jencks, whose analysis of "semantic groups" had first taken the lid off the problems involved in both post-modern and uncultured design. Actually Jencks singled out two principal "semantic groups" in society, the first of which comprised both the lower middle-classes and the stars of Hollywood and identified its own model of habitat with luxury, prosperity, dominance over nature and an architecture crammed with vulgar, consoling and bogus affectations. The second major semantic group lumped together intellectuals and aristocrats and was biased towards a more austere life-style, in harmony with nature, more rooted in local tradition, reserved and intimate. Both of these groups, according to Jencks, possess proven models of privacy that fit in with the theories of cultured design, and they often use builders or interior decorators merely as the constructors of realms that have already been imagined down to the last detail.

Mendini and Portoghesi represented the two extremes of this view of design, one nihilist, the other restorative. From both these points of view, the 1980 Biennale marked the official end of the pop era, that is to say the end of industrial culture as a shaping force behind the metropolitan landscape and the reform of society. Yet in many ways both Portoghesi's revival of style and Mendini's banal design brought the seventies to a somewhat problematical conclusion; they are still an integral part of that era in that they represent different paths from a fundamentally "critical" rather than speculative culture. Design, especially in the case of the banal, is expected to fulfil a didactic function, illustrative of a critical and polemical stance, rather than come up with new hypotheses for action. They are still, paradoxically, radical attitudes, aimed at aggravating the present historical situation through acts of planning; design and architecture are still used as ideological metaphors, critical allegories demonstrating an alternative, within the old culture of the death of design or its exit from history, in search of a tautological foundation of its own.

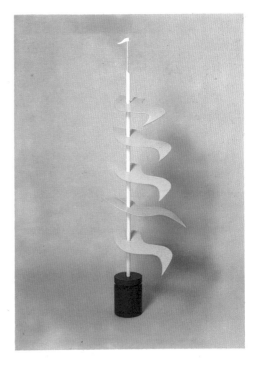

In the "Banal Rooms" everyday material life was reconstructed, full of "modern" culture: a serene domestic universe with no future.

333-334) Alessandro Mendini: "Mock Flowers", Zanotta, 1982.

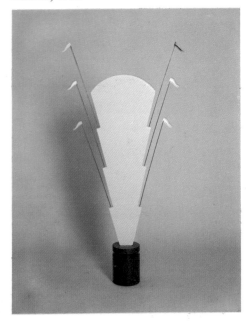

The Metropolitan Scene

XVI

Many of the experiences described so far, from the No-stop City to primary and banal design, can be lumped together to define a new metropolitan condition as the existential status of modern man, whether in a late-modern, post-modern or post-industrial society. It is clear that in describing our society as post-industrial, as both Lyotard and Deleuze have recently done, the intention is to give a label to the whole range of cultural and social changes that have left their mark on our civilization since the fifties. This has meant the de facto adoption of an intransigent and uniform ideological policy as an indispensable device for speeding up all the processes of integration in manufacturing and industrialization. Once its own quantitative position was secured, the phase of heroic expansion of the frontiers of the system, whether in terms of society or of territory, gave way to the current historical phase, the one to which the term post-industrial actually refers, characterized not by the disappearance of industry in the productive cycles of society, but on the contrary by the latter's complete and final takeover of the former — an ownership that is accompanied by the collapse of all the most intransigent and overbearing aspects of industrial culture. That culture no longer stands out as the pre-eminent factor in the production of culture, in so far as its completed expansion and genuine ownership of all the instruments of communication within society encourage a permanent internal manipulation of the production of languages by the media, and no longer by ideologies extraneous to the instruments.

There is no space left that is really outside the logic of industry and manufacturing, just as there no longer exists any ideology capable of presenting an alternative outside the system; there is no longer any nature to make comparisons with and no final goal at which to aim, simply because there is no reality outside the system, only a continuous present, in movement but with no progression.

From the 18th century to the Futurist era, culture and modern aesthetics have stressed the pre-eminent role of the city as a site for all social and linguistic changes: but it has always been a city that rose out of an alien setting made up of the countryside, nature and tradition. Inside this city art bore testimony to values from outside, both as a contrast with vanquished myth as in Marinetti's Nike of Samothrace and as mediumistic evocations of historical memories as in the painting of De Chirico.

Post-industrial culture excludes values and memories external to itself; it actually excludes the very assumption of "external", in this way building a model based on the absence of a beginning and of an end — an elliptic movement to be fed by the malaise of a continuous crisis without external disasters.

These new conditions of existence and work are fully expressed, in post-industrial culture, by the metropolis, which can no longer be seen as the outcome of abnormal growth of the city itself (the "dream of the village"), but represents rather an original, continuous and close-knit reality that, unlike the traditional city, has done away with any correlation or antinomy with nature, becoming nature itself, as in the all-embracing No-stop City, without a break, discontinuous and mobile; it is a sort of liquid space in which we are immersed like fish in the sea and which has no need to "represent the sea" in order to know it, since it forms part of our own bodily rather than mental experience. In the post-industrial metropolis art can no longer survive as critical discrepancy, i.e. as a gap between reality and plan, the sole workable possibility for the preservation of its "aura", as Heidegger saw it. In the industrial era art is reproduced in the same way as any other kind of object or merchandise: a film is made in the same manner as a car. Walter Benjamin, who was the first to come to terms with all this, concluded that art had permanently lost its "aura" but could still become an instrument to be used in

335) UFO Group: restaurant "Bamba-Issa no. 1", Forte dei Marmi, 1969.

336-337) UFO Group: restaurant "Sherwood", Florence, 1969.

338) UFO Group: boutique "Il Mago di Oz", Viareggio, 1969.

339) Gaetano Pesce: "Golgota" set, Braccidiferro, 1973.

340) UFO Group: stand at the Salone del Mobile (Furniture Showroom) in Milan, 1971.

341) UFO Group: restaurant "Bamba-Issa no. 3", Forte dei Marmi, 1972.

the "political understanding" of the world in the sense of Brecht.

No-one, not even the Futurists, conceived of an art belonging to the metropolis, seeing it always as a testimony to "external" values, the instrument of justice or of truth. In our perception, the metropolis has no beginning or end and art is a reality mixed up with institutions and merchandise: there is no critical discrepancy between these two categories, nor any difference in ideological strategy. Lyotard in fact defines the post-industrial metropolitan condition as a loss of all external referents, as the breakdown of criticism and of ideological sophistry. Life and space are becoming more and more artificial, social relations increasingly precarious and partisan and production itself more and more remote from society. Art no longer has any real goal, since the work of art reproduces the metropolis as it is, i.e. without transforming it into anything else. A repetition, therefore, that is superficial, banal and decorative.

342) UFO Group: "Inflatable Anas House", Florence, 1969.

343) UFO Group: "The House with Obstacles", Eurodomus, Turin, 1972.

344) UFO Group, "Tour of Italy", "Contemporanea" exhibition, Rome, 1974.

Art becomes a purely metropolitan phenomenon, an event without origins, just like many others that go on within the metropolis: typical examples of post-industrial metropolitan art are performances and autonomous environments, temporal and spatial events without origins or aims except that of creating an event and a space as a temporary spectacle. Examples of such autonomous environments are those created by the UFO group since the seventies, where staging and theatrical make-believe are indistinguishable: magic places, artefacts, in which the designer becomes user and at the same time recites his part from a private script. These are designs in which reality and make-believe — the staging and the new modes of behaviour induced by the staging — are totally superimposed. In this sense the "new theatricality" and New Design have gone through some interesting operational coincidences, within a society in which media performance and reality are mixed up without a break.

Every time that these correspondences have been set up, in other words when experimental theatre groups have worked in environments or autonomous settings produced by protagonists of New Design, an interesting re-definition of the concept of set-designing has occurred. In traditional set-design, which created a non-existent universe with close links to the theatrical performance, the scenery and the set were treated as given facts independent of the theatrical events, having their own autonomous spatial and cultural connotations. The breakdown of the narrative function of scenery resulted in a new kind of metropolitan realism in theatrical performances, in which this genuine dissociation of elements is re-assembled into an illusory but effective dramatic unity, raising the level of tension in the performance.

Mendini's sets for the Magazzini Criminali proposed in effect a progressive in-dependence from theatrical action, to the point of the "Mobile Infinito" ("Infinite Furniture"); the "Magazzini Criminali" acted on the site where this artefact was exhibited, making use of the dramatic force already created by setting up the "Mobile Infinito" in front of the faculty of architecture in Milan.

Thus, scenery is no longer a decorative setting for the theatrical performance, and the relationship is even turned on its head, so that the actors in Antonio Six-ti's *Casa per Giulietta*, with sets by Mendini, were required to play a wholly decorative role with respect to the staging, which did not ask for more than super-ficial interpretation. The same can be said for "Mussolini's Bathroom", a reconstruc-tion of the gymnasium that Luigi Moretti designed for the Duce in 1938 , which required nothing more from the performance of the "Out-off" group than theatrical animation.

This increasing autonomy of setting from performance has even led to the crea-

345-346) Andrea Branzi and collaborators: "Paradise and Records", Venice Biennale, 1980.

These condensed architectural "dramas" offer a realistic theoretical scenery where a certain idea is acted out which becomes a show in itself. In the case of "Town-Planning Interior", the idea was to show the passage from a decorated interior to a metropolitan scene.

348-349) Andrea Branzi, Studio Alchymia, collaborators: "Mussoloni's Bathroom" (reconstruction of Mussolini's gymnasium in the Foro Italico, by Italo Moretti and Gino Saverini, 1938), Centro Domus, 1982.

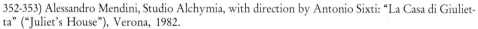
350) Alessandro Mendini, Franco Raggi, Daniela Puppa, Paola Navone: set for the Magazzini Criminali, "Nervous Breakdown", 1980.

The encounter with avant-garde theatrical groups gave rise to scenery drawn from pre-existent cultural phenomena. In other cases theatrical groups are called upon to animate existing environments with performances, happenings, etc.

352-353) Alessandro Mendini, Studio Alchymia, with direction by Antonio Sixti: "La Casa di Giulietta" ("Juliet's House"), Verona, 1982.

351) Alessandro Mendini, Studio Alchymia: window-dressing for the "Mali" firm, Florence, 1982.

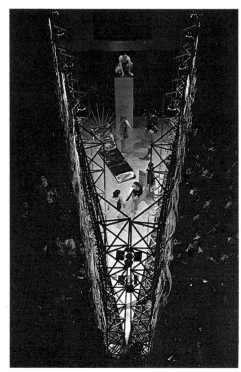

354) Alessandro Mendini, Studio Alchymia, with Magazzini Criminali: "Infinite Chattel", Faculty of Architecture, Milan, 1982.

tion of "mute scenes", places apparently intended to house theatrical performances that in fact never take place. This is the case with the reconstructions of "banal rooms", where no use is made of them at all (unless they are brought to life independently by the "Magazzini Criminali"), or even with the "Interno Urbanistico" ("Town-Planning Interior") set up in 1978 at the Palazzo dei Diamanti in Ferrara, or the "Paradiso e Records" ("Paradise and Records") in the church of San Lorenzo at the 1980 Venice Biennale. These mute scenes are not part of an experimental research into new models of housing, i.e. experimental sites where New Design recomposes avant-garde languages in the light of new modes of use, but genuinely autonomous theatrical experiences. In each case their function has been to express a literary hypothesis transformed into a real place, a metropolitan scene.

355) Studio Alchymia, Alessandro Mendini: "Decor Use", Fiorucci, Milan, 1980.

356) Alessandro Mendini, Studio Alchymia: "Dress Furniture", Fiorucci, Milan, 1982.

The New Handicrafts

XVII

Interest in handicrafts is a phenomenon that crops up regularly in the history of design and modern architecture, as a sort of confrontation with a production system that is seen as "lost innocence". Throughout the twentieth century, the fact that industrial work has been continually spurned has led to a perception of often non-existent values in handicrafts. People nostalgic for pre-industrial society, for example, are now looking to the values of craftsmanship for a new pattern of organization based on the rediscovery of the individual and on the myths of humanism.

The urban models of Leo Krier and the academic school of Luxembourg, for instance, resurrect the idea of an artisan city in which eclectic monuments are used to reconstitute an urban landscape abounding in symbols, where architecture may be saved by the sacrifice of social and technical progress and where it is given back the space to get across its own message, making a clean sweep of all the encum-

357) Andrea Branzi: "Gallery of Copyism", Studio Alchymia, 1979.

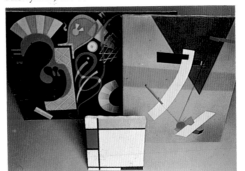

358) Andrea Branzi: "Metropolitan Couple", tapestry, 1977.

At the beginning of the eighties there was a revival of hand work (as in the case of the "Gallery of Copyism" where famous pictures were reproduced by hand). This was seen not so much as an alternative to industrial production but as being akin to applied arts.

359) Ettore Sottsass Jr.: "Even the Structures Tremble", table, Studio Alchymia, 1980.

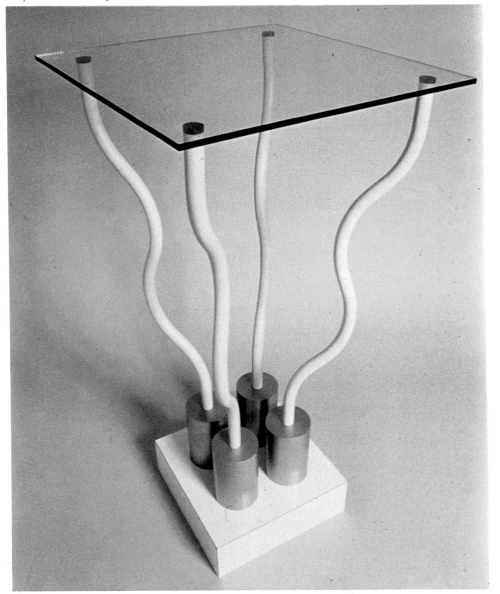

brances of modernism.

In this way handicrafts resume their place at the heart of a very broad concern with culture, as a touchstone for different hypotheses of historical development. But it turns out to be extremely difficult to isolate handicrafts as a category of production today; none of their supposed "purity" stands up to close examination. Complex and ambiguous relationships with manufacturing and the market have led on the one hand to a decline in the expressiveness of traditional products and on the other to an astonishing growth in the capacity for technological experimentation, unknown to industrial mass-production.

In his book *Dov'è l'artigiano*, Enzo Mari has attempted the first thorough examination of what goes by the name of handicrafts today, trying to retrace and rehabilitate the common thread linking those areas where "diffuse craftsmanship" is to be found in the industrial world. In the educational exhibition that he mounted for the Tuscan Region on the occasion of the 54th International Handicrafts Exhibition, Mari brought together the two extremes between which modern handicrafts are defined today, combining in a mathematical fashion the various factors that underlie differing patterns of production. He starts out with an example of the optimal state in which ownership of the means of production, design and execution coincide in the figure of a single operator: "An artist in modern society; a builder of arches in a primitive society." The other extreme is represented by total dissociation of all the different phases of the manufacturing process, in which designer, manager, executor and owner of the means of production are all different people, with separate responsibilities and fields of knowledge. As Mari puts it: "A manufacturer of domestic appliances in modern society, the constructors of pyramids in an ancient society." At this pole the involvement of the artisan has fallen to zero; but if just one of these conditions changes, one can fairly speak of an "ingredient of craftsmanship" in industrial production. The assumption of a clear-cut technical and ideological rift between handicrafts and industry does not stand up to the evidence of a vast program of functional collaboration between the two systems of manufacturing.

This is the setting in which the old controversy over the use of the machine that so exercised the greatest theoreticians of the last century, from Pugin to Morris, and then from Muthesius to Gropius, has been superseded by the technological flexibility of modern craftsmanship, which permits experimental processes that are beyond the grasp of the rigid structures of industry. Being an artisan does not mean not using machines in the process of manufacturing; on the contrary it means using all the machines in the workshop in rotation, maintaining direct control over all phases of production by passing — unlike the assembly line worker who

360) Enzo Mari: scheme of the exhibition "Where Are the Handicrafts?", Florence, 1981.

361) Enzo Mari: example of a stage in the preparation of a prototype for a mass-produced shoe (Calzaturificio Sheraton, Verona) (from the catalogue *Dov'è l'artigiano*, Electa edition, 1981).

362) Enzo Mari: models produced by an artisan workshop specializing in collaboration with industrial designers (Ditta Sacchi, Milan) (from the catalogue *Dov'è l'artigiano*, Electa edition, 1981).

363) Riccardo Dalisi: Neapolitan coffee-maker, 1981.

364) Riccardo Dalisi: funnel, 1982.

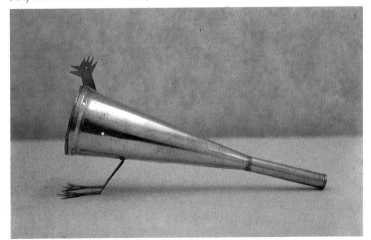

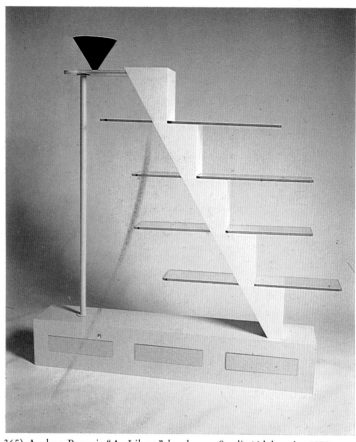

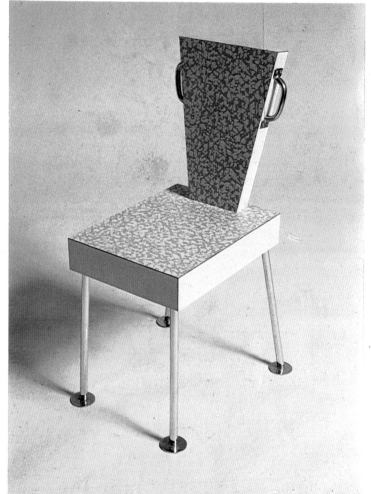

365) Andrea Branzi: "A. Libera" bookcase, Studio Alchymia, 1979.

366) Andrea Branzi: "Ginger" chair, Studio Alchymia, 1980.

367) Andrea Branzi: "Oskar" bookcase, Studio Alchymia, 1980.

368) Ettore Sottsass Jr.: high chair for dining, Studio Alchymia, 1980.

is confined to a single stage of construction — from one machine to another, just as the carpenter moves directly from the planer to the electric saw and the drill as the stages and methods of his own scheme of assembly require.

Making "by hand" today, if it does not coincide with the possession of the means of design and construction, means using the hand just like any other machine; it is no surprise that under such working conditions the category of handicrafts is often a cover for the most alienated section of the black economy.

The product of "diffuse craftsmanship" in a modern industrial civilization should not therefore be confused with the naïve or poor product. It is better represented by the experimental prototype with a high technological content: from the injection mould for the manufacture of plastic goods to the prototype of a formula 1 racing car. Such craftsmanship is indispensable to and indeed the basic premise of industrial manufacturing.

When on the other hand the artisan is employed in making handicrafts, i.e. producing goods aimed at a separate and alternative market to the industrial one, he is making use of cultural models far less susceptible to analysis, and the products that he offers have highly distinctive structural qualities, though they are often more symbolic than real. In fact the so-called arts and crafts are of considerable commercial importance today and are linked to a stable market with its own specific range of merchandise. People demand handmade goods, or goods that look handmade, precisely because they suppose it involves old and consequently better techniques of construction than those used in mass-production and also because they attribute a continuity with traditional culture and its methods to the design of this kind of product. The question of the technology and cultural models used in arts and crafts involves such a tangled and complex series of equivocations that it is difficult to unravel; perhaps the only feasible approach to making a critical examination of this question is one that involves going back to the period in which the market for handicrafts as a separate category from that of industrial products was formed.

One way to do this is to adopt the model of historical analysis recently proposed by Argan in connection with "peasant culture", which has also been the victim of widespread critical misunderstanding of an ideological origin. Argan holds that the origin of peasant culture lies in the courtly tradition of Byzantium, i.e. in a theocratic culture that, displaced by the emerging urban mercantile civilization, fled into agricultural territory, where it clung to stable values of living and working. Far from being spontaneous and primitive, it stands as a tradition of high cultural import with its own concepts of work and ethics that are in conflict with those of a mercantile civilization where the products of culture are viewed as goods of exchange with their own market value. So the peasant culture's system of symbols and techniques derives from Byzantine ideology, in which a system of im-

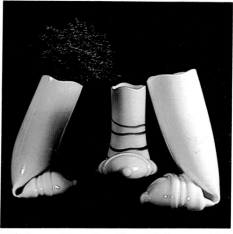

369) Gaetano Pesce: "per Venezia" glass vase, 1978.

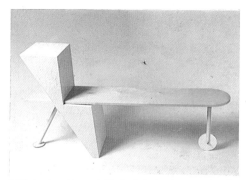

370) Andrea Branzi: "Seltz" chaise-longue, Studio Alchymia, 1980.

This group of objects is part of two collections by Alchymia called Bauhaus 1979 and Bauhaus 1980. They are the first achievements of the new craftsmanship, an experimental production in reduced series with the accent on linguistic and expressive research.

371) Michele De Lucchi: Girmi iron, prototype, 1980.

372) Michele De Lucchi: Girmi toaster, prototype, 1980.

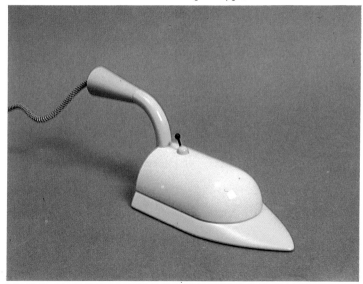

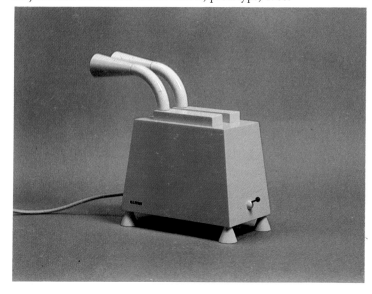

373) Lapo Binazzi: "Scarica Elettrica" lamp, 1975.

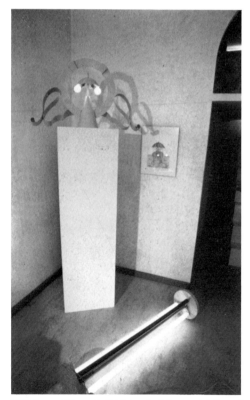

374) Lapo Binazzi: "Falciatrice" lamp, 1969, and UFO Group: "Paramount" lamp, 1971.

The idea of "custom-built" highly expressive objects can only be applied to single pieces using refined craftsmanship techniques.

375) Lapo Binazzi: appliqué masks, 1981.

mutable values was determined to exclude new technical and social experiences.

The same method of analysis can be applied to the process by which an artisan technology of marketable goods was formed over the last century, in an attempt to create an alternative to industrial mass-production and above all to the program of cultural adaptation and impoverishment that this involved.

Modern artistic handicrafts have been vaunted from their birth as an area where traditional values are conserved; dissociating themselves from any culture of design, the arts and crafts have ground out a range of products that are represented as lying outside the consumer market, responding to the real exigencies of age-old human needs rather than to the fashions of the market of induced needs. The supposed creativity of the artisan, or at least his "ancient wisdom", is contrasted with today's consumption-oriented technology. In reality the arts and crafts, shifting the responsibility for research into new forms of merchandise and consumption onto industy, stick to the pure and simple "reproduction" of existing models, i.e. those already shaped by tradition. The myth of artisan creativity crumbles before an analysis of the ways in which it functions on the market; all innovative processes are alien to it, and it only enters the market with formal models that are already stabilized.

Paradoxically, then, industry absorbs the experimental flexibility of a technological craftsmanship, utilizing it as a research phase within the industrial cycle, and at the same time eviscerates the creativity of artistic craftsmanship by transforming it into an alienated system for the reproduction of historical models for the market. The result is a total loss of political and cultural autonomy on the part of modern handicrafts, which are obliged to aid the development of markets and techniques in industry and at the same time make room for the latter on the market, renouncing any innovative role for its own artistic product.

In this way artisan production recycles even the modern style, though it is treated

as a historical style, interchangeable with other formal models drawn from tradition; in any case any ingredient of research or design is extraneous, and construction becomes synonymous with imitation.

Curiously, we are seeing today a repetition of this phenomenon that occurred a hundred years ago: within an advanced industrial society a theoretical debate of great significance is once again developing over handicrafts, seen as the area of confrontation between different theories about the development of architecture and the city. And this is taking place, again, at a moment when handicrafts are in the throes of an extreme crisis.

The crisis of the crafts as an independent field of research and design, together with the collapse of the myth of the artisan workshop, seriously complicates any research in this direction. We can approach handicrafts only as a privileged area within industrial production, where a particular organization of work permits the realization of products in which experimentation plays a greater part or the use of industrial materials that do not fall within the requirements of mass-production.

Handicrafts can be viewed, then, as a major experimental instrument, as an industrial area open to new patterns and new designs that mass-production would be unable to create owing to the rigidity of its technical and manufacturing structure. Possession of this instrument became, towards the end of the seventies, indispensable to the renewal of the culture of design. In 1979 Studio Alchymia of Milan presented the first "Bauhaus" collection, made up of prototypes and models by Sottsass, Mendini and De Lucchi, as well as myself: that moment saw the birth of a new formula of production and distribution to which we have given the name "new handicrafts".

The "new handicrafts", which were first put on show by Alessandro Guerriero at his Alchymia, possess certain very precise characteristics: the craftsmanship employed, given that production is made up of small runs or unique pieces, does not depend on the use of particular techniques, but rather on the speed with which the models — whose design makes no concessions to the possibility of future mass-production — are constructed by craftsmen using the most advanced techniques of modern joinery.

The explicitly cultural aspect of the models does not derive from "artisan culture", but rather from the way the latter is used as an area for experimentation. In fact the prototype and the limited run make no pretence of being an alternative to mass-production, but treat it as a possible subsequent phase to the experiments in design permitted by the new handicrafts. The "original", the model that can be reproduced only as a limited repetition of a prototype, is a consequence of the experimental nature of the design and not a theoretical premise. In this sense, the correct place for the new handicrafts is alongside, or before, mass-production and not in opposition to it, since by nature they involve an experiment not in technique or production but in expression.

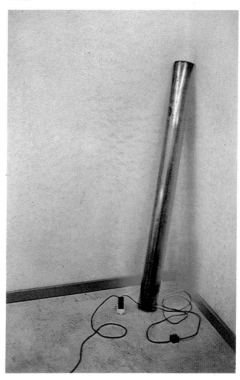

376) Lapo Binazzi, neon-lit copper shower-bath, 1982.

The new handicrafts are born out of a realistic appraisal of the present industrial production of furniture and in particular the essentially artisan nature of a large part of it. Often, in fact, the adjective "industrial" is intended as an indication more of a style than of a genuine mass-production of models. This is the result of a large number of factors, not least of which is the necessity of testing the commercial viability of a design before going into automated production, with the enormous amount of time and expense that this entails. What this means in practice is the production of handcrafted prototypes of potential mass runs that will require substantial modification if they are ever to go into mass-production. Simulated mass-production runs, i.e. those envisaged but not realized, make up a large part of the present-day furniture industry. The new handicrafts accept the positive side of this somewhat ambiguous situation, at least from the stylistic point of view, and turn it to advantage in a production that is free from the problems of mass scale and involves a high degree of experimentation and research. This makes clear the commercial rather than productive difference be-tween the new handicrafts and industry, where the one aims to sell a few prototypes of high cultural quality and the other aims to sell many prototypes of mediocre cultural value. There is no conflict here, only a difference in marketing strategies.

New Design

XVIII

There is an objective difference between New Design and traditional design: this is a question not so much of ideology or style but of changed market and production conditions. In fact what this book has dealt with so far is not an opposition movement but rather the history of research and experiments that derive from a completely different approach to the role of everyday objects in the domestic environment. In this new view considerable emphasis is given to the importance of creating an alternative to the rigid strictures that industrial design has over the years imposed on the expressive and functional potential of the objects themselves.

Taken as a whole, this research work has provided a wealth of languages, theories and instruments that can be used to cope with the transformation that design is undergoing in view of changes in the surrounding context and conditions. Classical design always referred to mass markets, and these are now disappearing. This is partly because standardization, with its urge to transform different types of behaviour and traditions into fixed universal models, had its roots in the existence of a large, homogeneous international market. Design was thus involved in thinking up objects that would suit everyone, whereas in fact they were also unsuited to everyone. These were products that were indiscriminately promoted throughout the whole range of the market.

Our present post-industrial society is characterized by the simultaneous presence of a variety of markets that correspond to different cultural groups, each with its specific behaviour, language, fashions and traditions, and each with a particular type of consumer requirements. Industry is therefore faced with having to devise a production strategy that relies not on the drastic semantic reduction that typified classical design but rather on a new and violent acculturation of the product; the product, that is, must actively select its own user, promote itself to a particular social group and must avoid apparently objective but substantially anonymous qualities.

377) Andrea Branzi: "Vallechiara" lamps, Croff Centro Casa/Latina Illuminazione, 1978.

379) Ettore Sottsass Jr.: "Valigia" light, Stilnovo, 1978.

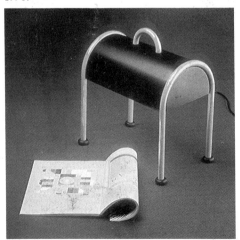

378) Achille and Pier Giacomo Castiglioni: "Allunaggio" seat, Zanotta, 1980.

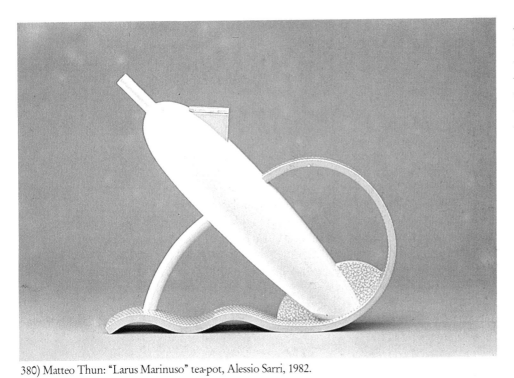

380) Matteo Thun: "Larus Marinuso" tea-pot, Alessio Sarri, 1982.

Memphis, born in Milan in 1981 from an idea of Ettore Sottsass Jr. and Barbara Radice with the support of Brugola, Artemide and Arch. 74 produces objects by avant-garde personalities including Hans Hollein, Arata Isozaki, Umeda Masanori, Michael Graves, Terry Jones, Sihiro Curamata, and Javier Marsical.

A new concept of product and environmental quality thus asserts itself, one which, beyond questions of performance and service, is intent on creating an emotional value — the only sort of value that is able to constitute a point of reference within the sphere of this new kind of consumption. This emotional value is created not by the object's functionality, but by its expressive level. This latter feature is made up of the object's basic materials, its shape, weight, smell, tactile characteristics and perceptual presence: from high-tech to high-touch. To make this move, design must take all the liberties offered by new technologies, using them as possibilities for new languages and new forms of use that can answer to the cultural needs of new social groups.

The critical culture produced during the seventies made a point of using design

381) Marco Zanini: "Cassiopea" goblet, 1982.

382) Ettore Sottsass Jr.: "Alaska" vase, Memphis, 1982.

383) Andrea Branzi: "Labrador" sauce-boat, Memphis, 1982.

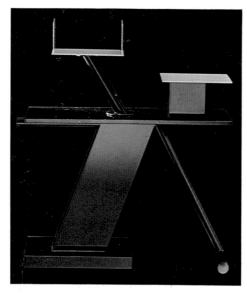

to underline the polemical and ideological nature of social systems and consumer society. By way of contrast, during the eighties a new and more mature form of culture has made itself felt, one that makes real proposals aimed at giving a certain area of design a cohesiveness it had lost. New Design emerged slowly, having made its way through the new professional and critical landscape in an attempt to establish a wider conception of design activity. Italian New Design has gathered strength to the point of being able to influence both the world of production and the parallel theoretical development. Ettore Sottsass Jr., presenting the first Memphis collection, wrote: "All that walking through realms of uncertainty..., all that talking with metaphors and utopia..., all that getting away from it all... has given us a certain experience; we've become good explorers. Maybe we can navigate dangerous rivers, penetrate jungles where no-one has ever been. There's no reason for getting worked up. We can finally make our way with ease; the worst is over."

Much of what was new regarding colour, decoration and expressive languages has now been adopted for many of the objects produced by Italian design in general. The International Furniture Fairs, from 1980 on, have taken on a new lease of life thanks to the new questions that have emerged. The barrier that for fifteen years separated "straight" design from the experiments of the avant-garde is beginning to diminish, or at least turn into a relationship involving the active exchange of experiences and languages between two culturally stable areas.

The importance of Italian New Design nevertheless goes beyond the mere renewal of the exterior aspects of current production. It reaches out across that wide range of activities that move from design to achitecture, and then on towards the city. In October 1983 Domus Academy was inaugurated in Milan. This is the first post-graduate design school, and it sets out from the theoretical nucleus of New Design while at the same time absorbing the innovative contributions of the most important designers in each given sector. Young architects and designers from all over the world have enrolled in this school, and teaching encompasses research into new models for living as well as design for the urban scene. The range of research work covered by New Design thus places it in a fundamental position as far as the redefinition of architecture itself is concerned. Of course this is not the first time this has happened: during the last century the applied arts led the debate that gave rise to modern architecture. As Giedion has pointed out, this debate in all

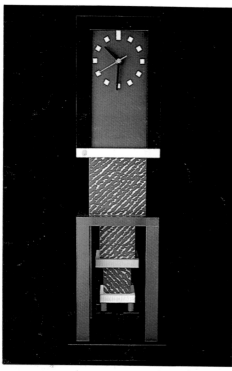

384) Ettore Sottsass Jr.: "Metro" furniture, Memphis, 1983.
385) George Sowden: "Metropole" clock, Memphis, 1982.
386) Michele De Lucchi: "First" high-chair, Memphis, 1983.
387) Andrea Branzi: "Century" divan, Memphis, 1982.

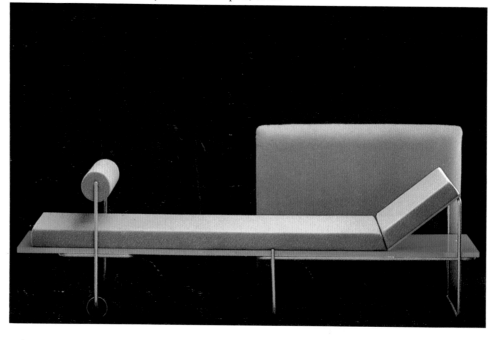

388-389) Paolo Deganello: "Bachbotton" armchair, Driade, 1982.

392-393) Alessandro Mendini: "Sabrina" armchair, Driade, 1982.

390-391) Achille Castiglioni: "S. Carlo" armchair, Driade, 1982.

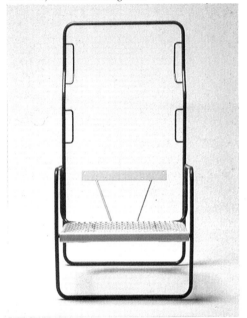 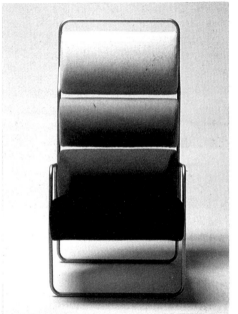

394) Massimo Morozzi: "Tangram" component tables, Cassina, 1983.

Furniture manufacturers like Driade are diversifying production line objects. Here an armchair with a basic structure has been interpreted by different deisgners using a variety of additions.

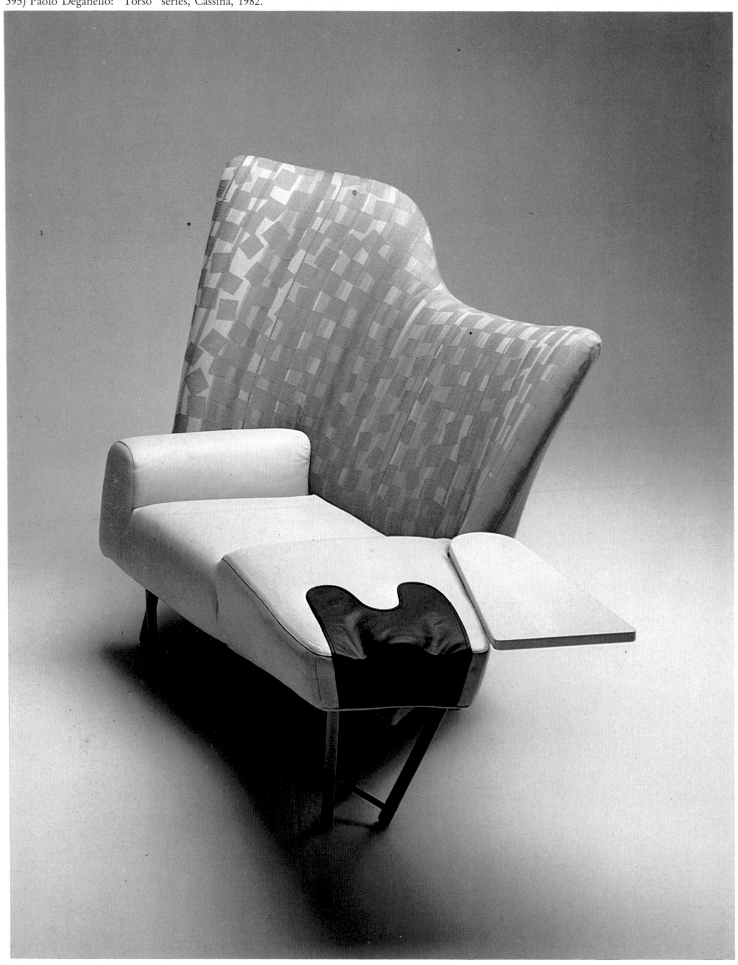

its complexity derives from the apparently marginal question of whether or not to make vases by machine. In fact, within an industrial civilization like ours, design has a great deal to do with the problem of man's relationship with his pleasure in doing things, with the problem of the emotional, symbolic and functional ties that link man in his habitat to his system of objects. At the Red House, William Morris was looking for the nucleus of a new way of living. His proposal was neo-mediaeval, one in which the craftsman's workshop was the centre of a different sort of society, and manual technique the way of achieving a renewed domestic civilization. The excessive development of architectural research certainly has not resolved, and actually has hardly dealt with, the problem of a new way of living, to the extent that all modern architecture has developed without any real awareness of how it is to be used. No wonder it has now reached a point of advanced social isolation.

The applied arts of the last century were full of signs and quotations, of metaphors and ornament. But they disappeared at the beginning of this century, suffocated by the unitary hypothesis of the Bauhaus with its insistence on the oneness of arts and techniques, with architecture, as the most important and most general instrument of control, acting as defender of a possible unity of purpose. "The ultimate goal of all the figurative arts is the complete building", wrote Walter Gropius in his manifesto of 1919. The disaster that followed was two-fold: on the one hand objects, which up till then had been autonomous signs that enriched domestic space quite freely, suddenly became part of a complete building in which they were only meaningful in so far as they were able to relate in dimension to their container; they thus became cold objects, lacking in any real cultural and therefore practical relationship with their users; on the other hand modern architecture was born on the basis of its belief in the utopian ideal of "unity of human arts and technologies", just when art, science, philosophy and economics began to operate in a discontinuous universe, in a small section of reality. Modern architecture is thus inevitably out of step with its own century. Far from being, as it claimed, the most advanced and integrated sector of the whole system, a mo-

396) Nathalie du Pasquier: "California" carpet, Memphis, 1983.

Technological research applied to design objects through the use of electronics and sophisticated plastics allows for a whole new range of expression by craftsmen and challenges the classical role of objects in decoration.

397) Daniel Wiel: morbid clock, 1982.

398) Nanda Vigo: "Light Trees", 1983.

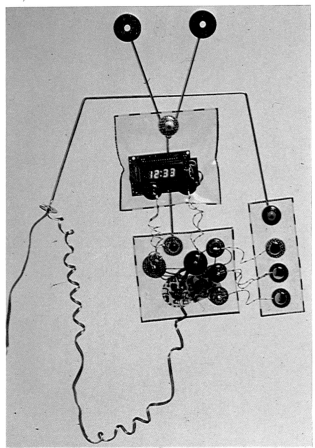

399) George Sowden: "Hilton" armchair, Bedding, 1976.

From the beginning, New Design was characterized by an effort to renew the language of domestic objects with new inspirations deriving from irony, curiosity, surprise and friendliness.

ment of synthesis and cultural unity, it was in fact as far removed as possible from the real world.

The inability of latter-day architecture to fit in with the modern world derives precisely from this historical schizophrenia. It is too advanced to form an autonomous domestic civilization of its own, and too backward with respect to the development of production and territorial communication. This incapacity is deep, painful and heroic as well. It is the outcome of a whole-hearted adoption of an atypical role, one that is out of step with history. And architecture was always convinced of being history's favourite child. The role adopted aimed at being central; instead it has always been a partial style and view of things with respect to the expressive wealth of surrounding society.

New Design is thus interested in putting together a different domestic culture, in recovering a system of ties and functions that cannot be explained in purely ergonomic or functional terms, that involve man in his relationship to his domestic habitat from a wider cultural and expressive point of view. The system of living thus conceived represents the threshold of a whole system of environmental and territorial design. There is no way modern architectural culture can carry on without having re-established a proper relationship with the user. The unliveableness of modern cities has usually been dealt with in collective terms by playing around with public spaces, when in fact it is the direct outcome of the crisis in the relationship between man and his own home.

Collective urban space today is bogged down with myths. For some time now efforts have been made to compensate for the dramatic lack of truly liveable domestic

400) Ettore Sottsass Jr.: "Flying Carpet" armchair, Bedding, 1976.

402) Sergio Cappelli, Patrizia Ranzo: "Auratour" agency, Naples, 1982.

Research undertaken by Gaetano Pesce has been recognized as an important point of reference, for its strength and continuity, for Italian New Design. At the same time he proposed both the dramatization of the objects of the new technology and the end of the repetition of mass-produced objects through the changing use of materials and the manual element.

403) Gaetano Pesce: "Dalila" chair, Cassina, 1980.

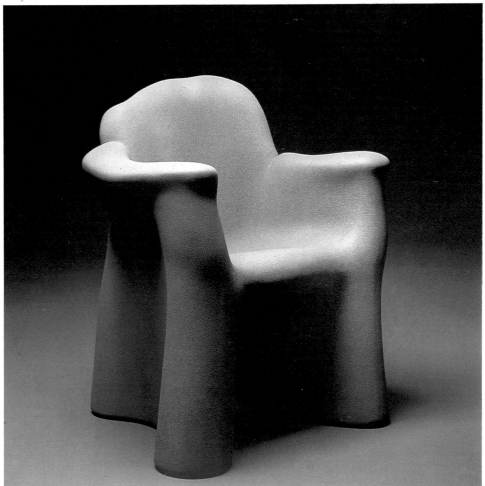

401) Gaetano Pesce: "Sit Down" armchair, Cassina, 1980.

404) Gaetano Pesce: "Sansone" table, Cassina, 1980.

Once again the internal environment becomes open with shelves and not closed cupboards, permitting an active participation in the domestic scene.

405) Gerard Taylor: "Airport", Memphis, 1982.

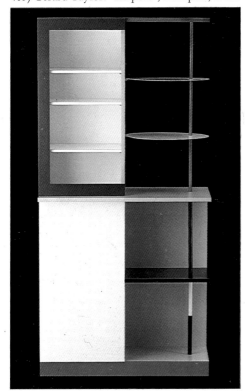

space by multiplying public space. From the Ville Radieuse to our latter-day town plans, modern urban planning has always believed that the various forms of collective urban life could make people forget the mediocrity of urban realities such as building typologies of the *Existenz-Minimum* sort. Urban space, pinned between wretched residential structures of little or no formal or cultural value, has often become a dead place that no amount of street furniture or stylistic change can hope to resuscitate. Often those empty parts of the city have been filled with a series of vital functions that once belonged to the domestic sphere, following a blind faith in the idea that all that is private is good and all that is public is bad. Dealing with the liveability of the home therefore means refounding the theorem of the metropolis itself, establishing a new way of setting about things that can make the outcome of design acceptable.

In 1914 Adolf Loos wrote: "On the outside a building should not speak; only on the inside should it reveal its richness." This statement is a forerunner of the ideas behind the No-stop City of New Design, the attempt to neutralize architecture as an artificial historic scenario and thus to promote the growth of kaleidoscopic systems of objects, languages and material that are better able to answer to the requirements of "poetic living", as Hölderlin would put it. In these interiors "in love", a new emotional tie can be created between man and the structures he lives in; the "hot house" can give rise to the new Metropolis. However, the focal point of this as we see it is not the recomposition of a unitary formal and linguistic code that sets out from the home and spreads across the city and territory as a whole; cultural or technical unity in contemporary design is not what we are after. As Mario Tronti puts it: "Let's leave big systems to little improvisors" and rather try to establish a system of new tolerance and new freedom for everyone.

There is no doubt that if architecture has a future, it must be not so much a new way of design but a new way of using the home — a way that comprises what is different, private, erroneous and at variance. Meticulousness of judgement and action should now be used not for breaking up the world into bits but for welcoming in other systems of thought and behaviour, for accepting debate that sets out from consciously partial positions. In the end the winner will be whoever can keep it up longest and has the most lucid ideas with which to follow and understand the world.

406) Antonio Citterio: "Max" divan, Flexform S.p.A, 1983.

Biographies

Alchymia

"Alchymia, the projection of images for the 20th century" started in Milan in 1976. In 1978 they presented their first collection of furniture, followed in 1979 by the collection "Bau.Haus uno" and in 1980 by "Bau.Haus due". They were awarded the Golden Compass in 1981 for design research. In recent years they have done many exhibitions. They have organized seminars and have also created videotapes, clothes, books, scenery for experimental theatres, objects, decorations, actions and architecture following the transition from radical to neo-modern design. They have written reviews and articles for the major international magazines. Their books include *In Praise of the Banal* with help from Barbara Radice; *Modern - Post-modern - Millennial* and *Architecture in Love* by Andrea Branzi; plus a *Catalogue of Decorative Furniture in the Modern Style, Rooms - An Idea for the Home,* and *The Unhappy Project* by Alessandro Mendini.

The collaborators of Alchymia are: Donatella Biffi, Pier Carlo Bontempi, Carla Ceccariglia, Stefano Casciani, Rina Corti, Walter Garro, Bruno Gregori, Giorgio Gregori, Adriana Guerriero, Rainer Hegele, Jeremy King, Yumiko Kobajashi, Ewa Kulakowska, Alessandro Mendini, Mauro Panzeri, Patrizia Scarzella.

Alchymia has produced objects by Ettore Sottsass Jr., Andrea Branzi, Alessandro Mendini, Michele De Lucchi, Franco Raggi, Daniela Puppa, Andrea Belloni, Paola Navone, Lapo Binazzi, Riccardo Dalisi, Trix and Robert Haussmann and others.

Archizoom Associati

Archizoom was founded in Florence in 1966 by Andrea Branzi, Gilberto Corretti, Paolo Deganello and Massimo Morozzi; in 1968, Dario and Lucia Bartolini joined this group. Their first work was in the field of architecture and urban research, where they explored some of the principal themes of radical architecture (including the No-stop City), and then they concentrated on the theme of innovative design and environmental projects, organizing exhibitions and products. They took part in the exhibition "Italy: The New Domestic Landscape" at the Museum of Modern Art in New York and have shown their work at many other individual and collective exhibitions of design around the world.

During their early years thay joined with Superstudio to organize the exhibitions of "Superarchitettura" at Pistoia and Modena (1966 and 1967), which gave rise to the debate on the culture of projects by the young. Their own research led in the years between 1971 and 1973 to the first projects of dressing design. They have always been interested in theoretical problems dealing with the new architectural culture and on this subject have written many articles for leading international magazines in this field. Their archives are preserved at the Archives of Communication of the Institute for the History of Art at the University of Parma, the curator of which is Carlo Quintavalle.

Lapo Binazzi

Lapo Binazzi was born in 1943 in Florence where he graduated and works at present. In the sixties he studied architecture, but he considers himself also a writer. In 1967 he started the group called UFO. He was part of the original group that founded Architettura Radicale. In 1968, together with the UFO, he invented the "Transient Urbans", gigantic blown-up objects that were placed in unlikely spots in the city area. His first work of architecture was "Casa a Castel Rigone" (1971) which, at the time, was clearly post-modern. In 1969 he did interior decoration for various shops. Since 1968 with the UFO he has taken part in many exhibitions, both in Italy and abroad. The most important were the Milan Triennales of 1968 and 1973, the Paris Biennale of 1971, Contemporanea at Rome in 1974, for which he personally created the design section, the International Biennale of Graphic Arts at Florence in 1976, the Venice Biennale of 1978, "Design by Circumstances" in 1981 at New York, "Design als postulat" at Berlin in 1973 and "Provakationen" in 1981 at Hanover. He had an important personal show at Alchymia in Florence in 1981. Among his other activities he has performed at the Centro Brera in Milan and at the Schema Gallery in Florence and has produced videotapes and films. He writes for various magazines including *Domus* and *Modo*.

Andrea Branzi

Andrea Branzi, architect and designer, was born and educated in Florence and now works in Milan. Until 1974 he was with Archizoom Associati, the first avant-garde Italian group. Since 1972 he has worked on the theoretical problems of New Design plus projects. Between 1974 and 1976 he took an interest in Global Tools, the first experimental laboratory for mass creativity. He was the General Coordinator for the International Design section at the 15th Milan Triennale and participated with personal shows in the 14th and 16th Triennales and the Venice Biennales of 1976, 1978, and 1980. His work has been shown at the New York Museum of Modern Art, the Victoria and Albert Museum in London, the Lijbanam Centrum in Rotterdam and in other cities throughout the world. In 1977 he helped organize the important exhibition "Italian Design of the Fifties" at Noviglio (Milan). He also worked and wrote the introduction of the book of the same title published in 1979 by Domus Editorial. He was a member of the C.D.M. (Milan Design Consultants) with whom he won the Golden Compass in 1979 for research into primary design. With the C.D.M. he also published two volumes on research into environmental decoration (*Decorattivo* 1 and 2, Idea Books) and three volumes on colour projects for industry ("The colours of energy" 1975, "Pre-synthetic colours" 1976, "Environmental colours" 1977, *Colordinamo*). In 1980 an anthology of his written works since 1972 was published (*Modern - Postmodern - Millennial,* Studio Forma/Alchymia). Numerous monographs on his work have been published by Space Design and Japan Interior Design. In 1982 and 1983 he was a contract lecturer at the Institute of Industrial Design at the Faculty of Architecture of Palermo; his collected lectures were published in the volume *Goods and the Metropolis* (Epos). He is educational director of the Domus Academy, the new international school of post-graduate study in New Design. Since January 1984 he has been director of *Modo,* the magazine of design and architecture.

Remo Buti

Remo Buti was born in Florence and at present lectures in the university there on Interior Architecture and Decoration. He was a founder of the avant-garde architectural movement in Italy and a co-founder of Global Tools. His projects have been shown at the 14th, 16th, and 17th Milan Triennales and at the Venice Biennale of 1978. He won the design competition for furnishing fabrics organized in 1970 by *Jardin de Mode* and, with others, the competition held at Cannes, "Construction et Humanisme".

Sergio Cappelli and Patrizia Ranzo

Sergio Cappelli and Patrizia Ranzo live and work in Naples. Their active careers started in 1973 when they took part in the Triennale in Milan. Their most significant projects over the last few years have been the BMW showrooms in Avellino, Naples and Caserta, and projects commisioned by the Borough of Naples for urban scenery and temporary architecture for "Summer in Naples" and "Piedigrotta". They have taken part in a number of design exhibitions in Italy and abroad and were among the winners of the "WIDI Competition" in California.

Casabella

This magazine dedicated to architecture and design was founded in 1928 and during its early years was directed by Edoardo Persico. After the Second World War the magazine, under the direction of Ernesto Rogers, became a point of reference for the new generation of architects (Vittorio Gregotti, Gae Aulenti, Aldo Rossi and others). In the years 1970 to 1976 it was directed by Alessandro Mendini, who used it as an international launching pad for the young avant-garde radical architects; regular items were written by Peter Cook, Ettore Sottsass Jr., Andrea Branzi and others. Mendini was succeeded as editor by Tomas Maldonado and then Vittorio Gregotti.

Achille Castiglioni

Achille Castiglioni was born in Milan in 1918. Right from his first experiments in 1940, his activity as a designer has been varied and intense, supported by intelligent practical and theoretical research. His work, in close collaboration with his brothers Pier Giacomo and Livio, with whom he has shared a professional studio from the beginning, has been a key to the worldwide success of the image of Italian design. From 1954 to 1964 his designs for "objects invented to allow the invention of space in the home" gained him a place in the 10th, 11th, and 12th Milan Triennales, and he has won the Golden Compass award six times. In 1969 he became lecturer in Artistic Design for Industry at the Faculty of Architecture of the Turin Polytechnic, where in 1977 he was given the Chair of Interior Architecture. To-day, as full professor, he lectures in Industrial Design and Furnishing at the Faculty of Architecture of the Polytechnic University of Milan. Eight of his designs are in the permanent collection of the Museum of Modern Art in New York. His latest creations are part of a continuous scientific research into the process of "integral" design, in the sense of the study of interdisciplinary relationships of the various operative phases aimed at linking up the languages of production and culture.

Cavart

The group known as Cavart was created in Padua in 1973 by Piero Brombin, Michele De Lucchi, Pierpaola Bortolami, Boris Premù and Valerio Tridenti; they were active during the period of Global Tools and the radical movement and organized projects, films, happenings and seminars, the best known of which is "Culturally Impossible Architecture", organized in the quarries at Monselice near Padua in 1975.

C.D.M.

C.D.M. (Milan Design Consultants) was founded in 1976 by Andrea Branzi, Gianni Cutolo, Alessandro Mendini, Clino Trini Castelli and Ettore Sottsass Jr. with the aim of creating a framework for large-scale projects such as landscapes, corporate images and other advanced research. C.D.M. did the project for the landscape and the corporate image of the Leonardo da Vinci airport in Rome, the information system for the new Italian Post Offices, the first centre of creative colorimetrics for the "Colorterminal", the Piaggio Colour System, part of the activity of the Montefibre Design Centre and other innovative projects.

Antonio Citterio

Antonio Citterio graduated from the Polytechnic University in Milan. Between 1972 and 1981 he collaborated with Paolo Nava on projects involving design and industrial strategy. He has produced many articles of furniture for important Italian manufacturers. He has also done interior decorating projects and has organized and furnished stands and exhibitions. He collaborated with the firm of Gregotti Associati on the restoration of the Brera Art Gallery in Milan.

Riccardo Dalisi

Riccardo Dalisi, born in Potenza in 1931, graduated in architecture at Naples University in 1957 and lectures there at present in Composition. Almost all of his works have been strictly connected to his profession of lecturer. In the seventies a working group which he organized in the poorer districts of Naples formed the central nucleus of a debate on "counter-design". He took part in the formation of Global Tools and together with Filippo Alison organized "Minimal Arts". His work has been published in various sources: *Unforeseeable Architecture*, a volume published at Urbino in 1970, documents his university courses, articles in design and architecture magazines, monographs and catalogues of personal and group exhibitions. He has taken part in three of the Triennale exhibitions in Milan and two Biennales in Venice. In 1981 he was awarded the Golden Compass for research. Noteworthy was his volume *Gaudì, Furniture and Objects* (Milan, 1979; English edition, 1980).

Almerico de Angelis

Almerico de Angelis, born in Naples, graduated in architecture in 1969; his interests lie in design, the image and interior decorating. In 1972 he organized an exhibition for the City Hall of Boston, Massachusetts, called "Naples and Its Region". In 1973 he started the movement called "For eventual architecture" and in 1974 the magazine *Che* based on studies of the use and significance of architecture. He lectures in Interior Design and Scenography at the Faculty of Architecture in Naples.

Paolo Deganello

Paolo Deganello was born at Este in 1940 and graduated in architecture at Florence in 1966. Together with Andrea Branzi, Gilberto Corretti and Massimo Morozzi, in 1966 he founded Archizoom Associati, which lasted until 1974. Then, in 1975, with Gilberto Corretti, Franco Gatti and Roberto Querci, he founded the "Group of Technical Designers", which took part in many architectural competitions. He has lectured at the University of Florence and at the Architectural Association in London. In 1975 he and Ennio Chiggio undertook publication of a series of essays entitled "Project Sketch Books". He has designed furnishing products for firms such as Planula, Marcatrè, Driade and Cassina. In March of 1981 his projects were included in the exhibition "Design by Circumstance" at the Clocktower in New York, organized by P.S. One and sponsored by the Institute for Art and Urban Resources of New York. In 1983 he designed a shop selling products for interior decoration for the Schöner Wohnen Company in Zurich, and he constructed a "Monument to the Snow" on the piazza in front of the shop. He has participated in many exhibitions of architecture and industrial design including the 14th through 17th Triennale exhibitions in Milan.

Michele de Lucchi

Michele de Lucchi was born in 1951 and graduated from the Faculty of Architecture in Florence. During his years at university he founded the Cavart group. He followed this with a period of lecturing as an assistant to Adolfo Natalini at the Faculty of Architecture and at the International University of Art in Florence. In 1977 he collaborated on the organization of the exhibition "Italian Design of the Fifties" in Milan. In 1979 he commenced a period as design consultant for Olivetti Synthesis at Massa and in 1984 at Olivetti in Ivrea. Together with Ettore Sottsass Jr. he designed the 45CR series and the support system for Modulo informatics. In 1982, again with Sottsass, he worked on the Icarus furnishing system for office automation. With Sottsass Associates he designed the furnishings and image of Fiorucci shops in Italy and Europe. He took part in the Triennale exhibitions of 1979 and 1983.

Jonathan De Pas, Donato d'Urbino, Paolo Lomazzi

These architects, all born in Milan in the thirties, have worked together since 1966 on architectural and design projects, organizing exhibitions, interior decorating and town-planning. In the sixties they concentrated on the design of furniture and temporary architecture using avant-garde techniques; they designed and saw built a series of pneumatic housing structures for both the Italian Pavilion at the Osaka World's Fair and the 14th Triennale in Milan; in 1967 they designed an inflatable armchair and called it "Blow". 1972 saw them at the MOMA exhibition "Italy: The New Domestic Landscape". They have built both industrial and residential buildings, furniture and utensils for the home and office, illumination and electronics. At the same time they have followed a line of research into the borders between architecture and design through, for example, their participation in "Italienische Model Design 1950/80" at the Stadtmuseum in Cologne. In 1979 they received the Golden Compass award. Their work can be seen at the Museum of Modern Art in New York, the Victoria and Albert Museum in London and the Pompidou Centre in Paris.

Domus

Domus, a magazine dealing with aspects of architecture, design, interior decoration and art, was founded by Giò Ponti in 1928; in the sixties *Domus* was edited by Lisa Licitra Ponti and then by Cesare Casati. From 1980 onwards guidance was in the hands of Alessandro Mendini, who gave it a new image as a forum for the new international design and for the new cultural-architectonic movements.

Domus Academy

The Domus Academy was founded in 1982 by Maria Grazia Mazzocchi, Valerio Castelli and Alessandro Guerriero. It offers the first postgraduate course of New Design. The scientific committee is composed of Giampaolo Fabris, Alessandro Guerriero, Alessandro Mendini, Pierre Restany and Silvio Brondoni; organization is in the hands of Mariola Fadini, and the director is Andrea Branzi. The aim is research into a new relationship between man and objects of everyday use and between man and planned structures, whether architectural or concerning the metropolis. The courses try to provide the professional "tools" needed for modern design, such as the use of calculators, a knowledge of industrial economics and the control of "soft" environmental structures. In the first year of activity basic subjects were: the History of the Culture of Planning (Andrea Branzi); Socio-Economic Forecasting (Francesco Morace); the Culture of Behaviour (Gianni Pettena, Pierre Restany); Industrial Technology (Valerio Castelli, Ezio Manzini, Alberto Meda, Carlo Alfonsi). Projects were: Primary Design (Clino Trini Castelli, Antonio Petrillo); New Habitative Models (Mario Bellini, Giorgio Origlia); Urban Outfits (Ettore Sottsass Jr., Marco Zanini); Design of Clothing (Gian Franco Ferrè, Giusy Ferrè, Daniela Puppa).

Nathalie du Pasquier

Nathalie du Pasquier was born at Bordeaux in France in 1957. From 1975 to 1978 she travelled extensively in Australia and India. She returned to Bordeaux in 1978 and studied drawing and design. In 1979 she went to live in Italy, first in Rome, then in Milan. In 1980 she joined the Studio Rainbow as a fabric designer. She designed the first fabrics for Memphis and in 1982 joined the creative staff of Fiorucci.

Anna Maria Fundarò

Anna Maria Fundarò directs the Institute of Industrial Design of the Faculty of Architecture at Palermo. She has published various historic and environmental studies of design. In 1982 and 1983, she organized the first courses on New Design run by an Italian university together with Michele Argentino, Marilù Balsamo, Anna Cottone and Alfonso Porrello, inviting as contract lecturers Ettore Sottsass Jr. and Andrea Branzi.

Alessandro Guerriero

Alessandro Guerriero was born in Milan in 1943 and studied architecture at the Milan Polytechnic. In 1976, together with others, he founded the Alchymia studio, of which he was the guiding light. In 1982 he took part in the foundation of the Domus Academy. Since December 1983 he has been director, together with Pierre Restany, of the magazine of design and interior decoration *Decoration International*, published in Paris.

IN

IN, an interdisciplinary magazine dedicated to architecture and design, was conceived in 1969 by Pierpaolo Saporiti together with Paolo Scheggi, Vittorio Cosimini and Ippolito Calvi. At the beginning of the seventies the magazine, directed by Pierpaolo Saporiti and with Ugo La Pietra as chief editor, published a series of issues dedicated to the international movement of younger architects. This was further elaborated in collaboration with Archizoom Associati and Superstudio in a series of issues dedicated to themes such as "The destruction of the object", "Destruction and re-appropriation of the city" and, later, "Dressing design". Apart from the names cited above, these numbers also included articles by Ettore Sottsass Jr., Raymung Abraham, The Archigrams, Franco Bisaglia, Jim Burns, Germano Celant, Giuseppe Chiari, Jacques Famery, the Street Farmers, Heinz Franck, Coop. Himmelblay, Hans Hollein, Fernando Montes, Leonardo Mosso, Max Peintner, Gianni Pettena, the Salz der Erde, the Strum Group, George Sowden and others.

Guido Janon

Guido Janon has been an important promoter of New Design in Italy and throughout the world. His early work was in editorial graphics, after which he founded the first Italian group dedicated to co-ordinated images; he worked with Giò Ponti on the first four editions of *Eurodomus*. He is a consultant for image and development for various important industries including Abet Laminati; in 1971 he organized the exhibition "The Neutral Surface" and in 1972 was among the organizers of the important exhibition "Italy: The New Domestic Landscape" at the MOMA in New York. He has been a consultant at the Montefibre Design Centre since its beginnings, a consultant for Fiorucci, Fiat and Confindustria, and has always looked after the relationship between these firms and advanced research in the design sector. In 1981 he was awarded the Golden Compass for his promotion and development of the relationship between design and industry. He organizes exhibitions and meetings on an international level on the new role of industrial production in interior design and in culture.

Ugo La Pietra

Ugo La Pietra was born in Milan in 1938 and graduated there in 1964. He was assistant lecturer at the Faculty of Architecture in Milan until 1974 and then, from 1967 to 1979, at the Faculty of Architecture in Pescara. Since 1977 he has been a lecturer in the planning course at the State Institute of Art in Monza. From 1971 to 1980 he directed the magazines *IN*, *Progettare in più*, *Brera Flash*, *Fascicolo* and since 1979 has been on the editing staff of *Domus*. He has worked on many exhibitions including "50 Years of Architecture" (Milan, 1980), the audiovisual sector of the 16th Triennale in Milan and "The Telematic House" at the Milan Fair in 1983. He has taken part in a large number of personal and collective exhibitions (more than 300 in Italy and abroad) and has written many articles, catalogues and books.

Libidarch

This group was very active during the period of radical architecture and then came together again to take part in recent exhibitions (including the Parc della Villette in 1983). The group was founded in Turin in 1971 by Edoardo Ceretto, Maria Grazia Daprà Conti, Vittorio Gallo, Andrea Mascardi and Walter Mazzella. They were continuously active up until 1975 doing research into the "poor" or "banal" urban image. In 1972 they made a videotape on "A proposal for the methodological definition of 'poor' architecture"; with these analytical instruments they took part in the 15th Triennale of Milan and the Biennale of Architecture at San Paolo. They have designed for the Busnelli industrial group some important works which have been widely publicized.

Giuseppe (Bepi) Maggiori

Maggiori is from Rimini and graduated in architecture at Florence in 1978. At present he lives in Milan. Together with Marco Zanuso Jr. he works for several furniture companies, and with Luigi and Pietro Greppi they founded a company making lighting systems called Oceano Oltreluce. He has exhibited at the 16th Triennale in Milan. He is in contact with young international designers with whom he organizes meetings and exhibitions, among them: "Camera Design" (Milan 1982), "For Sale" (Vienna 1982), "Mobel Perdu" (Hamburg 1982-83), "Consequenze impreviste: art, fashion, design" (Prato 1982), "Design Balneare" (Cattolica 1983), "Mobili mobili" (Lerici 1982), "Light" (Milan 1983). Since 1981 he has written on design and research for the magazine *Casa Vogue*.

Memphis

Memphis originated in Milan in 1981 as the brain-child of Renzo Brugola, Mario and Brunella Godani, Fausto Celati and Ernesto Gismondi, and in 1982 the group joined Artemide as partners. Memphis designs objects, fabric, silverware, carpets, marble goods, lamps, laminates; exhibitions have been held in Hanover, Dusseldorf, Stockholm, New York, Tokyo, London, Los Angeles, Jerusalem, Geneva, Paris, Edinburgh, Chicago, Montreal. Between 1981 and 1983 they also produced objects designed by: Martin Bedin, Andrea Branzi, Aldo Cibic, Michele De Lucchi, Nathalie du Pasquier, Michael Graves, Hans Hollein, Arata Isozaki, Terry Jons, Shiro Kuramata, Jarier Mariscal, Alessandro Mendini, Paola Navone, Peter Shire, Ettore Sottsass Jr., George Sowden, Studio Alchymia, Matteo Thun, Massanori Umeda, Marco Zanini, Thomas Bley, Graham Fowler, Rudi Haberl, Walter Kirpicsenko, Michael Podgorschek, Daniela Puppa, Christoph Radl, Gerard Taylor, Sue Timney, Daniel Weil, Issey Miyake, Fabio Bellotti, Robert Manjurian. The art director of Memphis is Barbara Radice.

Alessandro Mendini

Alessandro Mendini was born in Milan in 1931. Until 1970 he worked with Nizzoli Associates in Milan, where he collaborated with the group designing objects, buildings and experimental housing quarters including the Italsider in Taranto. From 1970 to 1976 he directed *Casabella*, an architectural magazine with a special interest in radical design, and the special numbers on fashion published by *Domus*. He founded and directed *Modo* and at present directs *Domus*. He has also designed on his own or with others furniture, objects and "small" architecture labelled "banal". He has been part of "Bracciodiferro" (Cassina) and Global Tools, a free school for individual creativity, and at present collaborates with Alchymia and other firms helping with image and design (Alessi). He writes and lectures in Italy and abroad. His works can be found in the permanent collections of the Gilman Paper Company and the Museum of Modern Art in New York, in the archives of the Pompidou Centre in Paris and Parma University. He writes reviews and articles for leading magazines. In 1979 he was awarded the Golden Compass for design. In 1983 a book of his was published entitled *The Unhappy Project* edited by Rosamaria Rinaldi, and in 1981 he wrote another book for Shakespeare & Company entitled *Goodbye Architecture*. Since 1983 he has been design lecturer at the "Hochschule für Angewandte Kunst" in Vienna.

Modo

Modo is an architectural and design magazine founded in 1977 and directed by Alessandro Mendini. Its editorial policy is to link the problems of planning to those pertaining to anthropology, custom, industrial techniques and craftsmanship. From 1980 to 1983 *Modo* was directed by Franco Raggi, who had been chief under Mendini. From spring 1983 to early 1984 the magazine was directed by a committee composed of Pierre Restany, Clino Trini Castelli and Andrea Branzi; from January 1984 onwards it is directed by Andrea Branzi.

Massimo Morozzi

Massimo Morozzi was born in Florence in 1941, and now lives and works in Milan. Until 1972 he was a member of Archizoom Associati, the leaders of Italian architectonic avant-garde. From 1972 to 1977 he co-ordinated the Montefibre Design Centre for the development of furnishing and textile products, and contributed to founding the disciplines of "design primario". The research carried out in this period on colour and interior decoration (*Colordinamo*, *Decorattivo*, Fibermatching 25 - the 1979 Golden Compass award) introduced the new techniques of the "soft" programme into the field of design. Afterwards working with the C.D.M. group (Milan Design Consultants), he developed co-ordinated image products (Rome Airport), product lines (Louis Vuitton) and the definition of new chromatic ranges and new materials. In 1982, under the name of Massimo Morozzi Design, he opened his own studio, directing his creative attention to the design of goods and services for the home.

Paola Navone

Paola Navone was born in 1950 and graduated at Turin University in architecture in 1973; her thesis, which was prepared with Bruno Orlandini, was published in *Casabella* as a document on radical architecture. She lives in Milan where she collaborates with the major architectural and design magazines. From 1974 to 1978 she worked at the Kappa Centre. At present she is directing research into decoration at the Domus Study Centre, and she also works as a consultant and designer for industries in the furnishing business, including Abet Laminates.

David Palterer

David Palterer was born at Haifa in 1949 and graduated in Florence where he now lives and works. He is Adolfo Natalini's assistant lecturer at the Faculty of Architecture in Florence and also holds a course in design at the Syracuse University there. He has taken part in many planning competitions and won several, including "L'interno dopo la forma dell'utile" at the 16th Milan Triennale, the International Interior Design Competition held by the magazine *Architectural Design* plus the project for the reevaluation of the old city centre of Parma (with Natalini's group).

Gaetano Pesce

Gaetano Pesce was born in La Spezia in 1939. While studying at Venice University in 1958 he started taking an interest in figurative art and showed his works in galleries in various Italian cities. In 1959 he helped found the "N Group" in Padua dealing with programmed art. With them he collaborated with "Gruppo Zero" in Germany and in Paris with the "Groupe de Recherche d'Art Visuelle", at the time called "Motus", and later with the "Gruppo T" of Milan. In 1961 he collaborated with "Hochschule für Gestalung" of Ulm in Germany (the "Bauhaus" of Max Bill), where he showed works in 1964. The same year, in Helsinki, he exhibited at the "Finnish Design Centre" and in 1965 held a conference at Jyvaskyla in Finland during the "Society in Architecture" congress. Personal and group exhibitions have been held in Bologna, Genoa, Milan, Naples, Padua, Paris, Rome, Turin and Venice. In 1972 he was asked, together with other architects, to design a room for the exhibition "Italy: The new domestic landscape" at the Museum of Modern Art in New York. In 1975 an exhibition was dedicated to his work at the "Centre for Industrial Creation" in Paris's Musée des Arts Decoratifs, entitled: "Le futur est peut-être passé". He lives and works in New York.

Gianni Pettena

Gianni Pettena was born in 1940 at Bolzano and graduated in architecture at Florence University where he works at present. He has always been interested in radical architecture. He has devoted much of his time to teaching and has lectured in universities in England, the USA, Germany, Switzerland, Spain and Austria. He has held peronal exhibitions in various cities in the USA and has taken part in many group exhibitions of architecture and design. He writes for several magazines, including *Domus* and *Modo*. He has written *The Anarchitect* (Florence 1977) and *The Invisible City* (a collection of articles on radical architecture), published in Florence in 1983.

Daniela Puppa

Daniela Puppa, who is a designer and architect, was born at Fiume in the district of Veneto in 1947. She graduated at the Milan Polytechnic in 1970 and has worked in various fields. In the publishing world she has contributed as a journalist and part of the editorial staff of *Casabella*, directed by Mendini, and also worked with *Modo*. She has taken part in various exhibitions, including the Venice Biennale of 1980 as co-creator of the individual exhibition "The Banal Object", in 1982 at Prato in the "Natural Object", in 1983 at the Triennale in Milan. In the world of the theatre she has been co-designer of some of the scenery used by the theatrical group Magazzini Criminali, in particular that for "Nervous Breakdown" in 1981. She is a designer and consultant in product design for furniture manufacturers, also for furnishing fabrics and lighting companies. She has also worked in fashion with Gianfranco Ferrè.

Barbara Radice

Barbara Radice was born in Como and graduated in Modern Literature at the Catholic University of Milan. For two years she was chief of the editing staff of *Data*, an art magazine, and in 1977 went into freelance journalism writing for magazines such as: *Modo, Casa Vogue, Domus, Donna* and *Japan S.D.* In 1978 she was guest editor for an issue of *Laica Journal* on Italy. In 1980 she edited the book *In Praise of the Banal* and in 1983 the book *Memphis*. Since 1983 she has worked for Memphis as art director and co-ordinator.

Franco Raggi

Franco Raggi, who is an architect and a designer, was born in Milan in 1945. He graduated at the Milan Polytechnic and since 1970 has worked in various fields: from 1971 onwards he was on the editorial staff of *Casabella*; he then became managing editor and subsequently editor of *Modo*, the magazine of design and architecture, where he stayed until 1983. He was planner and cultural co-ordinator of the 1973, 1979, 1983 Milan Triennales in the architecture and design section. In 1975-76 he was co-ordinator of the visual arts section of the Venice Biennale. He was co-creator of the exhibition "The Banal Object" and creator of "Summer Architecture", an exhibition held at Rimini. His designs and writings have been shown in various exhibitions both in Italy and abroad. He recently created "The House of the Triennale" which was shown simultaneously in Paris and Milan.

Cinzia Ruggeri

Cinzia Ruggeri, born in Milan, graduated at the Academy of Applied Arts. She became part of the Milanese artistic scene, taking part in personal and group shows. She decided to concentrate on fashion design and to that end went to Paris to serve a period of apprenticeship with Carven. She returned to Italy and worked as a stylist in her father's clothing firm where she organized the first project of research into style. Her trademark - Bloom - has been well known for many years now in the Italian ready-to-wear world. She has designed costumes for the theatre, designed womens' sportswear for Kim and designed a range of household linen for Castellini. She also acts as art director for the Italian Linen Board. Her creations have been collected by the Museum of Fashion in Parma. She took part in the Venice Biennale of 1981, the Milan Triennale of 1983 and the "Italian Re-evolution" exhibition held in California in 1982.

Denis Santachiara

Denis Santachiara was born in 1951 and his first experiences in designing were for the automobile industry, designing car bodies at Modena. He is self-taught and has always tackled advanced technology, electronics and telematics in a highly creative fashion. He has taken part in numerous design exhibitions and also in the 1983 Triennale exhibition in Milan where he showed a project called "The Dream House". He is now researching and working with firms dealing in plastics and furniture.

Ettore Sottsass Jr.

Ettore Sottsass was born in Innsbruck, Austria, in 1917 and graduated at the Turin Polytechnic in 1939. His professional activity started with the opening of a studio in Milan in 1947, preparing projects, participating in architectural competitions and building hotels, schools and housing developments in Italy. He has contributed to various Triennale exhibitions and his works have been shown in numerous personal and group shows in Italy and abroad. He is internationally recognized as one of the originators of the renewal of design and architecture after the functionalism of the period immediately before and after the last world war. In recent years he has worked as a design consultant for Olivetti. Following a lengthy lecture tour of English universities a laurea honoris causa was conferred on him by the Royal College of Art. He took part in the exhibition "Italy: The New Domestic Landscape" at the Museum of Modern Art in New York. In 1976 he was invited to exhibit a personal show for the opening of the Cooper-Hewitt Design Museum in New York and produced a collection of photographs of buildings in the desert or in mountain areas which expressed his reflections on the subject of design and architecture. In 1976 the Internationales Design Zentrum of Berlin organized an exhibition of Sottsass' work over the last twenty years, which was then transferred to the Biennale in Venice, to the Musée des Arts Decoratifs in Paris, to the Centro de Diseno Industrial of Barcelona, to the Israel Museum in Jerusalem and then to the Visual Arts Board in Sydney. In 1977, together with other colleagues (M.D.C.), he designed a whole system based on informatics for Fiumicino Airport in Rome. In 1978 he was invited by the authorities of the City of Berlin to submit a project for the re-building of the city's Museum of Modern Art. The year 1980 saw the formation of Sottsass Associates. For many years he has designed pieces of furniture for Memphis, of which he has been one of the guiding lights.

Sottsass Associates

Sottsass Associates is a design consultancy group founded in 1980 by Ettore Sottsass Jr. and three young architects, Aldo Cibic, Matteo Thun and Marco Zanini. They deal mainly with industrial design and interior decoration, working in varied fields: from mechanics to electronics and products for the home. Together with Michele De Lucchi, Sottsass Associates have furnished all the Fiorucci boutiques in Italy and the rest of Europe. In 1980 the group was asked to design and make various units of urban design for the City of Turin: a multi-purpose kiosk, a public toilet and spaces to be used for advertising. In 1981 they worked on graphic projects for Nava, Mandelli, Ungaro and Alessi; they also collaborate with Nathalie du Pasquier, Giovanni Sacchi and Erminio Rizzotti. In addition, they are working on various extraprofessional projects, amongst which is the planning of a collection dedicated to Memphis.

George Sowden

George Sowden was born in Leeds, England, in 1942 and graduated in 1964. For the following two years he travelled in the Middle East. In 1966 he took a design course and in 1968 founded a small business producing furniture. In 1970 he became a computer design consultant for Olivetti. In 1973 he took part in the exhibition entitled "The Invention of the Neutral Surface". In 1978 he started research into the decorated surface. He works with Memphis.

Nanni Strada

Nanni Strada was born in Milan but grew up in Buenos Aires. On returning to Milan she finished her studies in fashion. In 1964 she started her career designing knitwear with names like Avoncelli, Missoni and Cadette. She produced the first plastic sandals and injection-moulded footwear for Fiorucci. In 1970, after doing research in London into Oriental clothes and studying ethnographic texts by the German Max Tilke, Nanni Strada elaborated a theory of clothes design totally different from the traditional. The result is a roomy, simply cut geometric dress, suitable for all sizes and easy to manufacture. Another revolutionary clothing design is a dress made on the tubular machines used for knitting stockings; it needs very little finishing. This was shown at the Milan Triennale in 1974 and called "The Mantle and the Skin". She received the Golden Compass in 1979 for the first dress in the world made only of fabric. Her original ideas have led to many collaborations, as far away as China and Japan, where she has been involved with firms dealing in women's, technical, work and sports clothes. In September 1973 the Ministry for Light Industry in the USSR organized a symposium in Moscow where Nanni Strada showed a collection of knitwear dresses destined for the Soviet market.

Group Strum

The name of the group is derived from an abbreviation: "per una architettura strumentale" ("for instrumental architecture"); founded in Turin by Giorgio Geretti, Pietro Derossi, Carla Giammarco, Riccardo Rosso and Maurizio Vogliazzo at the beginning of the seventies, they have taken part in various exhibitions, including "Italy: The New Domestic Landscape" at the Museum of Modern Art, New York, in 1972. They have also organized seminars and written theoretical articles concerned with the political development of radical architecture.

Superstudio

Adolfo Natalini, Cristano Toraldo di Francia, Roberto Magris, Gian Pietro Frassinelli, Alessandro Magris. Superstudio began in Florence in December 1966 for the purpose of theoretical research into planning. Its members work in the field of architecture (preparatory plans, civil and industrial building) and design (system design, objects, furniture, consultancies), take part in national and international competitions, in exhibitions in Italy and abroad, hold courses and conferences in schools and institutes, publish articles, reviews and a series of printed publications. During the years 1971-1973 the studio produced a series of films on fundamental acts which were aimed at the philosophical and anthropological "re-building" of architecture in a series of adaptable processes. From 1973 to 1975 the studio was

part of Global Tools and since 1973 the group has been very involved in research and teaching activities both at the University of Florence and in other academic centres. Superstudio participated in the exhibition "Italy: The New Domestic Landscape" at the Museum of Modern Art, New York, in 1972; the 15th and 16th Triennale exhibitions in Milan and other important occasions from 1968 onwards. The exhibition "Superstudio: Fragmente aus einem persönlichen Museum" toured Europe in 1973-74; "Sottsass and Superstudio: Mindscapes" toured U.S. museums from 1973 to 1975. In 1978 and in 1980 the studio took part in the Venice Biennale.

Matteo Thun

Matteo Thun was born in Bolzano in 1952; he studied sculpture in Salzburg and took a degree in architecture at Florence University in 1975 which included the designing and making of a flying machine. He lives in Milan where he works with Sottsass Associates.

Clino Trini Castelli

Clino Trini Castelli was born in 1944. In 1958 he started work at the Centro Stile of Fiat at Turin; then he was in Milan with Olivetti, working with Ettore Sottsass. In 1967, together with Elio Fiorucci, he founded "Intrapresa Design". The year 1969 saw him back at Olivetti as a consultant for projects concerned with the corporate identity of the company. At the same time he designed fabrics for Abet Print. In 1973, with Branzi and Morozzi, he organized the Montefibre Design Centre. With these same partners (and at the beginning also Mendini and Sottsass) he started Milan Design Consultants in 1976. In 1978 he started the first centre in Europe for the promotion, documentation and planning of colour: the IVI Colourterminal. The following year in Turin he helped found "Habitaco" owned by Fiat-Comind, and he is still the design co-ordinator there. At present he works for the European and Japanese automobile industries on questions of colour, materials and equipment; he also collaborates with 3M on the development of decorative materials and advanced lighting systems. He is also a consultant for firms such as Visconti di Modrone, Ermenegildo Zegna, Dartington Mills, Vitra (Germany) and Herman Miller (U.S.A.).

UFO Group

This group was formed in Florence in 1967 by Lapo Binazzi, Carlo Bachi, Riccardo Foresi, Patrizia Cammeo, Vittorio Maschietto and, at the beginning, Sandro Gioli. They immediately became a focal point for radical architecture, developing their own original activity in the field of urban and environmental action. At the International Section of the Milan Triennale, 1968, they documented their work with ephemeral urban "blow-ups". This theme of town "happenings" was demonstrated in Florence in interior decoration and in lay-out of shops the years that followed. These were projects in which, from the first, there was a strict inter-change between architecture, stage design, furnishing and decoration, ephemeral decoration. The group used such materials as papier mâché, polyurethane, blow-ups, literary quotes and linguistic theorems. Projects included the Sherwood Restaurant in Florence and the Bamba Issa discothèque at Forte

dei Marmi in 1969. The theoretical work of the group is very important and they have intensified research into new written language and formal language. An important factor in this has been their friendship with Umberto Eco, who has collaborated with them from the start. In 1971 the group took part in the Youth Biennale in Paris; they also exhibited at the Contemporary exhibition in Rome, the International Graphic Biennale at Florence in 1976, the Venice Biennale of 1978 and many other exhibitions, shows and competitions. Their work has been widely published in important magazines; Domus has given them three front pages. They were founder members of Global Tools. Lapo Binazzi has directed most of the group's activity since 1972.

Nanda Vigo

She lives and works in Milan where she was born. In 1959 she graduated in architecture from the Institut Politechnique of Lausanne. She has always worked in the field of art and architecture in a highly individual way. Starting out with a group doing research into aesthetics, she then worked with architects in the U.S.A and had periods in advertising. Her work has always been closely connected creatively with artists such as Fontana, Castellani, Ponti, Le Parc, Ceroli, Baj, Pomodoro, Soto, Burri, César and Vasarely. She has taken part in numerous exhibitions, including Milan Triennales, and has held about 40 personal exhibitions. For many years she taught visual and graphic conception at the Institut Politechnique of Lausanne. At present she is lecturer at the Academy of Fine Arts of Macerata.

Marco Zanini

Marco Zanini is an architect who was born at Trento in 1954 and graduated at Florence in 1978 under Adolfo Natalini. From 1975 to 1977 he worked in Los Angeles for the Argonaut Company and did freelance work in San Francisco. From 1977 onwards he collaborated with Ettore Sottsass and in 1980 became a member of Sottsass Associati.

Zziggurat

Zziggurat is a group composed of Alberto Breschi, Giuliano Fiorenzuoli, Gigi Gavini, Roberto Pecchioli, formed in 1969 to deal with aspects of architecture. During their first years of activity they did research into architecture as a form of communication, with reference to myth, history and the subconscious ("Life, death and miracles of Architecture", a seminar exhibition at the Electronic Space in Florence). They have dedicated much time to research and took part in "Global Tools".

9999

9999 is a Florentine group of radical architects formed in 1967 by Giorgio Birelli, Carlo Caldini, Fabrizio Fiumi and Paolo Galli. The group presented a theoretical project at the exhibition "Italy: The New Domestic Landscape" in 1972 in New York; in 1972, in Florence, at the Super Space, a large dance hall managed by the group, they held a seminar on conceptual and behavioural architecture entitled "S-S-Space World Festival no. 1" which was attended by all the Italian radical groups plus some Austrian, British and American groups. In 1973 they published a book entitled Memories of Architecture.

Index

Abet, p. 88, 108, 110, 113, 114, 118, 120, 121
Accolti Giò, p. 40
Albers Anni, p. 109, 110
Albers Joseph, p. 20
Alberti Leon Battista, p. 109
Albini Franco, p. 37
Alchymia, p. 80, 119, 120, 121, 123, 126, 134, 135, 136, 138, 139, 141
Alexander Christopher, p. 116
Alfa Romeo, p. 108
Apelli & Varesio, p. 44
Arc. 74, p. 143
Archigram, p. 51, 54, 63
Archizoom Associati, p. 50, 52, 54, 55, 57, 58, 59, 60, 61, 62, 63, 66, 67, 68, 69, 70, 71, 72, 73, 75, 77, 78, 79, 80, 85, 86, 87, 93
Arflex, p. 42
Argan Giulio Carlo, p. 9, 139
Artemide, p. 143
The Art Journal, p. 12
Aulenti Gae, p. 48, 80
Auratour agency, p. 149
Bachi Carlo, p. 85
Baldessari Luciano, p. 33, 34
Balla Giacomo, p. 29, 32, 33
Bamba-Issa restaurant, p. 128, 129
Bartolini Dario, p. 79, 85, 93
Bartolini Lucia, p. 93
Bayer Herbert, p. 25
BBPR studio, p. 39, 41
Bedding Co., p. 148
Bellini Mario, p. 80, 118
Benjamin Walter, p. 128
Binazzi Lapo, p. 58, 85, 140, 141
Birelli Giorgio, p. 85
Birren Faber, p. 102, 105
Bloch, p. 92
Boccioni Umberto, p. 26, 27, 128
Bona Enrico, p. 85
Borsalino, p. 90
Borsani Osvaldo, p. 41
Boschini Luciano, p. 85
Bossi, p. 92
Bottoni Piero, p. 33
Bracciodiferro, p. 129
Brecht Bertolt, p. 129
Breschi Alberto, p. 85
Breuer Marcel, p. 22, 23, 24
Brugola, p. 143
Brunello Franco, p. 107
Brunori Bubi, p. 40
Bugatti Carlo, p. 16
Buti Remo, p. 85
Cage John, p. 80, 82
Caldini Carlo, p. 85
Cappelli Sergio, p. 149
Cardini Domenico, p. 52
Carlyle Thomas, p. 14
Carrà Carlo, p. 26, 27
Casabella, p. 83, 85
Cassina, p. 77, 145, 146, 149
Castelli Valerio, p. 45
Castiglioni Achille, p. 45, 75, 142, 145
Castiglioni Piergiacomo, p. 45, 142
Cavazza, Count, p. 16
C. & B. Italia, p. 75
C.D.M., p. 98, 99, 100, 101, 102, 104, 106, 107, 110, 111, 112, 115, 116, 117
Celant Germano, p. 33, 36, 63
Centro Design Montefibre, p. 93, 98, 99, 100, 101, 102, 104, 106, 107, 110, 111, 113, 115, 116, 117
Centrokappa, p. 45, 46, 47
Ceretti Giorgio, p. 52, 54
Charpentier R.F., p. 104
Chiesa Pietro, p. 38
Cifarelli Manuela, p. 45
Citroën Paul, p. 27
Citterio Antonio, p. 150
Coat Turin Adela, p. 115, 116, 117
Cole, p. 13
Collison G., p. 13
Colombo Joe, p. 78, 80, 122
Colordinamo, p. 103, 108, 104, 106, 107
Colorterminal IVI, p. 103, 120

Coppedè, p. 54
Corretti Gilberto, p. 85
Cova, p. 41
Croff Centro Casa, p. 142
Curamata Sihiro, p. 143
Dal Lago Adalberto, p. 85
Dalisi Riccardo, p. 81, 82, 83, 84, 85, 137
Darbo, p. 40
Data, p. 99
De Chirico Giorgio, p. 32, 128
Decorattivo, p. 115, 116, 117, 119, 120, 122
Deganello Paolo, p. 85, 145, 146
De Gregori Alessandro, p. 106
Deleuze Gilles, p. 128
Dell, p. 19
Dell'Orto Guido, p. 39
De Lucchi Michele, p. 139, 141, 144
De Pas Jonathan, p. 74, 75
Depero Fortunato, p. 29, 30, 31, 32, 33
Derossi Pietro, p. 52, 54
Der Sturm, p. 26
Design Center, p. 60
Design Quarterly, p. 96
Dieckmann E., p. 109
Diedron, p. 53
Dine Jim, p. 51
Domus, p. 55, 85, 90, 91
Domus Academy, p. 11, 144
Domus Moda, p. 90
Driade, p. 145, 150
Duchamp Marcel, p. 51
Du Pasquier Nathalie, p. 118, 146
D'Urbino Donato, p. 74, 75
Eames Charles, p. 49
Engels Friedrich, p. 14, 58
Eno Brian, p. 100
Feldman Morton, p. 80
Ferrè, p. 95
Fiat, p. 108
Fibermatching Meraklon 25, p. 111, 113, 114
Fiorucci, p. 88, 95, 135
Fischer Theodor, p. 17
Fisiolight, p. 98, 100, 101
Fiumi Fabrizio, p. 85
Flaubert Gustave, p. 61
Flexform, p. 150
Fornaroli Antonio, p. 39
Frassinelli Piero, p. 85
Galleria del Copismo, p. 136
Galli Paolo, p. 85
Gardella Ignazio, p. 48
Gatti, Paolini, Teodoro, p. 75
Giedion Siegfried, p. 17, 28, 144
Gilardi & Barzaghi, p. 43
GI.MO, p. 115
Ginsberg Allen, p. 55
Giovannetti, p. 76
Girmi, p. 139
Global Tools, p. 81, 83, 84, 85, 86
Gravagnuolo Benedetto, p. 88
Graves Michael, p. 143
Gregotti Vittorio, p. 47, 49, 85
Gropius Walter, p. 8, 17, 137, 147
Gualino offices, p. 33
Guenzi Carlo, p. 85
Guerriero Alessandro, p. 141
Haus-Ruker Co., p. 54
Heidegger Martin, p. 128
Hickethier, p. 104
Hilberseimer Ludwig, p. 25
Hölderlin Friedrich, p. 150
Hollein Hans, p. 51, 143
House and Garden, p. 103
ICA, p. 103
IN, p. 93
Isozaki Arata, p. 143
Jencks Charles, p. 78, 96, 127
Jolly 2 Gallery, p. 52
Jones Terry, p. 143
Jung C.G., p. 67
Kandinsky Vasili, p. 36, 122
Köhn, p. 9
Krier Leon, p. 136
Krizia, p. 95
Lambert Heinrich A., p. 104
Lancia, p. 108
Lanclos J. Philippe, p. 105
La Pietra Ugo, p. 55, 75, 76, 80, 85, 93
Latina Illuminazione, p. 142
Laveno, p. 43
Le Corbusier, p. 8, 51, 97

Le Figaro, p. 32
Léger Fernand, p. 18
Lenzi R. & M., p. 115
Levi Montalcini Gino, p. 33
Lynch Kevin, p. 30
Lingeri Pietro, p. 33
Lomazzi Paolo, p. 74, 75
Loos Adolf, p. 8, 72, 87, 115, 150
Lyotard Jean-François, p. 128, 129
Mackintosh Charles Rennie, p. 8
Mafia, p. 103
Magazzini Criminali, p. 131, 134, 135
Mago di Oz, boutique, p. 129
Magris Alessandro, p. 85
Magris Roberto, p. 85
Mainardi Sauro, p. 117
Maldonado Tomàs, p. 85
Mali, p. 134
Mana Art Market, p. 61
Mango Roberto, p. 40
Marchi Virgilio, p. 28
Mari Enzo, p. 85, 90, 137
Marinetti Filippo Tommaso, p. 28, 29, 30, 32, 33, 128
Masanori Umeda, p. 143
Maschietto Titti, p. 85
Matisse Henri, p. 80
Mayer Thobias B., p. 104
McDonald's restaurants, p. 51
McLuhan Marshall, p. 99
Memphis, p. 118, 143, 144, 145, 147, 149
Mendini Alessandro, p. 85, 90, 93, 118, 120, 121, 122, 123, 124, 126, 131, 135, 141, 145
Meneghetti Lodovico, p. 47, 49
"Metafisica", p. 33, 96
Modo, p. 124
Moholy-Nagy Laszlo, p. 19, 20, 26
Metabolism, p. 51, 63
Meyer Hannes, p. 72
Missoni, p. 95
Mollino Carlo, p. 44, 48, 49
Molnàr Farkas, p. 22, 23
Mondrian Piet, p. 36
Moretti Luigi, p. 131
Mormile Alfonso, p. 40
Morozzi Massimo, p. 52, 85, 112, 113, 121, 145
Morris William, p. 8, 13, 15, 17, 137, 147
Mosconi Davide, p. 92
Mucchi Gabriele, p. 38
Munsell System, p. 103, 105
Muthesius Hermann, p. 17, 137
Natalini Adolfo, p. 52, 85
Navone Paola, p. 45, 119, 120, 121, 124, 126, 134
Nespolo Ugo, p. 93
Nono Luigi, p. 80, 81
Olivetti & Co., p. 103, 108
Osca, p. 49
Ostwald Wilhelm D., p. 104
Out-Off, p. 131
Pagano Giuseppe, p. 33, 34
Pannaggi Ivo, p. 30, 33
Pantysol, p. 93
Paris Rudolf, p. 25
Pavese Cesare, p. 39
Paxton Joseph, p. 12
Pecchili Roberto, p. 85
Pesce Gaetano, p. 75, 85, 129, 139, 149
Pettena Gianni, p. 55, 57, 60, 85
Piaggio, p. 107, 108
Pianeta Fresco, p. 55, 60
Picasso Pablo, p. 22, 25
Pichler Walter, p. 51, 54
Piper, p. 52, 54
Pirelli, p. 39, 48
Pirelli - Sapsa, p. 42
Pivano Fernanda, p. 55
Politecne Cinematografica, p. 88
Poltronova, p. 48, 52, 73, 74, 75, 78
Ponti Giò, p. 39, 45, 47, 48, 122
Portoghesi Paolo, p. 121, 127
Prase E., p. 104
Pugin Augustus Welby, p. 13, 14, 137
Puppa Daniela, p. 119, 124, 126, 134
Racinet R. C., p. 14
Radice Barbara, p. 143
Raggi Franco, p. 85, 122, 124, 126, 134
Ranzo Patrizia, p. 149
Rasulo Prospero, p. 123
Rauschenberg Robert, p. 51
Ravegnate Mario, p. 40

Reiner Arnulf, p. 97
Reli - Tech, p. 113, 114
Ricci Leonardo, p. 52
Richter G., p. 104
Rietveld Gerrit, p. 8
Rilke Rainer Maria, p. 8
Rima, p. 40
Rinaldi Gastone, p. 40
Robbe-Grillet Alain, p. 80
Rogers Ernesto N., p. 8
Rosselli Alberto, p. 39, 46, 48, 80
Rossi Aldo, p. 55
Rosso Riccardo, p. 52, 54
Rubiani Alfonso, p. 16
Ruggeri Cinzia, p. 94, 95
Rünge Philipp Otto C., p. 104
Ruskin John, p. 13, 14, 20
Sabini Fabrizio, p. 117
Sacchi, p. 137
Santachiara Denis, p. 113, 120
Sant'Elia Antonio, p. 28
Sardella Bruno, p. 40
Sarri Alessio, p. 143
Savinio Alberto, p. 32
Savioli Leonardo, p. 52, 54
Scarzella Patrizia, p. 90
Schlemmer Oskar, p. 21, 22, 23
Schmidt Kurt, p. 18
Schwitters Kurt, p. 110
Scott Brown Denise, p. 51, 54
Sheraton, shoe manufacturer, p. 137
Sherwood restaurant, p. 128
Siegel Gustav, p. 9
Simon International, p. 85
Sixti Antonio, p. 131, 134
Sottsass Jr. Ettore, p. 45, 49, 55, 56, 74, 80, 83, 85, 93, 96, 100, 103, 108, 120, 136, 138, 141, 142, 143, 144, 148
Sowden George, p. 144, 148
Space Electronic, p. 52
Spadolini Giovanni, p. 79
Speer Albert, p. 35, 37, 74
Stilnovo, p. 142
Stonborough Margarethe, p. 98, 99, 100
Stoppino Giotto, p. 47, 49
Strada Nanni, p. 87, 91, 92, 93
Stratitex, p. 110
Strum, p. 80
Susini Antonio, p. 53
Superstudio, p. 52, 53, 54, 55, 60, 63, 64, 65, 76, 77, 80, 85, 93, 95
Tafuri Manfredo, p. 39, 73
Taylor Gerard, p. 149
Tecno, p. 40
Terragni Giuseppe, p. 33, 36
Terzic Mario, p. 86, 93
Thun Matteo, p. 143
Tilke Max, p. 87, 91
Toraldo di Francia Cristiano, p. 85
Trini Tommaso, p. 91, 92
Trini Castelli Clino, p. 93, 97, 99, 100, 112
Tronti Mario, p. 72, 150
UFO, p. 57, 58, 60, 85, 128, 129, 130, 140
Vallone Bruno, p. 40
Valtalina Giuseppe, p. 39
Venturi Robert, p. 51, 54
Versace, p. 95
Viganò Vittoriano, p. 45
Vigo Nanda, p. 147
Vincenzi Antonello, p. 40
Viollet-le-Duc Eugène, p. 13
Vuitton Louis, p. 112
Warhol Andy, p. 105
Wiel Daniel, p. 147
Wittgenstein Ludwig, p. 98, 99
Yamajiwa competition p. 73
Zampini, House, p. 30, 33
Zanini Marco, p. 143
Zanotta, p. 36, 74, 127, 142
Zanuso Marco, p. 42, 45, 46, 80
"900", p. 31, 33, 96
9999, p. 52, 54, 60